PRACTICAL GUIDE TO THE I CHING

"It is one of the most ancient of the Chinese texts. It is both an oracle and a major work of philosophy and wisdom. It carries 64 different hexagrams and their corresponding interpretations.

A mode of access to reality, considered divination manual, a guide to inner path, an expression of correlative though, a cosmological model, an ensemble of processes—developing certain techniques. It can help us—see more clearly, resolve doubts eliminate fears. It invites us to profit from lessons in life for steadiness (stability), harmony and meaning in our lives and for the whole of humanity."

PRACTICAL GUIDE to the I CHING

KIM-ANH LIM

New Age Books

ISBN: 81-7822-108-x

First Indian Edition: Delhi, 2004

First Published in 1998 by Binkey Kok Publications, Holland.

Published by
NEW AGE BOOKS
A-44 Naraina Phase-I
New Delhi-110 028 (INDIA)
Email: nab@vsnl.in
Website: www.newagebooksindia.com

Printed in India
at Shri Jainendra Press
A-45 Naraina Phase-I, New Delhi-110 028

CONTENTS

PREFACE

The *Book of Changes—I Ching*, or, according to the phonetic transcription instituted by the People's Republic of China, the *Yijing*—is a master work of Chinese thought, revealing, from sixty-four hexagrams, sixty-four mutations or fundamental changes to which all situations can be reduced. Although the term *Yi* in the word *Yijing* signifies change, it paradoxically also means immutability. Changing yet not changing: this is the *Yijing*'s supreme wisdom, which leads us, from a comprehension of sixty-four types of primordial evolutions, to the knowledge of what endures. If we could only fully realize this knowledge, stability and peace would reign over the land and in the heart of humanity.

The discovery in China, at the end of the last century, of oracular inscriptions on bones and tortoise shells, as well as documents unearthed by archaeological digs during this century—especially a version of the *Yijing* unearthed at the end of 1973 from a tomb at the Mawangdui site near Changsha in Hunan province—gave us a better understanding of the primitive text and its evolution. From a simple collection made up of the reunified divinatory oracles, the *Yijing* has progressively become the expression of a philosophical mind-set.

The *Yijing* is a "perennial philosophy," a mode of access to reality, to the way things are. There is not an area in Chinese culture that, in one way or another, does not make reference to this text, whether from a technical or philosophical point of view. Therefore, it can be considered as a divination manual, a guide to the inner path, an expression of correlative thought, a cosmological model, an ensemble of processes that have inspired the development of certain techniques in China, such as alchemy, through its encouragement of the observation and interpretation of nature and the evolution of life.

In the West, during the 18th century, the correlative mode of thought expressed by the *Yijing* especially impressed Leibnitz and Voltaire. At the beginning of the 20th century its divinatory aspect attracted renewed interest in the *Yijing* and C. G. Jung found within it an excellent complement to causal thought. This distinction would probably seem excessive to the Chinese mind, but the *Yijing* helped Jung with his development of the principle of synchronicity and became a tool in his exploration of the dynamic aspect of the unconscious.[1]

The *Yijing* can be used to know the future. But what it teaches, above all, are manners of comportment, appropriate reactions for any given situation. It urges us to surmount an obstacle in the best way possible: not by projecting into the future, nor by avoiding it, nor by opposing it, but by recognizing the obstacle's place, its significance and links with other elements in such a way as to help the situation evolve toward harmony. This type of thinking is situated outside of good or evil, for in the same way that yang is not better than yin, good is not better than evil, because one cannot be defined without the other. What is good for one person can be bad for another, just as "the good" in one given situation can have its origins in a bad one.

Masters who read the *Yijing* in China often warn against rejoicing if they cast a hexagram that represents a situation at its zenith, for after the zenith comes the nadir. This unequivocal acceptance of events is illustrated by a well-known story of the old man of the Chinese steppes.[2] One day, a man who lived on the Chinese border frontier lost a horse, and everyone went to console him. But the old man, who was an expert in divination, retorted that there was nothing for him to be disappointed about, for a misfortune can transform into fortune. Accordingly, two months later, the runaway returned, accompanied by a superb mare. All the neighbors came to congratulate the old man, who replied that there was nothing to be happy about because a fortunate event could be the source of tragedy. Some time later, his son rode the mare and broke his leg in a bad fall. The neighbors again came to comfort the old man, but he reminded them that, according to his experience, this misfortune could turn out well. When, several months later, the Chinese were at war with the barbarians on the frontiers, all the able-bodied men were enlisted, but the son, due to the divine grace of his broken leg, escaped the war. Thus father and son were able to spend their days together happily.

[1] See C. G. Jung, *Memories, Dreams, Reflections*, Aniela Jaffé, editor, Richard and Clara Winston, translators (New York: Vintage Books, 1989), p. 373-374

[2] Variations of this story are found in many cultures.

This philosophy of the relativity of happiness and misfortune is expressed by the proverb "in every cloud there is a silver lining."

But before assimilating this philosophy, to gain this lucidity in the face of life's vagaries, we can use the *Yijing* as a practical guide from which—far from getting pat answers and recipes—we can progressively learn to discern the subtle network of phenomena in the universe, the emotions and mechanisms of the human spirit which, according to the principle of correlative thought, are all linked together. When we are able to understand that all the elements of the universe have solidarity, we will have assimilated the most important lesson of the *Yijing*: to struggle against one thing, whatever it is, is to struggle against oneself. But it would be a misconception to think that not struggling means being passive. The *Yijing* simply suggests that we envision action within an ensemble of processes and links, in a way that makes the situation evolve toward harmony.

The *Book of Mutations* can help us see more clearly, resolve doubts, eliminate fears, especially one of the greatest—as it frequently resides in the unconscious—the fear of death. The end of life comes to everyone, but who knows, perhaps it could be the beginning of happiness; such is, in any case, the point of view of the Taoist Zhuangzi. One day he found a skull on the side of a road. He picked it up and placed it under his pillow. During that night, the soul of the deceased appeared to him in a dream, spoke to him about death and taught him that it would not want to come back to life for anything in the world, for the soul had attained an inexpressible happiness.

Instead of becoming distressed or joyful, instead of seeking knowledge of the future, the *Yijing* invites us to profit from lessons in life for, within the heart of its fluctuations, we can find stability, harmony, and meaning in our lives and for the whole of humanity. It is in this spirit that Kim-Ahn Lim reveals, with simplicity and clarity, how to work with the *Yijing*.

Catherine Despeux
Professor of Chinese Language,
Université de La Sorbonne, Paris

INTRODUCTION

In 1978 Arnold Keyserling introduced me to the *Yijing*. Son of Count Keyserling (the humanist who introduced C. G. Jung to Richard Wilhelm) and longtime disciple of G. I. Gurdjieff, Arnold Keyserling was, when I knew him, professor of philosophy and comparative religion at the University of Vienna in Austria. He also spent time in Paris, conducting seminars on the *Yijing*, which was a rare and unusual thing in those days.

More than fifteen years after this encounter, in a moment of a little distress and great confusion, I consulted the *Yijing*. Its response vividly clarified my whole situation, promptly appeased me and gave me a route of exploration so perfect that I wished that everyone could benefit from this remarkable tool. That is how, within a few days, the idea for this book was born.

I must add that as a professional astrologer, I consult the *Yijing* in areas where astrology reaches its limits and I offer it as a subject of study for my students. I am thus in a position to practice it intensively and reply to the problems that my students encounter.

Part One of this work concentrates on the history, philosophy, and practical use of the oracle. The *Yijing* was born in a civilization entirely different from ours and spans over 3,000 years of vicissitude. An overall grasp of its course, its environment, and its mechanisms allows you to use it as an effective and flexible tool and releases it from the burden of tradition and bookish knowledge. These first chapters will help you consult the oracle effectively and to understand the great translations of the *Yijing*.

Part Two contains an interpretation of the text of the sixty-four hexagrams. This interpretation is faithful to the traditional commentaries, yet is accessible even to those of use who are not scholars of Chinese.

PART I
HISTORY, THEORY, AND PRINCIPLES OF CONSULTATION

CHAPTER I
ABOUT THE *YIJING*

The *Yijing or Book of Transformations* is one of the most ancient of the Chinese texts. Both an oracle and a major work of philosophy and wisdom, it is composed of sixty-four different hexagrams and their corresponding interpretations.[4]

The term "hexagram" comes to us from translations of the 19th century (from the Greek *hex,* meaning "six;" *gramma,* meaning "letter," or "symbol"). In Chinese they speak of the *gua,* a figure which can either refer to a hexagram (a figure made of six lines placed one above the other) or a trigram (a figure made of three lines placed one above the other).

The lines (*yao*) of a hexagram can be either broken (— —) or solid (——). They represent, respectively, supple and firm, dark and light, weak and strong, yin and yang. Each hexagram has a particular distribution of yin and yang lines, which symbolize the dynamics of a situation.

A hexagram can also be viewed as a combination of two trigrams. The trigrams are the result of all the possible combinations of yin and yang lines grouped in threes. There are eight trigrams (the *ba gua,* or "eight figures") which symbolize eight elements and functions:

Heaven	☰	☷	Earth
Thunder	☳	☴	Wind
Water	☵	☲	Fire
Mountain	☶	☱	Lake

[4] Also referred to as *The Book of Changes, The Book of Mutations, The Canon of Changes,* or *Classic of Changes.* "*Yijing*" is the Pinyin spelling of "I Ching," which is the Wade phonetic system spelling. The author has used Pinyin as it is the officially recognized phonetic system of the People's Republic of China.

Sometimes, the yin and the yang lines change from broken to solid and vice-versa; these are the "mutable" or "changing" lines. They herald the "transformations," the main subject of the *Yijing*. Through these lines, by virtue of their mutability, each of the sixty-four hexagrams can change into any one of the other hexagrams. Because of the various combinations of mutable and non-mutable lines, the *Yijing* offers 4,096 answers or possible combinations (64 x 64 = 4,096).

Now, what is hidden in the term *"Yijing"*? Long ago the Chinese character for Yi symbolized the sun and the moon, and sometimes the chameleon. Nowadays, it is more commonly understood as being the imposition of the characters representing the sun (above) and rain (below). It can be translated as "change," "mutation," or "transformation." This transition from one state to the other is natural, flowing, and without constraint. It is in the order of things and operates without effort; much in the way that day and night alternate, and the chameleon changes colors. That is why Yi can also be translated as that which is easy, simple. But that is not all. Paradoxically, Yi also means immutable, for it is an eternal, unchanging truth that all is change: after day follows night, after rain comes fair weather. The rules to which changes submit are also immutable.

The character *Jing* symbolizes the underlying, hidden order of things. It evokes the weft of fabric and the currents of subterranean rivers. It applies to all that regulates and gives structure. Therefore Jing can be translated as a line of conduct, a rule, or law, and, for the subject that interests us, as a canonical or classical book.

The *Yijing* is therefore the "Book of Mutations," "Book of Transformations," "Classic of Changes," "Canon of Changes," etc. Although there are subtle differences in these translations, there is one point of convergence: the *Yijing* reveals the immutable laws which preside over natural movements, that which is inherent and constant in all phenomena.

Myths and History

In order to trace the origins of the *Yijing*, it is necessary, according to tradition, to go back to the very beginnings of Chinese civilization.

This is work that is as delicate as it is hazardous, for tackling such research on ancient China alone poses serious problems. A number of documents have disappeared, and the language has changed. In addition, history, while it attempts to apprehend the hidden order of the world to provide an inexhaustible source of teachings, has tended to be subjective toward events and the preservation of evidence. Chinese historians aligned themselves with a "tradition" as the sole access to the "truth," rather than collect and preserve the faint testimonies of the past. According to this tradition, for example, a sage appeared every 500 years, he attained a life-span of about 100 years, and a social apogee occurred around his 50th year. Alterations to the tradition were made so that certain events corresponded to mythical laws of the universe: a hero was added or deleted, a dynasty was relocated in time, and chronologies were re-adjusted. In addition, as the moral values of a reign or a personage were re-evaluated in order to serve as examples, certain elements were re-established, elements that were too shaky for history to be built upon. In the final analysis, the tradition itself is subject to the fluctuations of the dominant ideologies. This has led to concurrent chronological systems which in turn lead, in some cases, to discrepancies of more than a century for the same event or several different kings for the same dynasty.

Since we cannot count on everything that has been transmitted to us, we need to maintain a healthy skepticism. The history of China is very long and many of its episodes were lost in darker times. Fortunately, here and there, some of them re-emerged by chance. Archaeological discoveries have proven that the kings of the Shang dynasty did indeed exist. In short, everything urges us to be very careful, for the ideas about China's history that are set forth tend to reflect our present state of consciousness. The archaeological progress in China is relatively recent, and is slow in capitalizing on and transmitting its findings, but it promises yet many more revelations.

The Tradition

According to the Tradition, the *Yijing* was handed down to us by four sages: Fuxi, King Wen, the Duke of Zhou, and Confucius.

The first of them, Fuxi, was one of the eight sages at the source of Chinese civilization who transmitted their wisdom to humanity.

These eight sages are:

- the three August: Fuxi, Nüwa, and Shennong;
- the five Sovereigns: Huangdi, Chuanxi, Gaoxin, Yao, and Shun.

These personages had extraordinary physical features, which were sometimes erased for the sake of realism. Fuxi (whose lifetime is placed between 4477 and 4363 B.C.) was born after his mother, having bathed in the Lake of Thunder, walked in the footsteps of a giant. Fuxi is often depicted with two nubs on his forehead that look like the beginnings of a pair of horns. When he is united with Nüwa, the lower part of the two spouses is intertwined with a reptilian tail (perhaps a dragon's tail).

Some legends attribute many creations to Fuxi and Nüwa: Fuxi's emblem was the set square (symbol of the Earth), for he provided the elements for measuring and building everything. He taught the art of taming wild animals, of fishing, and cultivating silkworms. He determined family names and saw to it that the only marriages which occurred were between individuals with different names. Finally, he set up the basis of the *Yijing* by inventing the trigrams which would become, in time, the inspiration for writing. Nüwa, his sister and wife, had for her emblem the compass (symbol of heaven). She developed many plans to save the world from an earthquake which would have otherwise destroyed it. She dammed the rivers (one of the biggest calamities of ancient China). She intensified the blue of the sky by using rocks chosen from the five colors of the rainbow, which she fused together. She established the cardinal points and upheld the canopy of heaven by using for pillars the feet of a giant tortoise which she had amputated. They even say that she created humans and modeled them, in the first attempt, by hand, with yellow clay. This method proved too lengthy, so she decided to dip a cord in the clay and shake lumps off of it. The humans who were modeled from her hands constitute the people of high lineage, while those born of the drops of clay became the common people. Lastly, when she baked her creations, some were fired too long and had dark skin, and some were not fired long enough, and had pale coloring.

To return to the *Yijing*, it was while contemplating the sky, the earth, and the life forms on it that Fuxi invented the trigrams. Other accounts say that he was present at the creation of the world, and that a turtle or dragon appeared to him, on the back of which was drawn an array of black and white points called "The Table of the River." This table inspired the trigrams which he then placed one on top of the other to obtain the hexagrams. The development of the hexagrams, which is also attributed to King Wen, enabled him to encompass the whole universe, to a relationship with the gods, and to define the condition of all beings. In short, Fuxi's invention provided a way out of the chaos and apparent confusion of the cosmos.

This transmission of the fundamental elements of the *Yijing* took place around 4000 B.C. It was necessary, again according to the Tradition, to wait a very long time—until the 12th century B.C.—for King Wen and his youngest son, the Duke of Zhou, to complete this work.

King Wen and the Duke of Zhou were the founders of the Zhou dynasty, the longest and one of the most brilliant in Chinese history. During his lifetime King Wen was known simply under the name of Chang, Count of the West. It was his son, the Duke of Zhou, who posthumously gave him the title King Wen, "the Civilizing King," the name that carried him into posterity. King Wen reigned as a wise and enlightened man over the fiefdom of the Zhou. He kept each person there happy and prosperous, but he also revolted against the brutality and tyranny of Dixin, the sovereign of the Shang dynasty of which King Wen was a subject. One day, Wen sighed over a cruelty of Dixin's, who subsequently threw the exasperated vassal in prison. There he stayed for two years, and made good use of his time, meditating on the sixty-four hexagrams and writing a short judgment for each one. After long negotiations and paying a considerable ransom, Wen was finally liberated. More and more praised and followed by the people, he was proclaimed king. Already aged, he died some time later, leaving Dixin to bring about his own decline through his continued savagery and depravity. It was Wu, the eldest son of King Wen, who finally annihilated the bloodthirsty Dixin and established the Zhou dynasty. Wu was quite old when he attained power. He soon died, leaving the kingdom to a son who was too young. That was how the Duke of Zhou, Wu's brother and the youngest son of King Wen, came to maintain the regency in a manner as wise and enlightened as his father's.

While he was sovereign, the Duke of Zhou set an example for following generations. He influenced and inspired Confucius for whom he was a model and to whom he appeared in dreams. He assured the political continuity of his predecessors and studied the *Yijing*, while composing a short expression for each of the lines of the sixty-four hexagrams.

The name of the trigrams and hexagrams, the judgment for each hexagram, and the statement for each of its lines constitute the text of the ancient *Yijing*: the Zhou Yi (the Yi of the Zhou). The Commentaries were later added to the Zhou Yi.
It is said that Confucius (551-479 B.C.) devoted the end of his life to the study of the *Yijing* to the extent that he wore out the thongs that held his copy together. He also compiled the Commentaries, regretting not having been able to meditate on this sooner. He felt that the *Canon of Changes* would have helped him avoid many errors.

According to the Tradition, it took more than three thousand years to produce the *Yijing* as we now know it. More familiar historical reference points in the West will give us another perspective: around 4000 B.C. (the epoch of Fuxi), an urban civilization in Mesopotamia was dawning. King Wen was a contemporary of Ramses IX; as for the century of Confucius, it corresponded with that of Heraclitus, Pythagoras, and Socrates.

The whole of this Tradition was created by the Han Dynasty (206 B.C.–220 A.D.). Two points are worth noting here: first, is the direct link between the origins of the *Yijing* and the beginning of the world (without this profound connection, access to the primary, universal laws of change would be impossible); second, that Fuxi, King Wen, the Duke of Zhou, and Confucius were the enlightened guides, sages who, with their knowledge and their experience, had nourished humanity during the transitional periods of Chinese history. Fuxi is the August sage of the dawning of humanity, King Wen is the civilizing sage who, with the Duke of Zhou, established an exemplary dynasty, and finally, Confucius, the "Master of 10,000 Generations," is the one whose teaching strives to extricate humanity from confusion and ignorance. This succession of wise men gives the *Yijing* inestimable value and a lineage that hearkens to the wisdom of six millennia.

This is the Tradition; the historical reality itself gives a less magical, but nonetheless interesting, version of this genesis.

From Bone to Yarrow

China is so large and its history is so long and convoluted that many of its episodes have been forgotten, even by the Chinese themselves, sometimes for hundreds of centuries. As was the case with the six thousand terra cotta soldiers surrounding the tomb of the first emperor—rediscovered after having been forgotten for more than 2,000 years—and with a library of archives from the Shang Dynasty (1765-1122 B.C.).

Medical preparations based on the powder of "dragon's bones" were circulating around the 1900s. No one cared about their origin, until a writer noticed archaic Chinese characters on a fragment of bone that was not pulverized. This was the first step which led to the location of a special library—a diviner's of the royalty court in the last Shang capital. This site was partially brought to light during the Yellow River flood in 1899, but it was necessary to wait until 1927 when; thanks to a series of excavations, more than 100,000 carefully conserved oracular pieces were discovered. These objects, the bones of cattle and carapaces of tortoises, date from the end of the Shang dynasty (from about 1350 to 1150 B.C.). Today they bear witness to the everyday concerns (social, cultural, political, and religious) of this dynasty and, above all, yield a new understanding of the development of the *Yijing*.

The diviners began by searching for answers on the bones (primarily the shoulder blades) of bovines. This practice probably derived from the observation of how the bones of sacrificial beasts were cracked by fire. Refining their technique and their objectives, the diviners later decided to use tortoise shells. The tortoise, whose life-span seems extraordinarily long, has a form analogous to that of the world: its dorsal carapace is round like the celestial dome, its ventral shell is square like the Earth delimited by the four cardinal points, and the animal in the center is like humanity situated between heaven and Earth. Thus comprised, the tortoise was the ideal receptacle of the mysteries and secrets of the world. In order to make it speak, the ventral part of the carapace was carefully worked to control and limit the appearance of cracks, for too many of them would render the medium indecipherable. After a long and meticulous preparation where only the shell was conserved, the diviners made a vertical incision on the inside and thinned it down in small ovoid zones. Then, they put a brand or a hot metal shaft to it so that they obtained five major types of cracks. The date of the consultation, the names of the consultant and the diviner, the questions and answers, and the reactions that they inspired were carefully noted on the carapace. All of this was then preserved. This mass of information was used both to verify the diviners' prognostications and to recognize their failures, in order to draw out some general guidelines for divination. These commentaries are the origin of part of the Ancient Text of the *Yijing*; certain annotations found on the Shang carapaces are identical to it. The diviners also elaborated a system of codes to identify the cracks more quickly.

The transition from bone to tortoise shell was an important step in the evolution of divination but the link which led to the use of cut yarrow stems was decisive. The yarrow, like the tortoise, was chosen because it was endowed with the principle of immortality. This notion of immortality is very dear to the Chinese for they consider it the result of fully realized wisdom. The yarrow is a lively and enlivening plant with formidable regenerative powers that can be used in herbal medicine internally as a tonic and externally as an antiseptic coagulant. Its vigor is also demonstrated by the fact that it is very common in many areas of the world.

Iulian K. Shchutskii[5] proposes that divination with bones and tortoise shell dates back to an age where hunting was predominant, while the technique using the yarrow blossomed at the same time as agriculture. This hypothesis is based, among other elements, on the fact that the development of agriculture settled and augmented social organization; yet the *Yijing* refers to rural life and a feudal political and social system, the first to bring structure to China. Other sinologs think that the yarrow replaced the tortoise after the latter was practically exterminated by the diviners' heavy usage.

Be that as it may, for a long time, important questions were settled by comparing the answers given by the two methods. Later, the yarrow method gained such popularity that everyone totally forgot its origins until the discovery of the bones and Shang carapaces.

[5] *Researches on the I Ching* (London: Routledge & Kegan Paul, 1980) pp. 110-111.

The yarrow divination technique is traditionally attributed to a great seer at the end of the Shang dynasty, Wu Xian, "the influential shaman." The yarrow leads us directly to the *Yijing* by the definitive adoption of odd and even lines and an oracular text. The whole procedure engenders a simple mechanical system, rich with possibility.

Having arrived at this stage in our account, it is time to discuss the archaeological excavations carried out between 1972 and 1974 at the Mawangdui site (the Tumulus of King Ma) in Hunan. The excavations involve three tombs, those of the Marquis of Dai, who was the first prime minister to the King, the marquise, and their son, who died at the age of about 30. They lived during the former Han epoch. The marquis died in 186 B.C., the son in 168 B.C., and the marquise died a little while later from a heart attack. These funerary chambers, in very good condition, have revealed extraordinary material. The sarcophagus of the marquise, composed of six coffins enclosed each one inside the other, revealed a remarkably preserved corpse, covered in a red embalming fluid. Her tomb contained, among other things, rare lacquers, fabrics, dresses of extremely light silk gauze (one of them weighed no more than 49 grams), musical instruments, and pottery. The son's tomb contained a number of manuscripts including the *Daodejing, Yijing,* and other works, notably on astrology, astronomy, geography, and medicine. The *Yijing* discovered in this tomb, a manuscript on silk, is the most ancient specimen known to us. It dates from the beginning of the Han dynasty and generally corresponds to the current text. The most notable differences are found in the names of some of the hexagrams, in the order of the hexagrams, and the commentaries, part of which has not yet been revealed to the general public.

Another discovery, made in Fuyang, in 1977, unearthed a manuscript of the *Yijing* that was composed of bamboo strips, and is a bit more recent than the one from Mawangdui.

Today, the examination of oracular pieces such as the silk and bamboo manuscripts continues, and all the results have not yet been divulged. Furthermore, things that seem evident to us today sometimes take a long time to be truly understood. Such was the case when, in 1978, the archaeologist Zhang Zhenglang, thanks to the Mawangdui manuscripts, made the connection between the enigmatic words inscribed on a Zhou tripod (from the King Wen dynasty, discovered in 1188 A.D.) and the hexagrams.[6] He discovered and demonstrated that these inscriptions were archaic representations of the hexagrams. As a result, different archaeological items are attracting new interest, since we now know that they, too, contained primitive hexagrams.

The Lines

In order to refer to and use the information stored on their oracular pieces, the diviners instituted a system of codes for identifying the different types of cracks. These codes were retranslated into lines and then placed one on top of the other in groups of six, forming the archaic hexagrams.

As we shall see in the third chapter, even today the hexagrams are determined by a numeric combination:

8: yin	— —	unchanging	
7: yang	——	unchanging	
6: old yin	—x—	changing, becoming	——
9: old yang	—o—	changing, becoming	— —

Because of the work of Zhang Zhenglang, we know that certain primitive hexagrams took into account the numbers 1 and 5, but sometimes 2, 3, 4 were replaced by 1 and 6 in order to avoid confusion in writing (the characters two, three, and four are written by the superposition of solid lines). It seems that this system of codes varied from one period to another and from one kingdom to another. It is impossible, at this time, to guess how the system developed, or to know whether it concerned the *Yijing* we now know or one of its variants.

We now think that the codes led to the appearance of the lines, and these evolved into the extreme simplicity of yin (even) and yang (odd). Parallel to this, the diviners abandoned fire in favor of yarrow, written references left the bones and tortoise shells in order to be inscribed upon bamboo (the ancestor of paper), and scattered annotations

[6] Zhang Zhenglang, "Shishi Zhouchu qingtongqi mingwen shong de Yi gua." *Kaogu xuebao,* 1980.4, 404-415. Translated as "An Interpretation of the Divinatory Inscriptions on Early Zhou Bronzes." H. Huber, R. Yates, et al. *Early China* 6 (1980-81), 80-96.

took the form of an established text. Only then could we speak of the *Book of Mutations.*

The Hexagrams

The hexagrams did not belong exclusively to the *Yijing.* According to the *Book of Rites,* there were successively three systems of divination that related to these figures: the *Lianshan* (beginning with Hexagram 52), the Guizang (beginning with Hexagram 2)—these two have now disappeared—and the *Yijing.*

Zheng Xuan (127-200 A.D.), a scholar from the Han period, points out that the *Lianshan* was used during the Xia dynasty (2207-1766 B.C.); the *Guizang* by the Shang dynasty (1765-1122 B.C.); and the third, the *Yijing,* or *Zhou Yi,* during the Zhou dynasty (1121-771 B.C.).

According to the Tradition, King Wen determined the current order of the hexagrams. The silk Mawangdui manuscript gives us another: 1, 12, 33, 10, 6, 13, 25, 44, 52, 26, 23, 41, etc. This last arrangement is based on a simple structure: each upper trigram (in the order: HEAVEN, MOUNTAIN, WATER, THUNDER, EARTH, LAKE, FIRE, WIND) is combined successively with eight lower trigrams as follows: HEAVEN, EARTH, MOUNTAIN, LAKE, WATER, FIRE, THUNDER, WIND; each new series begins with the double hexagram. However, we do not find any references to the trigrams, in the Mawangdui manuscript.

The current, more complex order of the hexagrams is based on paired hexagrams where one is obtained by inverting the other and, when this reversal does not bring about any modification (as in HEAVEN and EARTH), by the mutation of all the lines. Wang Bi (226-249 A.D.), an inspired philosopher who we shall discuss later, recommended this arrangement because it demonstrates transformation by through the turnaround of yin and yang. His reasoning was upheld by the generations that followed.

The last puzzle of the hexagrams is their division into two unequal books:

- Book I, hexagrams 1 - 30 and
- Book II, hexagrams 31 - 64.

This division is traditionally attributed to King Wen. According to the Commentaries, Book I touches upon all that precedes manifestation, or the foundation of the manifestation, while Book II describes principles of the manifest and social life. It is very difficult to identify this logic in the succession of the hexagrams themselves, or in the text.

Alice Fano suggests that this division can be explained by a presentation of the hexagrams frequently seen in Chinese works: the hexagrams are turned 90 degrees and aligned so that they can be read from two points of view.[7] This disposition, made of two groups of 18 hexagrams corresponds to the two parts of the *Yijing* (see page 287).

The Trigrams

Legendary accounts affirm that the trigrams preceded the hexagrams. Archaeology proves the contrary. In fact, the first archaic representations of the hexagrams date from the end of the Shang dynasty (circa 1350 to 1150 B.C.), while the first trigrams date from the beginning of the Han (206 B.C.), putting them more than eight centuries later.

Although we know nothing of the true origins of the trigrams, their appearance seems to coincide with the philosophical development that took form around the *Yijing* during the Han dynasty.

Moreover, it is not certain that, in light of this development, the hexagram had been initially envisioned as 2 groups of 3 lines and not as 3 groups of two lines. In the latter case, we have, with the union of two solid or broken lines, different states of yin and yang:

Old Yang: ⚌

Old Yin: ⚏

Young Yang: ⚎

Young Yin: ⚍

The tripling of these two lines corresponds to the symbolism of the tortoise with its division of Heaven, Man, Earth:

7 Alice Fano, *Les Mutations du Yi King* (Paris: Albin Michel, 1994) p. 107.

Heaven

Man

Earth

Easily understandable, and with a great wealth of symbolism, the trigrams, especially since the time of the Neo-Confucians, have enriched the message of the hexagrams. Their relatively late appearance makes them no less interesting; it is precisely because of the considerable value and numerous applications that diviners and philosophers found in the trigrams that the Tradition gave them historical precedence over the hexagrams. Now, the trigrams are some of the most frequently-seen Chinese symbols in every field of knowledge (notably medicine), even outside the limits of Chinese territory.

It is also worth pointing out that the names of certain hexagrams are phonetically identical. In order to distinguish them, in the spoken language, the Chinese commonly designate them by the constituting trigrams. This custom certainly contributed to the increased use of the trigrams, as did resorting to a table of upper and lower trigrams in order to find the hexagram or hexagrams obtained from consulting the oracle.

The Ancient Text

The "Ancient Text" as opposed to the "Commentaries," is made up of:

- the name of the trigrams and hexagrams;
- the judgments for each hexagram;
- the statements for each of the lines.

We have noted that this text is called the Zhou Yi, "the Yi of the Zhou," however some researchers have pointed out that Zhou can mean "universal," "complete," "circular." Also, the name of King Wen could be an echo of the appearance of writing, for it can be translated as "The Scholar King," or "Civilizing King." Zhou and Wen could then be associated with the *Yijing* without making reference to a dynasty or a sovereign.

Because the meaning of some ideograms have been lost and the historical references of the *Yijing* are not always identified, it is often difficult to determine the origin of all the elements of the Ancient Text. By and large, we think that it comes from sources as spread out in time—from about the 12th to about the 8th century B.C.—as in the range of derivative material (oracular pieces, collections of poetry, proverbs, etc.). This slow construction of the *Yijing* is also found in the names of the hexagrams. Of the 64 hexagrams in the silk manuscripts of Mawangdui, 29 of them have the same names we now know, and 35 are different. The names that were first attributed to the hexagrams initially had only an identifying role (the first word of the text belonging to the hexagram). Later, in the period when the trigrams appeared, some of the hexagram names acquired greater symbolic value.

The Commentaries

The Commentaries are traditionally attributed to Confucius, but this was contested from the 11th century A.D. onward. The main arguments put forth were:

- The content and form of the Commentaries are so disparate that it is impossible to attribute them to one man, or even to the same period.
- Confucius had always refused to write down his knowledge. His teaching was oral. What has come to us from him has come through his disciples.
- Confucius had many times declared that he did not wish to deal with anything that had to do with divination, the mysteries, or the beyond.
- The only reference to the *Yijing* made by Confucius is the following statement: "Give me a few more years, so that I may have spent a whole fifty in study or the *Yi*, and I believe that after all I should be fairly free from error." Unfortunately, the ideogram *Yi* is sometimes also transcribed in such a manner that it does not refer to the *Yi* in the *Yijing*, but to a *Yi* that means "also" or "again." Which gives us: "Give me a few more years, so that I may have spent a whole fifty in

study, and I believe that after all I should be fairly free from error."[8] This is more in line with Confucius' philosophy.

• According to the Tradition, Confucius studied his copy of the *Yijing* so much that he wore out the cords that held it together three times. The text in the Mawangdui manuscript also indicates that Confucius found a passion for the *Canon of Changes* at the end of his life. But how then can we explain that his disciples often cite the other Classics and keep quiet about the one that is said to have been their master's center of interest during the last years of his life?

It is highly probably that Confucius had none of the involvement with the Commentaries that the Tradition attributes to him. Nevertheless, in examining the historical evolution of the *Yijing*, it is possible to conceive that Confucius knew the *Zhou Yi* and had read it, if only for the interest that he had for the cultural legacy of the Ancients, but it is doubtful that he was interested in its oracular aspect.

The Commentaries, known as "The Ten Wings" (Cyrille J. D. Javary points out that the ideogram for "wing" gives the notion of aid, assistance[9]) are the vestiges of ancient works. Some of them have only partially survived. Of the Seventh Wing, for example, all that is left addresses only the first two hexagrams.

The ensemble of the Commentaries is by different anonymous authors, and was compiled between the 5th century B.C. and the 1st century A.D., and some parts of the Seventh and Eighth Wing predate Confucius.

Not all of these Commentaries have equal import. Among them, "The Great Commentary" *(Da Zhuan)*, also known as "Commentary on the Appended Judgments" (*Xi Ci Zhuan* or more simply, *Xi Ci*), has a particularly important role. It probably dates from the 4th and 3rd centuries B.C., and sets out the laws of yin and yang and those of the numbers. The *Yijing* owes it a good part of its prestige.

[8] Arthur Waley, in *Confucianism: The Analects of Confucius, Sacred Writings series*, Jaroslav Pelikan, ed. (New York: Book-of-the-Month Club/HarperCollins, 1992) points out that the Ku version of Book VII, paragraph 16 of the Analects (where this quote is found) introduces the reference to the *Book of Changes*, while the Lu version (on which Waley's translation of the Analects is based) does not. p. 126n3.

[9] Cyril J. D. Javary founded the Centre Djohi for studying and exploring the *Yijing*, and is the author of several books, including *Understanding the I Ching*, translated by Kirk McElhearn (Boston: Shambhala Publications, Inc., 1997).

It is also noteworthy that in the traditional Chinese presentation of the *Yijing*, the Ancient Text and the Commentaries are kept strictly separate. This rule has often been transgressed in order to group all of the information, no matter what the source, hexagram by hexagram. This arrangement has made life easier for many readers, but not, with reason, for the purists.

Contents of The Ten Wings

• 1st and 2nd Wings: "Commentary on the Decision" or "Commentary on the Judgments" *(Tuan Zhuan)*.

These commentaries develop the meaning of each of the 64 hexagrams and their accompanying Judgments or Formulas. The 1st Wing corresponds to Book I (Hexagrams 1 to 30), the 2nd Wing to Book II (Hexagrams 31 to 64).

• 3rd and 4th Wings: "Commentary on the Images" *(Xiang Zhuan)*, respectively the Great and Small Images.

The 3rd Wing (the Great Images) examines each hexagram by its constituting trigrams to explain the name of the hexagram and draw from it a line of conduct.

The 4th Wing (the Small Images) contains commentary on all the lines of the hexagrams.

• 5th and 6th Wings: The "Great Commentary" *(Da Zhuan)* or "Commentary on the Appended Judgments" *(Xi Ci Zhuan* or *Xi Ci)*. This commentary is divided into two parts, without any apparent logic. It reveals the philosophical basis of the *Yijing*.

• 7th Wing: "Commentary on the Words of the Text" *(Wen Yan)* or "Commentary on the Words and the Writings" *(Wen Yan Zhuan)*.

This Wing pertains to only the first two hexagrams. The text for the other hexagrams was either lost or may have never existed.

• 8th Wing: "Commentary on the Gua" *(Shuo Gua Zhuan)*, translated by Wilhelm as "Discussion of the Trigrams." The term *gua* (figure) can refer, in Chinese, to either the trigrams or the hexagrams. This Wing is composed of eleven chapters dealing with the trigrams and hexagrams, and in particular attributes to them a wide variety of symbolic images.

• 9th Wing: "Commentary on the *Gua* in Order" *(Xu Gua Zhuan)* or, according to Wilhelm, "Sequence of the Hexagrams." It justifies the order in which the hexagrams appear.

- 10th Wing: "Commentaries on the Gua in Disorder" *(Za Gua Zhuan)*. This Wing is incorporated by Wilhelm into the "Miscellaneous Notes on the Hexagrams" found in Book III of his translation.[10]

From the Chinese Empire to Louis XIV

More than 3,000 years after its birth from the oracular cracks, the *Yijing* collected, on the thread of its lines, experiences transcribed in the form of advice, predictions, poems, and historical and mythological references. Century after century, it was continually enriched by its internal structure, by magic squares and other reflections on the numbers and ideas in the *Yijing*.

In order to grasp the evolution of the *Yijing* and its enormous impact on Chinese thought, it is necessary to linger on an event that had an unparalleled political and cultural effect: the creation of the Empire. Before the Empire, China had a feudal regime comprised of more or less powerful kingdoms. Their sovereigns abandoned themselves in constant warring in order to conquer and absorb their neighbors. King Zheng (Kingdom of Qin, the origin of China's name) ended up the winner of this game when, in 221 B.C., he annihilated the last bastion of resistance, after having dominated all of the other states. He had no intention of dividing up his power and proclaimed himself emperor. He took the name of Qin Shihuangdi, thus reclaiming for himself the Three August and the Five Sovereigns: *Huangdi* signifies "August Sovereign," *Shi* "first," and Qin is the name of his native land.

Qin Shihuangdi (260-211 B.C.) immediately set about establishing a solid foundation for his empire: a powerful administration carried out his authority, he harmonized the currencies, weights, and measures to enhance trade and commerce, and he decreed the writing of the country of Qin as the official script. This last initiative, while politically and economically necessary, discouraged the comprehension of the ancient texts. In addition to this, following the advice of his closest counselor, Qin Shihuangdi ordered the burning of all writings that were deemed to be dangerous—annals, political, historical, and philosophical treatises—and he had all the scholars who dared to

[10] Richard Wilhelm, Cary F. Baynes, translator, *The I Ching or Book of Changes* (Princeton: Princeton University Press, 1967) p. xix.

infringe these interdictions buried alive. He also burned the books that he had authorized (agriculture, medicine, and other technical works), after they had been transcribed into the official script. The *Yijing*, only a modest book of divination, was not suspected of subversion and escaped total destruction. Even though these measures were severely enforced only between 213 and 207 B.C., considerable political troubles kept the books from reappearing until much later. Some of them were rediscovered, secreted away in walls, others were resurrected from the memory of the old scholars. Many were definitely lost. Because of the change in the written language and the disbanding and disappearance of the schools that had formerly handed down the oral teachings, during the following centuries there was no other solution than to transcribe the archaic characters into modern characters, leaving us with "interpretations" rather than "translations."

Although he was an outstanding politician, his contemporaries, was well as generations to follow, remembered Qin Shihuangdi's reign as one of misery, terror, forced work, and death. His evil, tyrannical, and megalomaniac spirit would not tolerate any limits to his power. On one occasion, furious that Heaven had not recognized his omnipotence, he desecrated a sacred mountain by stripping it bare and painting it red when a pilgrimage he made to it turned into catastrophe. Thousands of peasants and scholars lost their lives when he decided to construct the Great Wall; their bodies were walled-up in the edifice in order to increase its martial power. He also had a gigantic palace built for him where he walked about without anyone knowing where he could be found. The passageways were designed after the Milky Way, and the most influential families were forced to live there. To his temporal power he wanted to add immortality and it was definitely by consuming the "elixir" of one of the numerous magicians that surrounded him that he came to a brutal end, far from his palace, during an inspection of his vast empire. His remains were transported in a mad rush to the capital, proceeded by wagons of fish to mask the odor of his decomposing body. His funerary rites were revealed to have equaled his reign when in 1974, a farmer who was digging a well disengaged a clay head; this lead to the discovery of a terra cotta army, the one that defended the tomb of Qin Shihuangdi; and was forgotten by the Chinese themselves for more than 2,000 years. Of this army, standing in battalion formation, we have uncovered 1,000 soldiers. Ultrasound probes allow us to estimate their number at close to 6,000. Yet, powerful though he was, Qin Shihuangdi's dynasty did not survive him for very long. His son was confronted with general hostility and he was not up to the task of maintaining his succession.

The Han (206 B.C.–220 A.D.) were next to come into power, restore peace and order and, above all, create a common philosophy that conveyed an ideology which remained virtually unquestioned until the advent of Communism. In order to establish this cultural identity, Emperor Wou (140–84 B.C.) instituted the notion of "Classics" or "Canonical Books." He decided, to the detriment of the other schools, to favor the scholars—the Confucianists—and took as the Classics six works reputed to be fundamental in the teachings of Confucius:

The *Shujing* - The Analects;
The *Shijing* - The Classic of Poetry;
The *Yuejing* - The Classic of Music;
The *Liji* - Memoirs on the Rites;
The *Chunqiu* - Chronicles of Spring and Autumn in the Land of Lu;
The *Yijing* - The Classic of Changes.

After the upheaval of the first empire, it was necessary to relocate these books (which was accomplished, except for the *Book of Music*, which was definitely lost), to try to restore them to their original integrity, and to attribute official commentaries to them. When all of this was done, the books became required study for the high government officials. The number of classics varied from dynasty to dynasty: five in the Han, seven at the beginning of the Three Kingdoms, nine in the Tang, thirteen in the Song.

Alone among the classics to have escaped the wrath of Qin Shihuangdi, the *Yijing* was, until the Han, the only ancient text that was freely accessible. Because its structure and its language permitted all intellectuals to find within it a large amount of material to reflect upon, it is totally natural—even though it was never taught by Confucius—that it took its place among the reference works of the new empire. The Han had endowed it with a solid symbolic structure (with, in particular, the appearance of the trigrams), as well as an official history and identity. From this renovation, the study of the *Yijing* was articulated around two fundamental axes: divinatory and philosophical (the laws of change applied to the human condition), and cosmological (the *Yijing* as a representation of the universe). Thus, thanks to the Han, the *Yijing*—the most historically and ideologically contestable of the Classics—rose to the ultimate stature of "The Classic of Classics."

After the Han, political instability, the retreat of the Confucianists, and the expansion of Buddhism brought about a relative disinterest in the *Yijing*. It is nevertheless necessary to mention the impact of the young (he died at 23) and brilliant Wang Bi (226-249 A.D.). This Neo-Taoist scholar wrote great commentaries on the *Daodejing* and the *Yijing*, and his innovative spirit distinguished itself among the official versions. Wang Bi's treatise on the *Yijing*, the *Zhou Yi Lue Li* (General Remarks on the Changes of the Zhou), is the oldest treatise to be passed on to us intact. Much of his study was upon the metaphysical aspect of the *Yijing* and his works served as a reference for many schools.[11]

The Song dynasty (960–1279 A.D.), a period of great cultural development, saw the revival of Confucianism. During this epoch the philosopher and cosmologist Shao Yong (1011-1077 A.D.) developed a theory of the universe based on the *Yijing*. His reflection relied on metaphysical considerations and on a theory of numerals which inspired him to create a diagram that, seven centuries later, captured the attention of the German philosopher and mathematician Gottfried Wilhelm von Leibnitz. After Shao Yong came the Cheng brothers (Cheng Hao, 1032-1085 A.D. and Cheng Yi, 1033-1108 A.D.) designated by the name of Cheng Zi and, most importantly, Zhu Xi (1130-1200 A.D.) whose philosophy became the only one to be officially recognized, beginning with 14th century. This period formed a bridge between the ancient and modern texts, and it was during this time that people began to use coins for interrogating the oracle.

During the Qing Dynasty (1644-1911 A.D.) the Manchurian Emperor Kang Xi (1662-1722 A.D.), whose reign was the longest in Chinese history, had an important influence on the development of the *Yijing*.

11 See Richard John Lynn, translator, *The Classic of Changes: A New Translation of the I Ching as Interpreted by Wang Bi*. (New York: Columbia Univeristy Press, 1994).

Kang Xi actively favored trade with the West. He was passionate about mathematics and the sciences and appointed to his court knowledgeable Westerners chosen from among the Jesuit missionaries. This policy of cultural exchange was upheld by Louis XIV (1643-1715 A.D.) with whom Kang Xi corresponded. In 1715, the Emperor ordained the compilation of the *Zhou Yi Zhe Zhong,* "The Correct Arrangement of the *Yijing.*" This *Yijing* owes a great deal to the intellect of Zhu Xi and was drafted by a group of scholars directed by Li Kuangti (1642-1718 A.D.). It became the reference work for all the Western translations. The reign of Kang Xi in China and that of Louis XVI in France came to be the point of departure for and expansion of the *Yijing* in the West.

Fuxi and the eight trigrams.

How the Yijing Came to the West

In order to better evaluate the importance and the contribution of each version of the *Yijing* and its commentaries, it is important to understand the problems that the translators and commentators of the ancient Chinese texts encountered. There are three factors to take into account: the age and development of the Chinese language; historical uncertainties; the particular features of Chinese language and expression.

Translation Difficulties

*The Age and Development of the Chinese Language.*Chinese is spoken by the largest number of people in the world and its literature is the oldest. The only examples we have of writing that predate Chinese are Sumerian, which go back approximately 5,000 years, but all the languages that issued from Sumerian disappeared even before the Christian era. The oldest Chinese characters that we know of date back 3,500 years and the language that they convey, although certainly more evolved, still exists today. The *Yijing* is significantly linked to the birth of writing, the first traces of which show up on the oracular bones and Shang carapaces, and there certainly seems to exist a parallel between the graphics of the cracks and the appearance of Chinese ideograms. The inscriptions on the Shang oracular pieces are in no way literary, but sinologues were surprised to find a wealth of vocabulary in them. From these pieces, between 4,000 and 5,000 words have been inventoried so far, and about 2,000 of them have been identified.

In its primitive form, Chinese writing was composed of stylized drawings which have been found engraved on bones, metal caldrons, on coins, and stones (jewels, steles, etc.) When the Chinese traded the stylus for the brush and adopted writing surfaces such as silk, bamboo, and paper, they gave birth to calligraphy and enriched the variety of their characters.

The elementary Chinese word is a monosyllabic ideogram. It is associated with other elementary words, while keeping its original substance, in order to designate more elaborate ideas. These words are written with straight or curved lines; the most complex words contain more than thirty lines. The ideograms are far from being completely stylized drawings because as their meanings evolved to encompass more concepts, their forms became more abstract. There are about 30,000 characters in the Chinese language today, and it is necessary to master close to 4,000 in order to read a newspaper.

The last great reform in writing is very recent. It began in 1956 when the government of the People's Republic of China decided to simplify the writing and establish an official transcription for it in the Roman alphabet. Since then, the Chinese ideograms contain an average of five to six lines, which allows the composition of the same text with half as many lines than it would have required in 1956.

Historical Uncertainties. As we have seen, certain events, like the creation of the Empire—with its burning of books, persecution of scholars, and establishment of the official written language—had particularly disastrous consequences for the preservation of documents and directly affected the cultural heritage of the Chinese. Translators are constantly confronted by uncertainties that the complexity of Chinese history throws upon the ancient texts. Doubts over a historical reference, the ramifications of a word, of an expression, of a notion, are always there to complicate the process. The operative choices can be revealed as judicious or can be contradicted by new archaeological discoveries, by more careful cross-checking, or by a new understanding. This has already happened and will happen again to the *Yijing*.

The Particular Features of Chinese Language and Expression. The Chinese language dispenses with conjugation and declension, and relies on the context of the phrase to give indications of tense and number. It also does without punctuation. In ancient China, there was an oral tradition that was responsible for transmitting the rhythm that gave meaning to the written language. This tie was broken with the creation of the Empire, which left many questions in its place.

Our Western writing is phonetic, that is, it is written (in most cases!) according to its pronunciation. As for our vocabulary, its function is to designate strictly defined notions in the most precise manner. For us, a language is valued if it is rigorous both in its words and in its grammatical structure. Chinese writing, on the other hand, ignores sound but draws and creates images in referring to its sub-

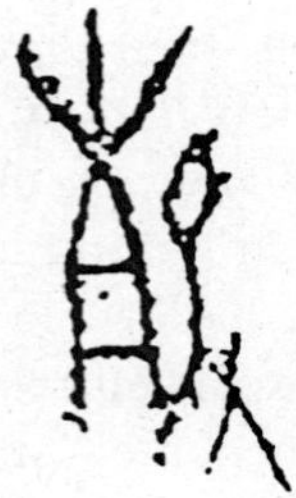

1

2

3

Fig. 1 Inscription on bovine shoulder blade bones (2nd millennium B.C.).
Figs. 2 and 3 Rubbings of inscriptions on metal, Zhou dynasty (11th–3rd centuries B.C.).

4

5

6

Fig. 4 Inscription on metal, Qin Dynasty (221–206 B.C.).
Fig. 5 Calligraphy of Chu Suillang, Tang Dynasty (618–907).
Fig. 6 Modern writing.

ject; the word is effective if it suggests and evokes. One Chinese word can include many meanings, whether or not it is used in the same context. Among these meanings, the translator must take a stand.

The evocative power of the Chinese word also inspires a style of expression that is full of imagery. The author does not seek to present an idea as a sort of isolated, abstract entity. He submerges the reader into a total representation of the situation. This prose often seems disjointed to us and very far from the obvious structures and rigorous demonstrations of which we are fond and in the habit of using. Thus the historical annals overflow with poetic themes and proverbial anecdotes—incessantly the same but put in the service of different causes—while the philosophical works are flooded with aphorisms. It is easy to imagine the inherent difficulties in translating a writing style that has such a wealth of imagery. The Chinese have themselves experienced many troubles in facing the complexity of their fundamental texts. This explains, in part, the profusion of commentaries in all genres.

Finally, we cannot discuss translation without approaching the delicate issue of phonetics. While the Chinese words are rich with meaning, their pronunciations are singularly close to each other, in spite of inflections which are also varied and difficult to transcribe. The phonetic transcription of these sounds has always posed many problems. In summary, here are some of most common phonetic styles:

The missionary alphabet: that of the first translations;
E.F.E.O.: phonetics of the French School of the Far East (L'École Française d'Extrême Orient);
Wade: Anglo-Saxon phonetics;
Pinyin: transcription of the People's Republic of China (the only one declared official by China).

Therefore "*Yijing*" can be written as:

Y King	Missionary alphabet;
Yi Tsing	E.F.E.O.;
I Ching	Wade;
Yijing	Pinyin;
I Ging	German phonetics;
Yi King	A compromise between the missionary alphabet and E.F.E.O.;

Yijing A compromise between the most common term in France (Yi King) and the Pinyin alphabet (*Yijing*).

This is only an example but it applies to the entire Chinese vocabulary. So one must be extremely vigilant, when going from one work to another, when determining whether or not two similar transcriptions refer to the same subject

In our time, the generalized use of Pinyin (which means "the spelling of sounds") greatly harmonized the system of spelling. Pinyin was officially instituted in 1958 by the People's Republic of China. It was recognized by the United Nations as the official transcription in 1979. Originally, Pinyin was put in place by the Chinese for the Chinese, in order to facilitate teaching their language to their children. Even though the spelling of Chinese names is made appreciably (but not definitely) easier, it does not really correspond to our pronunciation. Also, Pinyin uses five accents to indicate modulations that determine the meaning of the words. These accents disappear in most works because of the limitations of suitable typewriters and word processors.

In this book, I have used Pinyin, except for the names that are already anchored in our vocabulary, such as Confucius.

The Dissemination of the Yijing

It is difficult to understand China without referring to the Classics. It was therefore totally natural that beginning with the 12th century A.D., the *Yijing* gained the attention of the first missionaries who disseminated documents concerning the *Yijing* throughout Europe. Later, Father Joachim Bouvet (1656-1730), the mathematician and Jesuit missionary sent by Louis XIV to the Emperor Kang Xi, wrote: "This work [the *Yijing*] contains the principle of all sciences, and, put more precisely, it is a fully developed metaphysical system."[12] Thanks to Father Bouvet, the philosopher and mathematician Gottfried Wilhelm von Leibnitz (1646-1716) discovered the *Yijing* in 1701. Leibnitz had mastered Greek and Latin and studied theology, logic, and law, in addition to philosophy and mathematics. He was also a diplomat,

[12] From a letter in a dossier on Father Bouvet, at L'Académie des Sciences. Paris, France.

theologian, philosopher, and lawyer, but it was his mathematical discoveries that were claimed by posterity. Leibnitz's encyclopedic knowledge, theory of syncretism, and, above all, his research on a "universal characteristic" inspired him to closely examine the *Book of Changes*. He believed he found his true calling within it, noting that the hexagrams reproduced the numbers 0-63 written in binary code. He compiled a small treatise titled "The Binary System of the Chinese Emperor Fo Hi"[13] and proposed to Kang Xi the creation of a World Academy of Sciences.

Like Father Bouvet and Leibnitz, numerous thinkers searched for the common denominators between the Chinese and European cultures. This outlook, even though it was the cause of many misunderstandings, fostered a real desire to share knowledge. It is interesting to review those that marked the beginnings of the introduction of the *Yijing* in the West, knowing that the oracular aspect of the work was rarely put forward.

The first translation, into Latin, was undertaken by a Jesuit, Father Jean-Baptiste Régis. Completed in 1736, it was not published until a century later in Germany in 1834 (Volume 1) and in 1839 (Volume 2). The second translation, which was rendered in English, was that of Reverend James Legge. It was completed around 1855, but sunk into the Red Sea with the boat that transported it. Against all odds, it was finally retrieved and published in 1874. The presentation adopted by Legge corresponds to the 1715 Chinese edition.[14]

Paul-Louis-Felix Philastre, in 1881, published a French translation. In addition to the traditional text, it contained the Song dynasty commentaries written by Zhu Xi (Tshou Hi) and the two Cheng brothers designated by the name Cheng Zi (Tsheng Tse). This very interesting translation was reissued by Editions Zulma.[15]

The 1923 German translation by Richard Wilhelm was requested and supervised by a Chinese philosopher and descendant of Confucius, Lao Hai Hsuan (Lao Naï Souan 1843-1921), who Wilhelm respected as his "venerable Master." This version was translated into English by Cary F. Baynes, a student of Carl G. Jung, and was pub-

[13] This treatise also resides at L'Académie des Sciences.

[14] James Legge, translator, *The I Ching: The Book of Changes* (New York: Dover Publications, 1963). First published by Clarendon Press.

[15] Paul-Louis-Felix Philastre, translator, *Le Yi King* (Cadeilhan: Editions Zulma, 1992).

lished in 1950. The Wilhelm-Baynes translation saw its true fruition with the publication of the second edition in 1961, which included a preface by Jung himself, who lent it his knowledge and notoriety so that it received the attention that it deserved; this proved to be a success. With the help of Wilhelm and Jung, and carried forth by the Hippie movement, the *Yijing* was gently released from the circle of the initiated.

Today, in every discipline, works about the *Book of Changes* are multiplying. After the silence of the Cultural Revolution, international conferences and research groups were organized and gradually spread throughout the world. If, from the point of view of mathematics, the *Yijing* cannot be seen as a binary numeration, its combination of solid and broken lines nevertheless constitutes what Leibnitz was searching for: a universal language. It is a language that is useful in any field of application because it is so easy to analyze a hexagram by examining its internal rapport between yin and yang. The notions of dark and light, of feminine and masculine, of passive and active are comprehensible to the entire human species. That explains how the *Yijing* passes from one domain of knowledge to another, from civilization to civilization, and from one millennium to the next, becoming enriched by the nuances belonging to each science, culture, and epoch, without losing its identity.

Returning to the subject of the translations, new currents are emerging which are distinguished by the desire to rid the ancient text of the weight of too many commentaries. This is the point of view of *Le Yi King Mot à Mot*[16] by the Djohi Center work group and *Les Signes et Les Mutations*[17] by Wang Dongliang. Certainly, modern translators have benefited from recent archaeological and linguistic advances, but the older translations, such as Philastre's should not be overlooked.

[16] Centre Djohi, *Le Yi King Mot à Mot*, Collection Question de (Paris: Editions Albin Michel, 1994).
[17] Wang Dongliang, *Les Signes et les Mutations* (Paris: Editions L'Asiathèque, 1995).

Overview of Chinese Philosophy

Although it is hardly possible to summarize Chinese thought without altering its meaning and reducing its import, I shall try to give an overview of Chinese philosophy as it relates to the *Yijing*. "Confucianism" and "Taoism" may be somewhat familiar words, but what they encompass is often quite foreign to Westerners. However, for lack of completely grasping its profundity, perhaps we can get a general feel for the salient points of Chinese philosophy.

In ancient times, the Chinese had a multitude of gods linked to the different elements of their environment—water, stars, mountains, animals, etc. They tried to obtain the gods' good graces as well as those of ancestral spirits by attending celebrations (rituals, sacrifices, diverse offerings) some of which could only be conducted by the sovereign himself, the Son of Heaven.

Consequently, the religious sentiment evolved, but did not persist in the durable form of one god or a pantheon. It is commonly held that in China, philosophy had a place of importance comparable to that of religion in the West.

The Chinese rarely use the terms "philosopher" and "philosophy." They have "masters" who transmit a "way" (Tao), for Chinese philosophy concerns itself with the sharing and transmission of a way of life and wisdom rather than with elaborating theories or the foundations of concepts.

Generally, three elements characterize Chinese philosophy:

- *Concern over good government*

This was a major preoccupation of most Chinese philosophers. Many of them, at the peril of their own lives, intervened in the decisions of sovereigns and princes in order to counsel them or reprimand them. Naturally, the Confucianists tried this and so did the Taoists, but to a lesser degree.

- *A moderate interest in metaphysics*

The Greek and East Indian philosophers always had a great passion for metaphysics. The Chinese however, hardly concerned themselves with the creation of the universe or its primary principles; their conception of the world depended on a logic of correspondences and analogy. They searched to discover and prove the intimate ties that exist between the phenomena of the universe and those of humanity.

• *The union of humanity and the universe*

Sanctity cannot be disassociated from a total fusion with natural forces. The analogy that the Chinese philosophers drew between the cosmos and human nature inspired this fusion. This point of view had an important influence in the development of Chinese wisdom and medicine.

The official history of Chinese philosophy begins with Confucius. Ideas and masters circulated long before he did, but the lack of documentation and a Tradition that was very careful about historical appearances designated him as the first master. In any case, it was the century of Confucius and Laozi that determined the great treatises of Chinese philosophy; only the introduction of Buddhism and, much later, Western philosophy, broke this continuity.

Confucius and Confucianism

Confucius is the Romanized name that the first Western missionaries gave Master Kong (Kongzi) or Kong Fuzi (Kong was the family name of Confucius; Fuzi signifies "master" or "venerable master"). The term Confucianism ensued, but the Chinese refer to it as the School of the Learned Ones.

Of everything that is said about the life of Confucius (551-479 B.C.), nothing is certain. Not a single reliable document has survived time and many legends are attached to this personage. Tradition has it that he was born to a family of high nobility in the Shang dynasty. His father, governor of the land of Lu, was about 70 years old when he took an adolescent for his third concubine. She soon bore him a son, Confucius, but some years later, her husband died, leaving her destitute. Even though Confucius was a poor, young orphan, it seems that he was able to benefit from the solid education of the nobility. At 19, he married and had a son who died at 50, and a daughter about whom we know nothing. Confucius occupied different posts in the administration of the land of Lu. Everyone who met him was impressed by his great height (he was close to six and a half feet tall), his seriousness, and his desire to teach and restore virtue. In the course of his

Confucius (Kongzi), about 550-480 B.C.

Laozi (Lao Tseu), about 6th-5th century B.C.

travels he met Laozi (Lao Tseu) whom Confucius described as a dragon, such was the impression he made on him. Laozi counseled Confucius in moderation, modesty, and urged him to give up his crazy and unproductive ideals of peace and social virtues. Around the age of 50, either because of some political intrigue or because the values that he dispensed did not receive any response, Confucius exiled himself, abandoning his official duties. He then led, with his disciples, an adventurous and dangerous life, searching from one state to the next for a prince who had enough virtue to listen to and apply his teachings; this was in vain. He returned to his homeland only to die there.

During Confucius' lifetime, many masters wandered all over the country, highly educated noblemen who had lost their fortunes and influence as a result of the social and political upheavals that took place in China at this time. In effect, Confucius lived through the decline of the Zhou dynasty (the longest, and one of the most brilliant). In his opinion, only a return to moral values and a virtue similar to that of King Wen and the Duke of Zhou could restore order.

Confucius did not intend to found a school or a new philosophy. He felt he had a divine mission: to transmit the way of the ancient ones. He did not consider himself a sage but simply as someone who persevered without lassitude and taught others without discouragement. He was also, it seemed, the first master whose teaching was open to everyone.

Even though he attributed moral power to Heaven and respected the cult of the Ancestors, he kept his distance from all that was mysterious—spirits, divinities, destiny, etc. The Taoists often reproached him for taking into account only moral or cultural values, but for him, as for the Taoists, the true influence of the sage had no need of action, and the most profound teaching could not be transmitted through words. Something existed, inaccessible on the ordinary level, and could not be expressed through words, why speak of it? So he kept silent.

Confucius, without neglecting the classic texts of aristocratic education, liked to take occasions from everyday life to demonstrate practical wisdom. He was more attached to a concrete morality than to ideas. His teaching was flexible and adapted to the needs and capacities of his disciples. Not a single opportunity was rejected when it came to education, although Confucius' teaching method did give rise to occasional contradictory discourses.

To Confucius, it was essential to develop loving-kindness, uprightness, justice, equity, and respect for one's superiors and the elderly. One must be wary of base impulses, and value the rites of education. One must instruct and cultivate oneself and refine one's understanding and perceptions, never fearing to ask a question, even to one's inferiors. It was equally important to distinguish between justice and profit. Thus the superior being undertook an action if it was just and necessary, without being concerned for its success. The ordinary or inferior person was motivated only by the lure of personal gain. This explains Confucius' tireless work in spreading his message, even though his efforts were not rewarded.

Confucius ascribed considerable importance to community. If one's company was well-chosen, it aided one's personal development, fostered self-respect and the respect of others, and offered a thousand and one occasions to examine oneself. Confucius' Analects show that he knew how to make good use of the communal life that he led with his disciples.

The philosophy of Confucius could be described as a flexible, living, original, and confident wisdom. It was very far from the rigidity and dull conformity with which it was later vested.

Like the majority of the philosophers of his epoch, Confucius did not leave behind a single written work, but, belatedly, his disciples made a compilation of his talks, called the *Lunyu*, "The Selected Sayings" or "Analects" of Confucius. Along with many other documents, these Discourses were lost during the creation of the Empire, then reconstructed during the Han Dynasty.

Confucius had, in his lifetime, a renown sufficient enough to keep his teaching alive well past his death. Many of the princes that he encountered were impressed by his exceptional qualities and, unable to persuade the master to stay with them, included in their courts the best disciples who had studied with him. In this way, Confucius' teachings continued to be propagated. Among the numerous scholars that proclaimed his teachings, three are noteworthy: Mencius, Xunzi, and Dong Zhongshu.

Mencius (371-289 B.C.), which is the Romanized name for Mengzi (Master Meng), lived a century after Confucius passed on. Like him, Mencius descended from nobility and was orphaned at an early age. According to Mencius, the basic nature of the human being is good. We only need to develop, through appropriate education, our four innate qualities—compassion, shame and repulsion for evil, modesty, and a sense of right and wrong—for these generate the four Confucian cardinal virtues of kindness, equity, respect for ritual, and moral discernment. Mencius advocated traditional economic and social ideas while being careful to protect the peasants from princely tyrannies. He placed the sage above everyone, including sovereigns. A brilliant scholar, he composed seven works that were incorporated into the "Four Books" of orthodox Confucianism.

According to Xunzi (300-220 B.C.) human nature is predominantly evil, but intelligence renders us permeable to education that can improve it. In order to overcome our brutal and egotistical tendencies, we have recourse to music (which was always a favorite of the Confucianists, including Confucius himself), dance, and most importantly, ritual, of which Xunzi was a master. For Xunzi, heaven was no longer a moral power; it was the expression of the forces of nature (this belies the Taoist influence). The impact of Xunzi on orthodox Confucianism was more important and enduring than that of Mencius.

Nearly four centuries after Confucius, Dong Zhongshu (179–104 B.C.) played an active part in the establishment of Confucianism as the official doctrine of the Empire. He lived during the reign of Emperor Wou (Han Dynasty) and inspired him to choose his high functionaries from among the scholars, which were the Confucianists. This began the institution of entry exams for the mandarin, where, at the exclusion of other schools, the Five Classics were studied according to their "official interpretation." Dong Zhongshu was an erudite master. He adapted and propagated different theories that Confucianist defenders of the "ancient texts" would not accept:

- cosmology and metaphysics based on the Earth, Heaven, Yin, Yang, and the five elements (note that the theory of the five elements is absent from the *Yijing*);
- a mythical history where Confucius represented a dynasty ("a king

without a kingdom");

- an esoteric interpretation of the teachings of Confucius.

During this period, Confucius was endowed with the aura of a veritable god (miraculous birth, prophecies, extraordinary gifts, etc.), which had negative consequences for his teachings; the proverbial pendulum swung Confucianism into rigidity, conformity, bookishness, and preoccupation with ritual.

The 400-year reign of the Han (206 B.C.–220 A.D.) was followed by 400 years of great political and social instability during which Confucianism was eclipsed by Taoism and especially Buddhism. With the Tang (618-907 A.D.), Confucianism experienced a timid revival which only affirmed itself in the Song dynasty (960-1280 A.D.). This movement, called "Neo-Confucianism" by Westerners and "Daoxue" ("Study of the Way") by the Chinese, combined two currents of thought. Born of a reaction to the dual influence of Taoism and Buddhism, it forced the Confucians to expose themselves on their adversaries' terrain: metaphysics and cosmology. During this period, philosophers of great talent expressed themselves, and the *Yijing* generally occupied much of their speculations.

With the Manchurian dynasty of the Qing (1644–1911 A.D.) a more critical approach to the texts appeared, encouraged by the reigning emperors who preferred to see the scholars occupied with philological work rather than with recipes for good government. They denounced the apocryphal writings and reestablished what they could in the matter of dates and presumed authors.

One might be surprised by the considerable role of Confucianism in Chinese political and cultural life. However, Fung Yu-Lan explains, that what the West calls the Confucian school is in reality the School of the Scholars. The Scholars were not only thinkers but were also well-versed in the cultural legacy of the ancients; other philosophical groups in China could not offer such a synthesis. The Confucians taught the literature of the past and continued the great cultural traditions, thus giving them the best interpretation possible. In an agricultural country, where the people were respectful of the past, these scholars could not help but become the most influential group.[18]

[18] Fung Yu-Lan, *A History of Chinese Philosophy, Volume 1: The Period of the Philosophers.* Derk Bodde, trans. (Princeton: Princeton University Press, 1955).

Taoism

The beginnings of Taoism are difficult to pin down for we know practically nothing about the men and the works that were its source. While Confucius taught incessantly and worked unhesitatingly for the public good, the Taoists laughed at his efforts and advocated solitude and non-action. Several men are noted for originating Taoism: Laozi (Lao Tseu), Yangzi, Leizi, and Zhuangzi (Tchouang Tseu).

Laozi means "Old Master." He was old on more than one account: according to legend, he lived for more than 160 years and was born with white hair from having meditated in his mother's womb for 80 years. He had been the archivist at the Zhou court before he retired to the solitude of the mountains. He came to a mysterious end: leaving the kingdom on the back of a water buffalo (numerous paintings depict him this way), he wanted to embark upon a mountain pass. But the guardian of the pass, who was an experienced astrologer, had predicted the arrival of the Old Master. When Laozi arrived, the guardian begged him not to leave without giving him a final message. That is how Laozi came to dictate the text which would become a masterwork of Taoism, the *Daodejing* (Tao Te King). After he was done, Laozi continued on his way toward the west and disappeared forever.

The *Daodejing* (the "Classic of the Way and of Virtue"), in the form that we know today, could have dated from the third century B.C., but many clues suggest that a work of similar depth was in circulation before this date. Although we have numerous translations of it, the *Daodejing* has the reputation of being nearly untranslatable due to its complex and profound text.

Of Yangzi (or Yangzhu), we have only scattered commentaries. The dates of his life-span are completely uncertain, ranging from the 6th century to the 3rd century B.C., depending on whether one accepts him as a disciple of Laozi, a contemporary of Mozi (a philosopher from the end of the 5th century B.C.), or of Mencius. He is often noted for his individualism and pessimism.

Liezi had often been considered to be a purely mythological personage, but there is no more reason to doubt his existence than that of Laozi. His birth took place sometime around 450 B.C. He had been a disciple of Laozi and had attained such a level of interior realization that he was able to ride the wind. One of the classics of Taoism, the "Canon of Perfect Emptiness," is attributed to him. The name of this work was settled upon by a decree in 732 A.D. but the work itself dates from the 4th or 3rd century B.C.

After Laozi, the Taoist Zhuangzi (Tchouang Tseu ca. 363-286 B.C.) is the most well-known to Westerners. He lived in isolation and misery, refusing the honors and responsibilities that his renown attracted. He left behind a book that carries his name and that seems to be, for the most part, attributable to him. It is a very popular book and well-appreciated as much for its ideas as for its lively and snappy language (in Chinese!). Unfortunately, translations cannot render the reading pleasure that, according to all accounts, is offered by the *Daodejing* and the *Zhuangzi* in their original language.

There are many contradictions within the same Taoist work and among Taoism's different founders. However some general concepts can be drawn out.

First is the concept of *Tao*. The Tao is primordial, eternal, indeterminate; virtually impossible to define and name. All that is, is penetrated by the Tao. It is emptiness but everything manifests from and organizes itself by the Tao. This organization responds to invariable laws which give, to those who know them, wisdom and extraordinary powers. Among these powers is immortality; this is acquired by restoring and conserving vital energy, through the cultivation of longevity techniques. These special powers are illustrated by saints as well as centenarians such as Laozi, or by persons who are liberated from human constraints, like Liezi, who could ride the wind.

Among the invariable laws of nature, two should be remembered: "movement" and "return."

In the Tao, everything is movement and all movement is reabsorbed by the Tao. From this comes the power of the sage who rests in the Tao. Birth and death, for example, are part of these incessant fluctuations; they alternate, give rise to different forms, but do not have a pre-eminent importance.

Return, which is "movement of the Tao," is the principle according to which an energy grows, expands, and passes its point of balance and transforms into its opposite. The Sun arrives at its zenith and declines; misfortune succeeds fortune, but upon misfortune rests prosperity. This idea has had a considerable influence on Chinese philosophy in general, and on the *Yijing* in particular.

In order for a person to return to the Tao, solitary meditation is indispensable. It provides an escape from civilization and culture which can hide and deform the true simplicity and spontaneity of nature and establish distinctions where unity is necessary. In fact, civilization and culture multiply, to the great misfortune of humanity, knowledge and desires. For Laozi, there was no worse disaster than not being satisfied with what one possesses, and no greater fault than having the desire to acquire.

It is also important to understand action and non-action. Cultivating non-action allows one to avoid corruption and to diminish the demands, desires, and honors which would only abbreviate one's existence. A tree, whose wood does not interest anyone, can last 100 years, for the woodcutter does not even notice its presence.

The Taoist master does not intervene, yet he achieves everything. He rejects nothing and no one, and all beings come to him and are effortlessly enriched. Non-action brings about success for it does not counteract the true and fundamental nature of things. The Taoists recommended that princes follow this example, for imposing prohibitions and advocating virtue would only increase offense and pervert the people.

The Tao (which translates as the "Way") is universal, but there is also the *Te*, which signifies "power" and "virtue," the power inherent in the nature of each thing or each being. The Tao is that which is the most simple in the universe, the Te is that which is the most simple after the Tao. Human beings should not separate themselves from either the Tao or their Te.

After original Taoism came what Westerners call "Neo-Taoism" (3rd and 4th centuries A.D.). Two of the most remarkable philosophers of this epoch—Wang Bi (226-249 A.D.) and Guo Xiang (unknown-312 A.D.)—wrote commentaries on the "Three Books of Mystery" or the "Three Metaphysical Books" which were the *Daodejing*, the *Zhuangzi*, and the *Yijing*. For them, Confucius was a veritable saint, for he knew the Tao but refused to speak of it; he was "inwardly a saint, outwardly a king." He knew the relative and absolute truths, while Laozi and Zhuangzi were only concerned with the absolute. Not all of the thinkers of Neo-Taoism held this point of view but those who opposed it were not, for the most part, hostile toward Confucianism.

It was also during this period that the distinction between "philosophical Taoism" (which we just explored) and "religious Taoism" appeared. The religious Taoists organized themselves into monastic communities inspired by Buddhist models, mainly with the intention of slowing down the spread of Buddhist monasteries. Taoism took from Buddhism the notions of karma (the law of cause and effect) and reincarnation, while retaining and developing classical Chinese techniques such as the cultivation of longevity.

Finally, to conclude this section on Taoism there is an anecdote which illustrates the power of one who is in harmony with the Tao. It was an event that Richard Wilhelm witnessed.

The Chinese village in which Wilhelm lived was prey to an interminable drought. At the end of their resources, the villagers decided to call upon a "rainmaker." Upon his arrival, the old man got out of his carriage, sniffed the air with disgust, and shut himself up in an isolated cabin. He asked to be left alone and that his meals be left in front of his door.

Three days later, not only did it rain, but it snowed (never seen during this time of year). To Wilhelm's intrigued questions, the rainmaker explained: "You see, I come from a place where the people are in order—they are in the Tao; so the weather is also in order. In arriving here, I saw that the people were not in order, and they contaminated me. Therefore I stayed alone until I was again in order and then, naturally, it rained and snowed."[19]

The Tao

Up to this point we have only talked about the Tao in relation to the Taoists, but this word does not belong to them alone. Tao literally means "road," or "way."

[19] Jacques Castermane, "Au coeur de l'écologie, le coeur de l'Homme" (Lyon: *Revue Terre du Ciel* N°. 13, July 1992), pp. 15-19.

even further, in the calendars that regulated the secular and religious life of ancient China. Back then, the year was not divided according to astronomical indicators like the equinoxes or the solstices but according to seasonal rhythms. The flowering of a plant, the beginning or end of an animal's hibernation, and the migration of a bird were the subtle indicators of the seasonal changes. The notions of yin and yang arise from a natural and pragmatic classification, not from an abstract mental construct. The primitive definition of yang signifies that which is in sunlight and yin signifies that which is not in sunlight. Yang evokes all that is warm, light, active, and arduous, while yin refers to the cold, darkness, winter, and inertia.

In the *Xi Ci* (one of the Commentaries of the *Yijing*) we find the first metaphysical development concerning yin and yang. It served as food for thought for many scholars. However, in the most ancient texts of the *Yijing*, there is no mention of yin and yang but of Dark and Light, and later Yielding and Firm.

Here are some qualities that can be attributed to yin and yang:

YIN	YANG
Dark	Light
Earth	Heaven
Feminine	Masculine
Cold	Warm
Weak	Strong
Supple	Rigid
Substance	Essence
Dependent	Independent
Passive	Active
Rest	Action
Immobilization	Movement
Even	Odd
Interior	Exterior

It is important to avoid distinctions like good/bad, useful/useless or, especially with the *Yijing*, good luck/bad luck. A flexible and enthusiastic, or active and energetic attitude is never good or bad in itself. By

even further, in the calendars that regulated the secular and religious life of ancient China. Back then, the year was not divided according to astronomical indicators like the equinoxes or the solstices but according to seasonal rhythms. The flowering of a plant, the beginning or end of an animal's hibernation, and the migration of a bird were the subtle indicators of the seasonal changes. The notions of yin and yang arise from a natural and pragmatic classification, not from an abstract mental construct. The primitive definition of yang signifies that which is in sunlight and yin signifies that which is not in sunlight. Yang evokes all that is warm, light, active, and arduous, while yin refers to the cold, darkness, winter, and inertia.

In the *Xi Ci* (one of the Commentaries of the *Yijing*) we find the first metaphysical development concerning yin and yang. It served as food for thought for many scholars. However, in the most ancient texts of the *Yijing*, there is no mention of yin and yang but of Dark and Light, and later Yielding and Firm.

Here are some qualities that can be attributed to yin and yang:

YIN	YANG
Dark	Light
Earth	Heaven
Feminine	Masculine
Cold	Warm
Weak	Strong
Supple	Rigid
Substance	Essence
Dependent	Independent
Passive	Active
Rest	Action
Immobilization	Movement
Even	Odd
Interior	Exterior

It is important to avoid distinctions like good/bad, useful/useless or, especially with the *Yijing*, good luck/bad luck. A flexible and enthusiastic, or active and energetic attitude is never good or bad in itself. By the same token, nothing is entirely yin or yang. It all depends on the circumstance. For example, a man is yang in relationship to his wife, but he is yin vis-à-vis his superior or his elders.

Yin and yang oppose each other in a way, but they also alternate, completing and perfecting one another. Their true significance resides in the inner dynamic that joins them. That is how they reveal the process of transformation. One quality pushed to its extreme transforms into its opposite: destitution is the beginning of prosperity. The germ of yin is in yang and the germ of yang is in yin. Transformation is natural and easy, and not sudden and brutal, for all change is, in reality, the fruition of an evolution that began long ago, underground, inside. We can see this in the celebrated symbol of Taiji "The Supreme Ultimate," with its contrasting points in each of the two halves.

Destiny and Divination

According to the Tradition, when a king took the throne or abdicated, when a dynasty extinguished itself and another was born, extraordinary natural events manifested concurrently, for a person's actions, especially a person's virtue, had a direct impact on the environment. The sovereign who was called and considered to be the Son of Heaven did not have the unconditional support of his awesome Father. Pride, a weakened integrity, or inconsiderate desires could strip him of his "Heavenly mandate" and throw him in the deepest depths. In order to avoid such a disaster, it was the king's duty to dispel his doubts with the help of divination. The diviners therefore occupied an elevated position in the royal court and were invested with high and heavy responsibilities. They were revered as much for their virtues (they had to have pure hearts) as for their capacities. It was the duty of the diviners to clarify the twists and turns of divine will by analyzing anything that could serve as indicators. They had to understand the messages transmitted by Heaven and deduce the appropriate conduct. To this end, numerous divination methods were used, which the ancient Han classified into six categories:

1. Astrology
2. The almanacs (they enabled the determination of periods of warmth and cold and, therefore, life and death).
3. The five elements (their natures touched upon everything in

Taiji "The Supreme Ultimate"

The contrasting points visible in each of the two halves symbolize the germ of yin in yang, and the germ of yang in yin.

the universe and with a masterful knowledge of how they interacted, one could be sure of every revelation).

4. Divination by tortoise shell or yarrow (the most practiced by the sovereigns of high antiquity).
5. Diverse divinations, notably:
   – physiognomy, which was popular and frequently practiced around the 4th century B.C. and in the royal court around the 10th and 11th centuries A.D.
   – dream interpretation (used in conjunction with tortoise shell divination).
6. A system of forms (placement and disposition of houses, tombs, etc.).[21]

Sustained by their philosophical principles, the Chinese were in no way fatalists. They applied themselves to modifying the seemingly ineluctable by trying to reach an understanding of the demands of the times and act according. The diviners officiated so that their sovereigns could apprehend the will of Heaven and conform themselves to it. The Taoist sages transcended their human condition with wisdom and appropriate practices. The Confucianists developed what was good and virtuous so that inner influence gave birth to outer influence. This attitude was reinforced around the 4th and 5th centuries with the introduction of the Buddhist concept of karma, the law of

[21] Known today as Feng Shui.

cause and effect. The *Yijing* inspires us to sound-out the past and explore the present, rather than to divine a hypothetical future. With the *Yijing*, we do not have to be pawns, manipulated by our desires and contradictory tendencies; we can discover the harmony of the universe.

The Key Principles of the Yijing

The "Classic of Changes" reveals the immutable laws that govern the natural, inherent, and constant movement of phenomena. With this in mind, in order to survey the key ideas of the *Yijing*, we should define that which, in changing, does not change:

- Movement: in the Tao everything is movement and all movement returns to the Tao. Continuity is the fact that which moves, changes, and transforms itself.
- Yin and yang: everything always expresses itself in varying degrees of yin and yang, light and dark, active and passive, etc. But yin will always be yin, and yang will always be yang. Light will always be luminous, darkness will always be opaque, the sky will always be above and the Earth below.
- Return: In yin there is always some yang, and in yang there is always some yin. Yin and yang coexist. Yin calls yang and yang calls yin. That is why, when they attain their peaks, yin transforms into yang and yang transforms into yin.

We can add two other concepts that are constantly developed throughout the hexagrams. The first is that there is no change more profound and more important than that which ameliorates and develops character, for if one wants positive exterior effects, one must try to generate a true inner light. The second is the importance given to union. Everything in the universe prospers and grows because of union, that is why there is no worse obstacle than that which creates disunion or prevents reconciliation.

Within each hexagram reside veritable pearls of wisdom and meditation. If, for example, you want to turn your attention to the creative role of time, you could refer to Hexagram 1; if it is joy that intrigues you, Hexagram 58 will speak to you of its possibilities and limits. You can consult the "Succession and Connection of the Hexagrams" in the appendix to get an idea of the contents of each one.

Lastly, in addition to these fundamental ideas there are three key personages mentioned in the *Yijing*: the ordinary man, the noble man, and the sage.

• The little, ordinary, common, or inferior man is impervious to the *Yijing*. He lacks elevation or ideals. He sacrifices everything for his personal well-being and is hardly concerned for others, unless it is for his own gain. In the symbolic scheme, he represents something that represents an obstacle that hinders us from attaining our goal. This obstruction can be of an exterior nature, when circumstances or persons oppose us, or of an interior nature, when we lack wisdom, generosity, reflection, depth, etc.

• The noble man—also translated as the good man, gentleman, honest man, the superior man, or the accomplished man—is free of the base drives of the ordinary man, but still has not attained the freedom of the sage. That is what he wants, and that is why he allows himself to learn from people and circumstances. It is to him that the *Yijing* speaks.

• The *Yijing* was transmitted by the sages and the sage evidently does not need the *Yijing*. He is in the Tao. The law of changes is no secret to him. The sage is beyond the theater of this world; when he participates in it, it is only for the good of others, without being taken by any illusion whatsoever. Symbolically, he represents success experienced dispassionately, without falling into the traps of pride, attachment, or excess.

In speaking of "man," we are implying man or woman. The interrogations of the *Yijing*, even the most ancient, were conducted for men as well as for women, and touched upon political as well as domestic concerns. If there was any discrimination, it was rather at the social level, because initially the *Yijing* was reserved for the aristocracy. However, it was quickly democratized, and when the first Confucianists spoke of the noble man, they were talking about the nobility of the heart rather than that of rank.

CHAPTER II
LINES, HEXAGRAMS, AND TRIGRAMS

You do not need to read this chapter in order to consult the *Yijing*, but it will help you get a better understanding of the oracle and its complex responses.

The Lines

While most Chinese characters are written from the top to the bottom, the hexagrams are constructed from the bottom to the top. The physical and spiritual development of a person, like the growth of the yarrow, goes from the inside, the bottom, toward the outside, the top. The interrogation of the oracle comes from a person—from the earthly condition, below—in order to approach heaven above. As for the advice received, it allows the ordinary person, below, to discover and embark upon the way of the sage, above.

The Succession of the Lines

A hexagram is also read from the bottom up:
• An action begins, a person arrives, an energy manifests with line 1 at the bottom.
• An action is at its pinnacle, a person retreats, an energy dissipates with line 6 at the top.
This movement is often expressed by symbolic images such as the parts of the human body (the feet—line 1, to the head—line 6, as in Hexagram 31), the progression of the flight of a dragon (Hexagram 1), or a wild goose (Hexagram 53).

Hierarchy and Functions of the Lines

The Commentaries explain the succinct ancient text and elaborate the foundations of the hexagram lines' organization, which echoes the feudal hierarchy. Within it we find the high functionary, the minister, and the sovereign, or prince. To each function there are corresponding powers, capacities, and duties that are more or less contradicted or favored by the surrounding lines and the positions they occupy.[22]

In addition to examining a line according to its position within the hexagram, we can examine it according to its place in the trigram:

- The 1st and 4th lines, at the bottom of each trigram, are at the beginning of a renewal, positive or negative. Their positions are vulnerable.
- The 2nd and 5th lines, in the center of each trigram, have primary roles. They have an enviable freedom of action to the point where the other lines often seek to establish relationships with them, because of their favorable influence.
- The 3rd and 6th lines occupy delicate positions because they are leaving their respective trigrams. They conclude a stage and mark a transition.

1st Line/Place

The first line initiates movement. Here, everything begins and prepares itself.

This place is yang because strong inner determination is needed for the movement to be established upon sane and solid foundations.

Here, one needs to be extremely vigilant, for the first steps are always delicate, nearly dangerous, and they determine everything that follows.

Because it is at the bottom of the lower trigram, this position sometimes represents the intermediary who is the link between the people and the sovereign. The text of this line often advises prudence and vigilance.

2nd Line/Place

This is the place of the high functionary, of the official representative of the sovereign, the 5th line. Like the sovereign, it is in the center of its trigram. Although this position gives it a degree of autonomy and capacity for action, this line must keep the princely directives of the 5th line in mind, because it still only occupies the lower trigram.

This position is yin because the high functionary must efface himself before his sovereign. This subordination necessitates adaptation, flexibility, self-control and self-sacrifice all the more so because the

[22] The personification of graphic symbols may seem strange to Westerners, but if you can think of the lines as alive with yin or yang personalities or functions, you will get a better understanding of their meanings and the implications of their relationships within the hexagram as well as how they relate to your situation.

high functionary is geographically isolated from the sovereign. This line is often favorable.

3rd Line/Place

This line is on the frontier of the lower and upper trigrams. It marks the passage from the interior, lower trigram, to the exterior, upper trigram. This position is critical because, at this pivotal moment, it is easy to leave the true path. If one has strayed, one must immediately regain the correct path. This determination to go toward good relates to the yang quality of this position. This highly risky position is often unfavorable.

4th Line/Place

This is the place of the minister. It is a position that is appreciated for the possibilities it can foretell, but it is also a delicate one because of its direct contact with the great power of the sovereign. This proximity to high risk impedes independence and initiative and amplifies the effect of the smallest action. Impropriety carries heavy consequences, and successes must be received with humility in order to avoid offending the prince.

This is often a positive line, the text of which contains a warning, for it is also, like the third line, at the boundary of the two trigrams.

This position is Yin, for a good minister must be prudent and bring the sovereign discrete, open-minded, and effective help.

5th Line/Place

This line represents the sovereign. It is generally the most favorable position in the hexagram. At this stage, the situation is in full bloom, bearing its fruit. This place is yang for here, the strength and enlightenment that the sovereign has acquired through his position and personal qualities are actively manifested.

The sovereign is the Son of Heaven. His caliber is great but so are his obligations. The Classic of History states that the five benefits that a sovereign must dispense to his people are: health and longevity; wealth; peace; the maintenance of excellent virtues; and total fulfillment of each person's lot in life!

6th Line/Place

At this stage, the dynamic process represented by the hexagram reaches its finale. Two outcomes are possible: that of the fool who has lost his way through his own fault, or that of the sage, liberated and detached. This position is Yin, for in both cases action is no longer called for. The sage has no need to intervene to manifest his realization for the good of others. The fool, since he could not correct himself in time, must not move because of the risk of getting himself into deeper trouble.

All the lines occupy the ideal position in Hexagram 63, After Order. Its opposite is Hexagram 64, Before Order. Contrary to what one might imagine at first sight, the judgment for Hexagram 64 is more favorable than that for Hexagram 63 because when all is perfect, things break down so they can be renewed, and the cycle goes on forever.

Relationships Between the Lines

As we shall see, each line relates in varying degrees to the others. The relationship can either compensate for deficiencies or accent certain tendencies toward excess. In any case, these relationships explain how a weak line can, in the end, show itself as strong, or conversely, how a line in a critical position can sometimes receive unexpected, positive help.

Most of these relationships are based on mutual cooperation but there are some rivalries. When one line does not relate to any of its fellow lines, this is usually a bad sign, for isolation leads to stagnation. However, isolation is favorable when nothing can be done and when it keeps the luminous principle beyond the reach of the dark principle.

The relationships between the lines are codified. They may depend on similarities between the positions of the lines. The lines that have the same position within their trigrams have analogous functions. This complicity arouses mutual helpfulness, especially when, in these pairings, a yang position is associated with a yin position:

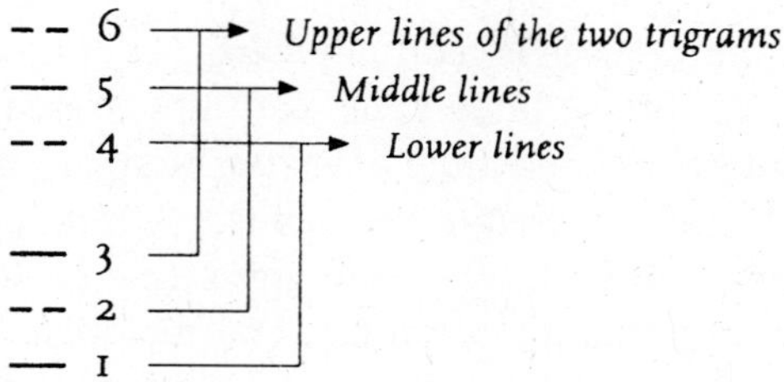

Neighboring lines also have close exchanges. They can cooperate with and lean on one another. However, a yin line can place itself on top of a yang line only when the urgency of the situation justifies it.

Generally, all relationships between the lines are possible, and their repercussions will depend on the hexagram in which they are situated. The most frequent and influential are naturally those established with the sovereign, the 5th line.

We cannot, in the scope of this book, study the interactions between the lines in detail. They are complex and vary from hexagram to hexagram. Those of you who wish to go deeper into this subject can refer to the translation by Philastre and to Jean-Philippe Schlumberger's book *Yi King—Principes, practique et interpretation published* by Editions Dangles.[23]

Qualities of the Lines and Mutations

The *Yijing* is built upon two lines—solid and broken. Richard Wilhelm thought that the differentiation between the solid and broken lines of the *Yijing* reflects the simplest responses:

Yes ——, the yang line
No – –, the yin line

When a hexagram is cast, each line, yin or Yang, will occupy a weak (Yin) or a strong (Yang) place in the hexagram. If the 5th line is Yin, we have a weak (Yin line) sovereign (5th place) in a strong position,

[23] For English readers, see *The Complete I Ching: The Definitive Translation by the Taoist Master Alfred Huang* (Rochester, VT: Inner Traditions International, 1998). This translation is especially valuable for his explanation of the relationships between the hexagram lines, or *yao*.

since the 5th place is naturally Yang.

The quality—Yin or Yang—of the line cast and its suitability with the yin or yang attribute of its position, are not intrinsically good or bad. A weak sovereign can be positive if it benefits from the support of strong lines (as in Hexagram 14), or if the general situation demands flexibility, humility, and diplomacy. On the other hand, a yang line in a yang place could introduce excess energy to the detriment of the harmonious progress of events.

A line, once it has arrived at its peak, transforms itself into its opposite; it undergoes a transformation:
The yang line (7, ——), when it becomes "Old Yang"
(9, –o–), changes into yin (– –).
The yin line (8, – –), when it becomes "Old Yin"
(6, –x--), changes into yang (——).

The changing lines, or "mutations," emphasize the most important aspects of the situation, and are thus crucial. You should pay special attention to them.

The transformation can be fortunate, neutral, or dangerous, according to the position that the line occupies and the hexagram in which it is inscribed.

When there is a mutation, old yang (9) loses its initiative and power while it gains in receptivity and gentleness. Old yin (6) undergoes the opposite process.

The Hexagrams

The Succession of the Hexagrams

We have seen, in the first chapter, that the order in which the hexagrams follow each other in the *Yijing* is based on paired hexagrams; the second hexagram is obtained by inverting the first. When the inversion does not bring about any modification, then all of the lines mutate. For example:

N°1 Heaven

䷀

N°2 Earth

䷁

N°27 Nourishment

䷚

N°28 The Great in Excess

䷛

N°29 Danger

䷜

N°30 Clarity

䷝

N°61 Inner Confidence

䷼

N°62 The Small in Excess

䷽

This sequence emphasizes the principle of "return," when a culminating principle changes itself into its opposite. However, the question of why one pair of hexagrams follows another remains unanswered. However, the Tenth Wing (Za Gua Zhuan) of the Commentaries gives, *a posteriori*, a brief but interesting philosophical explanation of the passage of one figure to the next (see page 114, "The Sequence and Connection of the Hexagrams").

Rulers of the Hexagrams

When a line has a position and quality that holds a preponderant role in a hexagram, it is called the "ruler" of the hexagram.

There are two types of rulers: constituting and governing. The constituting rulers can be good or bad and can often be detected by examining the "constitution," itself, of the hexagram. For example, a single yin line in a hexagram (such as Hexagram 9) is the constituting ruler because it has a determining role in the physical makeup of the hexagram. Whether or not it is adapted to the situation has no importance. The governing rulers "govern" because they are at the right place at the right time, with good qualities (for example, the 6th line of Hexagram 36). Governing rulers can be discerned by examining the overall meaning and composition of the hexagram.

Each hexagram can have from one to two constituting and governing rulers. More often the two types of rulers are mixed but Hexagram 42, Augmentation, has four rulers: two governing and two constituting.

Design of the Hexagrams

A culture founded on figurative script cannot help but be sensitive to the visual design of some of the hexagrams. Some hexagrams have particularly eloquent forms that reveal their general meanings. For example, Hexagram 27, Nourishment recalls the image of an open mouth. Its symbolism revolves around the manner in which a person finds nourishment and nourishes others, physically and spiritually. In Hexagram 20, Contemplation, we can see the image of a tower, in Hexagram 21, Cutting Through Separation, a line blocks the closing of a mouth, in Hexagram 23, Usury, the roof of a house threatens to collapse, in Hexagram 50, Cauldron, the first and fifth lines recall its feet and handles.

Hexagrams and Timing

Those of you who wish to determine the date of an event can look to the twelve hexagrams that correspond to the twelve months of the Chinese year. These hexagrams illustrate the different stages of the arrival and departure of light and dark (see Table 2.1).

• The yang line represents light. It is at its maximum intensity (6 yang lines) at the moment of the Summer solstice (fourth Chinese month or May-June).

• The yin line represents darkness, the maximum of which is attained at the Winter solstice (tenth Chinese month or November-December).

• The two hexagrams of the equinoxes are: Hexagram 11, Prosperity, for the Vernal equinox, when Earth in the upper trigram, and Heaven in the lower trigram encounter one another and favor growth. At the Autumnal equinox, everything freezes, bringing Decline, Hexagram 12, when Heaven in the upper trigram and Earth in the lower trigram become more and more distant from one another.

Table 2.1. The Chinese and Western Months and Corresponding Hexagrams

Hexagram	*Chinese Month*	*Western Month*
䷊ N° 11 Prosperity	1st	February/March
䷡ N° 34 Great Strength	2nd	March/April
䷪ N° 43 Resolution	3rd	April/May
䷀ N° 1 Heaven	4th	May/June
䷫ N° 44 Approach of the Malleable	5th	June/July
䷠ N° 33 Retreat	6th	July/August
䷋ N° 12 Decline	7th	August/September
䷓ N° 20 Contemplation	8th	September/October
䷖ N° 23 Usury	9th	October/November
䷁ N° 2 Earth	10th	November/December
䷗ N° 24 Return of the Light	11th	December/January
䷒ N° 19 Benevolent Attention	12th	January/February

The Chinese year does not correspond exactly to the Western year. Our calendar is calculated exclusively on the progress of the sun, of which the four most powerful moments are the two solstices and the two equinoxes. The Chinese calendar is luni-solar, based on the cycle of the Moon (twelve lunations of about twenty-nine days), to which the Chinese periodically add, in order to keep the solar year, a thirteenth month. Therefore, if you want to use the table above with exactitude, you would need to verify, for the year in question, the precise dates of the months. This information can be found in any good Chinese astrology book. However, since the Chinese calendar repositions itself on the course of the sun in order to follow the rhythm of the seasons, we can also dispense with the Chinese calendar by adapting the twelve hexagrams to our twelve months. That would give us the correspondences illustrated in Table 2.2.

The trigrams of the *Yijing* can also be synchronized with our 24-hour cycle:

☰ HEAVEN *Noon* *South*

☱ LAKE *Approx. 9:00 a.m.* *Southeast*

☴ WIND *Approx. 3:00 p.m.* *Southwest*

☲ FIRE *Approx. 6:00 a.m.* *East*

☵ WATER *Approx. 6:00 p.m.* *West*

☳ THUNDER *Approx. 3:00 a.m.* *Northeast*

☶ MOUNTAIN *Approx. 9:00 p.m* *Northwest*

☷ EARTH *Midnight* *North*

Table 2.2. The Hexagrams and the 12 Months

Month	*Hexagram*
January	䷗ N° 24 Return of the Light
February	䷒ N° 19 Benevolent Attention
March	䷊ N° 11 Prosperity
April	䷡ N° 34 Great Strength
May	䷪ N° 43 Resolution
June	䷀ N° 1 Heaven
July	䷫ N° 44 Approach of the Malleable
August	䷠ N° 33 Retreat
September	䷋ N° 12 Decline
October	䷓ N° 20 Contemplation
November	䷖ N° 23 Usury
December	䷁ N° 2 Earth

Noon and midnight are fixed astronomical references, the others are variable, in our latitudes, according to the seasons. The sun rises at 6:00 a.m. and sets at 6:00 p.m. at the Vernal and Autumnal equinoxes. If you would like to be even more precise, you could also take into account the difference between the solar hour, indicated by the position of the sun, and the legal hour. In the United States, you have to take into account which time zone you are in.

The Trigrams

A wealth of literature has developed around the eight trigrams, dealing with the relationship and interaction between the trigrams, and then philosophical, medical, and cosmological applications, etc. Here, we shall limit ourselves to the essential concepts that will help us better understand the answers of the oracle, using three categories of symbolism:

- the rapport between the yin and yang lines;
- the natural element (heaven, wind, water, etc.) attributed to each trigram;
- the trigram's correspondence with the members of the nuclear family. We have seen how the lines of a hexagram relate to social organization; here's how the familial organization is portrayed by the trigrams:

The Father:		Heaven	☰
The Mother:		Earth	☷
The Sons:	- *Eldest*	Thunder	☳
	- *Middle*	Water	☵
	- *Youngest*	Mountain	☶
The Daughters:	- *Eldest*	Wing	☴
	- *Middle*	Fire	☲
	- *Youngest*	Lake	☱

The father and mother are the generative trigrams, indispensable to one another. The sons, because of their male nature—yang—manifest a certain independence while the daughters—yin—follow movement. The youngest defer to the oldest, and the sisters defer to the brothers.

The single yang line of the son trigrams is found: on the bottom of the trigram for the eldest; in the center for the middle; and for the youngest on top. The single yin line of the daughter trigrams follows the same pattern.

It may seem surprising that the numeric minority should determine the "sex" of the trigrams, but in the hexagrams, the minority rules; when a line is in the minority, its role is the determining one.

Symbolism of the Eight Trigrams

HEAVEN ☰

The Chinese name of this trigram can be translated as: Heaven, sovereign, man.

Its image is *Heaven.*

Its three yang lines are strong, firm, luminous.

Heaven represents strength, virtue, integrity, justice, and luminous qualities. It is the time in which change is inscribed.

In ordinary people, *Heaven* is hardness of character and stubbornness.

EARTH ☷

The Chinese name of this trigram can be translated as: *Earth,* woman, obedience, repose.

Its image is *Earth.*

Its three lines are yin, weak, malleable, dark.

Earth is self-sacrifice, suppleness, equanimity, submission, maternal and nourishing values.

In ordinary people, *Earth* is passivity which becomes laziness and indulgence of his or her faults.

THUNDER ☳

The Chinese name of this trigram can be translated as: shock, earthquake, disruption, movement, lightning flash, a clap of thunder.

Its image is *Thunder.*

A single strong and luminous yang line arrives: *Thunder* is movement. It chases away darkness—the two yin lines—and pushes it aside with such force that everything trembles.

Thunder is also called the Arousing. Its formidable rumbling spreads terror around for miles, but the fear that it causes inspires us to check the uprightness of our intentions and actions. *Thunder* chases away torpor; it is impulse and activation.

Thunder is also associated with the image of thunderbolts or lightning; it is the spark that ignites explosives.

In the familial hierarchy, *Thunder* is the eldest son. After the parents, he has the most power and responsibility.

In ordinary people, *Thunder* is hastiness, excessive excitement, or, on the other side of the coin, the fear that immobilizes body and spirit.

WIND ☴

The Chinese name of this trigram can be translated as: submissive, docile.

Two images are used to describe this trigram: *Wind* and *Wood.* *Wind* is the dominant image but Wood appears in a series of hexagrams (Hexagrams 28, 46, 48, 50, 53).

The point in common between *Wind* and *Wood* is gentle penetration. *Wind* penetrates by blowing about and infiltrating everything, wood plunges its roots into the earth while unfurling its foliage in the sky. This penetration is synonymous with expansion and in order for this process to occur and bear fruit, it takes time, patience, and perseverance.

In this trigram, with the single, weak, yang line, darkness arrives and is confronted by two strong, luminous yang lines. Wind represents the gentleness (yin) that can penetrate and gradually dissolve rigidity (yang), as well as gentleness in character and means employed against rigid exterior and interior obstacles such as rudeness, and egotism.

In ordinary people, *Wind* is indifference and indecision that impedes the completion of an endeavor.

WATER ☵

The Chinese name of this trigram can be translated as: abyss, precipice, pit, brutal captivity.

Its image is *Water.*

The solitary strong line, yang, is in the middle of the negative yin lines. The light is right in the middle of darkness, and that is very dangerous.

Water represents danger—an unfathomable danger—but it also possesses the means for escape. *Water* flows without tiring, filling all the holes, wearing down all the rocks. It takes its time to overcome obstacles so that it can continue on its way. That is why it symbolizes a persevering and patient character, as well as a profoundness which leaves nothing to hazard.

Water is a vital element. It is therefore associated with food, drink, and all that is materially or spiritually nourishing. This trigram also symbolizes the refreshingly beneficial rain that liberates tensions accumulated before the storm.

In ordinary people, *Water* represents inner gloominess as well as being stubborn and entrenched in bad habits.

FIRE ☲

The Chinese name for this trigram can be translated as: to set apart, to meet.

Its image is *Fire*, but sometimes it is also the sun or lightning.

The single yin line in the center clings to the strong yang lines enclosing it. This is the image of a flame that lives off its fuel.

The image of *Fire* reminds us that we depend on the beings and ideas to which we cling. We must recognize this dependence and its importance in order to adapt our behavior, for unless we embrace luminous values that endure with a steady radiance, we will quickly burn out like straw fires.

Fire is also intelligence that enlightens everything, leaving nothing in shadow. It distinguishes the value, quality, and function of things and beings. The clarity of *Fire* shows the escape route away from confusion and amalgamations. It favors order as well as the expansion of good and repression of evil.

In ordinary people, intelligence leads to excess examination, criticism, and suspicion.

MOUNTAIN ☶

The Chinese name of this trigram can be translated as: immobile, steadfast, firm.

Its image is the *Mountain*, which can be easily seen in the graphic design of the trigram.

The solitary yang line has arrived at the summit of the trigram and dominates the other weak yin lines. Because it has nowhere further or higher to go, the line is naturally immobilized.

This immobilization is in harmony with the times. It is the calm, closure, and tranquillity that provides shelter from physical and mental agitation, and holds back precipitation and hesitation born of doubt.

The *Mountain*, covered with sparkling snow, symbolizes purity and the radiance of a well-rooted personality.

In ordinary people, *Mountain* is inertia, rigidity, lack of cooperation, and the inability to adapt. It is also anger which rises as high as the *Mountain* but can be frozen by its own immobility.

LAKE ☱

The Chinese name of this trigram can be translated as: exchange.

Its image is the *Lake* but also the Cloud or the mists that rise from the lake.

Two yang lines, strong within the trigram—that is, at the bottom—outwardly manifest as gentleness, joy, and serenity represented by the weak yin line above.

Lake or Cloud symbolizes sweetness and joy. These are not trivial qualities; they are the peaceful and soothing expression of veritable inner strength. Joy is tonifying and stimulating, for it drives along enthusiasm and cooperation. With joy, even heavy burdens become easy to bear.

The water of *Lake* has a fertilizing action. That is why *Lake* is associated with the mouth, the speech through which joy is expressed, and the knowledge that nourishes and elevates humanity.

In ordinary people, joy does not have the benefit of inner strength and becomes a sudden emotion that causes loss of self-control and wounds the heart with desires and passions.

Upper and Lower Trigrams

A hexagram can be read by looking at the placement of its six lines or its two trigrams:

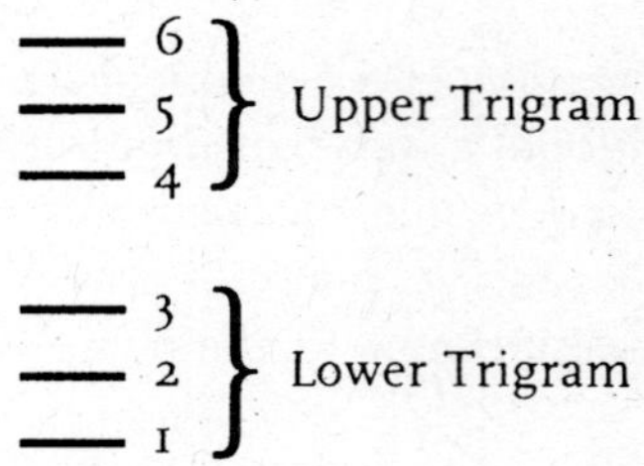

The following attributes correspond to each trigram:

Upper Trigram	*Lower Trigram*
Leaving	Arriving
Above	Below
Ahead	Behind
Outside	Inside

These functions determine how the hexagram can be read. For example:

Hexagram 4 IMMATURITY:
Upper trigram *Mountain*
Lower trigram *Water*

Water, in the lower trigram, springs forth from the foot of the Mountain, the upper trigram. Here the danger (Water) is within (lower trigram). In order to face this danger, one must be inwardly (lower trigram) persevering (one of the qualities of Water), and outwardly (upper trigram) calm (Mountain).

If we switch these two trigrams, we have Hexagram 39, OBSTACLE:

Upper trigram *Water*
Lower trigram *Mountain*

Water is blocked and accumulates at the summit of the Mountain. The obstacle is outside—*Water* in the upper trigram—so one must be inwardly calm (lower trigram *Mountain*) and outwardly persevering (upper trigram *Water*).

Even though the Commentaries do not analyze all the hexagrams by their constituting trigrams, you can easily do this yourself, for the symbolism is very easy to work with.

Movement of the Eight Trigrams

Each of the eight trigrams is animated with a natural movement: ascending, descending, penetrating, immobilizing.

The upper and lower trigrams also have movement: ascending for the upper trigram and descending for the lower trigram.

The combination of these movements determines the degree of fusion or repulsion between the two constituting trigrams of a hexagram.

HEAVEN : Rising ↑
EARTH : Descending ↓
THUNDER : Rising ↑
WIND : Rising and penetrating ↖↑↗
WATER : Descending ↓
FIRE : Rising ↑
MOUNTAIN : Immobilizing and pushing down ⤓
CLOUD/LAKE : Rising (the Cloud or the Mist rises from the Lake) ↑

Example: Hexagram 12 DECLINE:

Upper trigram *Heaven* ☰
Lower trigram *Earth* ☷

The natural, ascending movement of *Heaven* is amplified by its superior position in the trigram: *Heaven* rises higher and higher. *Earth* and its naturally descending movement is amplified in the lower trigram. In this configuration the two trigrams become further distant from one another. Separation is accentuated and prohibits exchange or understanding, leading to DECLINE.

On the other hand, with an upper trigram of *Earth* and a lower trigram of *Heaven*, we have PROSPERITY (Hexagram 11):

䷊

Heaven has a naturally rising movement and therefore it elevates itself from the lower trigram. *Earth*, naturally descending, escapes from the upper trigram in order to descend toward Heaven. In this way, the two elements meet each other and harmoniously associate their complimentary qualities.

Relationships between the Eight Trigrams

Each of the eight trigrams has, due to its symbolic meaning, a privileged relationship with one of the other trigrams. They form energetic pairs or complimentary functions:

HEAVEN and EARTH
THUNDER and WIND
WATER and FIRE
MOUNTAIN and CLOUD/LAKE

The Chinese Tradition transmitted two arrangements of the ensemble of trigrams. The first, attributed to Fuxi, is called "The Anterior Order of the World" or "Earlier Heaven." It is linked to the compass rose and associates the trigrams according to the pairs that they traditionally form:

Earlier Heaven:

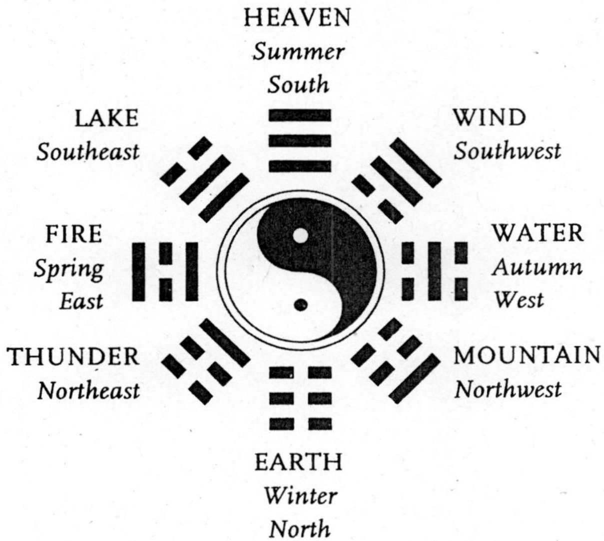

Note that, unlike us Westerners, the Chinese place south above and north below, east to the left, and west to the right. These choices are totally self-explanatory: at noon (the most easily recognizable astronomical moment), the Sun, which is at the height of its course, is, for our hemisphere, in the south. That is why most of us appreciate houses that have "southern exposure." Following this logic, the sun rises in the east (to the left) and sets in the west (to the right). That is how the four corners of the Earth—the symbol of which is the square—were determined.

The second arrangement is attributed to King Wen. This is the "The Interior Order of the World" or "Later Heaven." A great mystery surrounds this diagram for we have no information that reveals the logic behind this arrangement.

Jean Choain[24] proposed a theory on the logic of this arrangement founded on the elements of Chinese medicine. Other tentative explanations have been brought to light, but we can only hope for future archaeological discoveries reveal the true reason for this arrangement.

[24] Jean Choain, *Introduction au Yi King*. (Monaco: Editions du Rocher, 1991).

Arrangement According to King Wen:

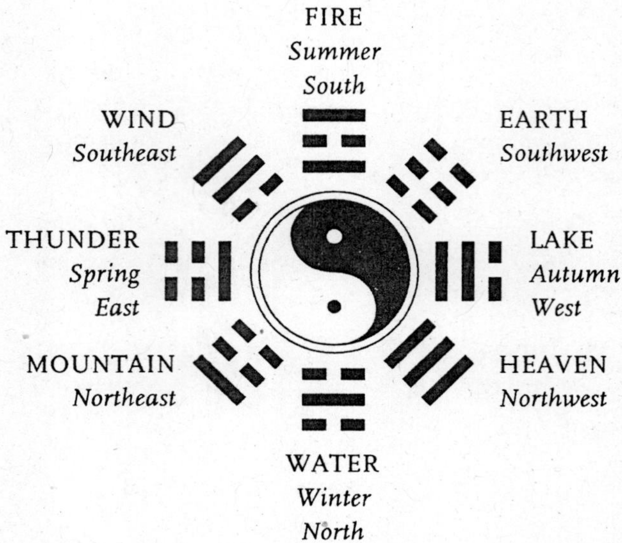

The Nuclear Trigrams

The nuclear trigrams—which in Chinese are called *ba gua*, or "intersected figures"—are obtained in the following manner: ignore the first and the last line of the hexagram, and you can see an upper trigram falling from the fifth line and a lower trigram rising from the second line. The trigrams obtained in this way overlap in the center of the hexagram:

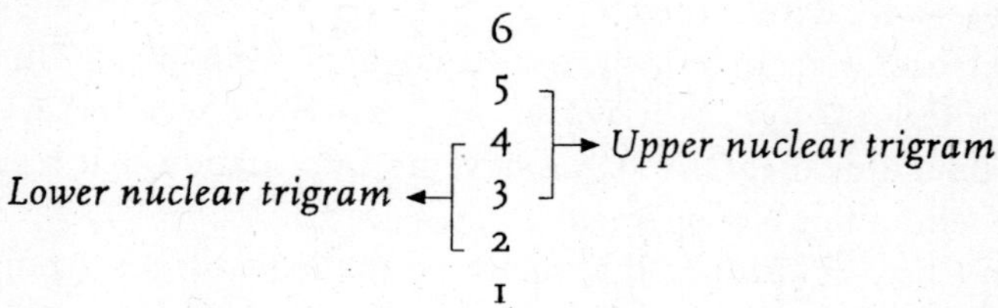

The Commentaries sometimes refer to the nuclear trigrams in order to explain the difficult aspect of a hexagram that, on the whole, is mostly good or the favorable side of a critical situation. In effect, their presence can accentuate, inhibit, or equalize the characteristics of the constituting trigrams.

For example, let's look at Hexagram 18, RESTORING WHAT HAS DETERIORATED:

Upper trigram	MOUNTAIN	☶
Lower trigram	WIND	☴

Upper nuclear trigram	THUNDER	☳
Lower nuclear trigram	LAKE	☱

The *Wind* blows at the foot of the *Mountain*, playing havoc with everything it encounters. Outwardly there's inertia (upper trigram, *Mountain*) and inwardly, indifference (lower trigram, *Wind*, which leads to a slow deterioration of the situation. Fortunately the ascending movement of *Thunder* and *Lake* (the nuclear trigrams) provides a way through this situation, using enthusiasm (*Thunder*) and joy (*Lake*).

The function of each of the lines can also be determined by its rapport with the nuclear trigrams:

- The first and sixth lines are isolated and outside of the situation because they are not included in either of the nuclear trigrams.
- The second line also lacks strength and autonomy because it is at the bottom of the lower nuclear trigram.
- The third line is simultaneously in the middle of the lower nuclear trigram and at the beginning of the upper nuclear trigram. This double identity underlines its pivotal role and critical position.
- The fourth line is on top of the lower nuclear trigram and in the middle of the upper nuclear trigram. This is a favorable position which foretells good potential.
- The fifth line is at the summit of the upper nuclear trigram, thus affirming its leading role.

Lastly, here is an interesting little curiosity: each of the eight trigrams shows up sixteen times as a nuclear trigram. If we place these on top of each other, we obtain sixteen nuclear hexagrams, numbers 1, 2, 23, 24, 27, 28, 37, 38, 39, 40, 43, 44, 53, 54, 63, 64. Each of the trigrams is represented four times. If you reproduce this operation in order to find the nuclear hexagram in these sixteen hexagrams, you will find four hexagrams: the first and last two of the *Yijing* (Hexagram 1, 2, 63, and 64).

In divinatory interpretation, it is not necessary to put any disproportionate importance on the nuclear trigrams or nuclear hexagrams. The fact that they are considerably fewer in number shows more that they define great families than they emphasize a particular situation.

CHAPTER III
CONSULTING THE *YIJING*

Many Western researchers, upon discovering the *Yijing*, have minimized or denied its divinatory origins and function and ascribed to it a wide range of other uses: as a collection of poems, proverbs or magical formulas; as a method of calculation; as a treatise on logic, astronomy, politics, military strategy, etc. This denial and misappropriation has different sources:

• The images and the text of the *Yijing* seemed so enigmatic to the first explorers that they were greatly perplexed by it and suggested the most fantastic hypotheses.

• The whole work so deeply penetrated each domain of Chinese knowledge that it could almost appear legitimate for each domain to claim the *Yijing* as its exclusive property.

• The systematic rejection of divinatory practices put the *Yijing* in a bad light.

• Finally, it was truly difficult to conceive that a system with a purely oracular origin could acquire so much influence and be used in so many diverse applications.

A Method of Divination?

Today, the mantic origin of the *Yijing* is without a doubt. Iulian K. Shchutskii thinks that it was used exclusively for divination up until about 602 B.C.,[25] after which time it became the subject of intellectual speculations. In spite of everything, even in China, the divinatory aspect of the *Yijing* gave rise to many reservations; we find traces of this beginning in the 3rd century B.C. This disassociation from the divinatory aspect of the *Yijing* has lasted centuries and there are still those who reject the *Yijing* as an oracle on principle, or practice divination without calling it such.

[25] Iulian K. Shchutskii, *Researches on the I Ching*. (London and Henley: Routledge & Kegan Paul, 1980) p. 193

We have seen, in the first chapter, how the Chinese integrated divination into public and religious life. The Chinese also maintained the critical and pragmatic attitude toward divination, they have always shown. Because of this, the oracular pieces were saved to compare them subsequently with real events. For the Chinese, the process of divination was not a question of gods or of magic, and even less of blind faith; they tried, tested, elaborated upon, and compared their methods. They sometimes even recommended against using divination for important questions. This shows how objective the Chinese could be vis-à-vis their oracles.

The more the *Yijing* was developed as a path of wisdom and a philosophy of change, the more it was set apart from simple divination. Philosophical maturity led to an understanding of the oracle where the questioner was neither passive nor credulous in the face of the oracle's responses, but was the actor responsible for his or her destiny. However, we should beware of hypocrisy: using the *Yijing* to explore the present is no less magical and irrational than using it to predict the future.

Symbols

The *Yijing* utilizes a symbolic language, the only one that allowed the holy sages to transmit their wisdom. Originally, the "symbol" was a sign of recognition. Two people broke a coin or tore a bill in half, each taking away a piece, and these two pieces had to be reunited so that the two parties could recognize each other as the proper interlocutor. Contrary to the sign, which covers some precisely defined notions, the symbol is impossible to pin down because it harbors an inexhaustible multitude of meanings. It rises above the concrete, the real. The symbol possesses different levels of meaning, and within it resides the art of a teaching that remains secret even through no part of it is actually hidden. The properties of the symbol are such that it is the means of expression for religion, esoteric teachings, and, naturally, oracles.

An object or an image is symbolic when it refers to something more vast than its immediate significance. The more universal the object or the "something" that the symbol represents, the more widespread it is. Such is the case with the Sun, the Moon, the ocean, and the Earth. But the fact that a symbolic image is adopted by different cultures does not mean that it contains the same meaning for everyone. Water often represents, to us as well as to the Chinese, the unfathomable, danger, and impenetrable mysteries. However, the West also attributes to it inconsistency—water has no defined form and depends on its container—while in the *Yijing*, its attributes are perseverance, patience, and a character that knows neither obstacle or alteration. Water is stopped by nothing, it fills, without losing any of its essence, all the hollow spaces and uses every projection. In your approach to *The Book of Changes*, sometimes you will learn some new symbols—for example, tortoise, symbol of the universe—and change, or widen your perception of others, like the symbol of water.

Some people use the words "emblem" and "symbol" interchangeably. Their meanings, however, are different. An emblem (from the Latin *emblema*, "retrieved element, mosaic") is a remote representation, an abstract of its source, while there is an analogy, a similarity of nature or form between a symbol (from the Latin *symbolus*, "sign of recognition") and that which it represents. An emblem is often the fruit of coincidence, of hazard, and it is for this reason, contrary to the symbol, an emblem has only one meaning. For example, the cock is the emblem of France because the Romans had baptized the Gauls and the cock (*gallus*) with the same name, probably because of the belief that this bird was native to Gaul.

So, the *Yijing* rests on a symbolic language with which we will attempt to familiarize ourselves.

How To Cast The Yijing

There are two traditional methods for consulting the *Yijing*. The first—the most ancient—calls for fifty yarrow stalks. The second, which is also ancient, but more simple, uses three coins.

General Instructions

• A hexagram is always constructed and read from the bottom up. The first number obtained corresponds to the first line and is placed on the bottom of the hexagram. The second result corresponds to the second line and is placed above the first, and so on.

6th place ——— ⎫
5th place ——— ⎬ *Upper trigram*
4th place — — ⎭

3rd place — — ⎫
2nd place ——— ⎬ *Lower trigram*
1st place ——— ⎭

• The numbers obtained from the cast of the yarrow stalks or coins determine the types of lines (solid, broken, mutable). These numbers can only be 7, 8, 6, and 9:

7: Young Yang ——— non-mutable
8: Young Yin — — non-mutable

6: Old Yin — — mutable, becoming ———
9: Old Yang ——— mutable, becoming — —

Traditionally, when it is mutable or changing, old yin is written: -x-, and old yang: -o-, but for convenience, these graphics are often omitted, and the mutable lines are indicated by their original numbers 6 or 9.

• A line is defined by the number obtained from the cast and by its position in the hexagram. For example, a third non-mutable yin line would be designated as "Eight in the third place" and "Seven in the fifth place" would indicate a fifth non-mutable yang line. In some texts, you will see the lines defined as "Third eight" or "Fifth seven."

• Once you have converted the six numbers into lines, check the table in the appendix (page 304) in order to find the number and name of the hexagram or hexagrams obtained.

• When there are no mutable lines, the answer consists of a single hexagram. Focus on the general text for this hexagram, and do not pay attention to the text for the lines.

• When there is one or several mutable lines (all six can change), consider the general text of the first hexagram, the commentaries on the mutable lines of the first hexagram, and the general text of the second hexagram.

Casting with Yarrow Stalks

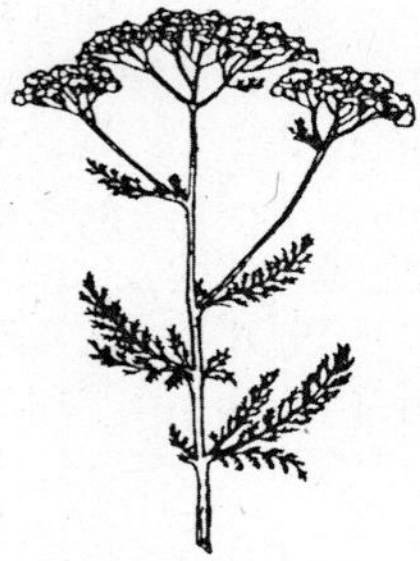

Pink or white umbells; the whole plant has a strong fragrance. 15 to 20 inches in height. Each plant contains from 4 to 5 stalks.

ACHILLEA MILLEFOLIUM (Carpenter's Weed)

Preparing Your Own Yarrow Stalks

The yarrow is a very common plant. It is found in terrain with high clay or limestone content, or in areas that tend to be dry. Its name, *Achillea Millefolium,* comes from the Greek hero Achilles who is said to have discovered its properties. There are many different varieties of yarrow. Millefolium is the most well-known, and it is the one you will use. You will need several plants for 50 stalks. Make your cuttings as long as possible—12 to 15 inches long. You prepare your stalks by choosing the straightest and thickest stems and clipping off the leaves and flowers (the stalks will shrink in the drying process).

How to Cast the Yarrow Stalks

This method was instituted in the 12th century B.C. by Wuxian, a diviner who lived during the end of the Shang Dynasty. At first, it might seem complicated, but it is really simple because it is very repetitive. With practice, you can obtain a hexagram in about fifteen minutes.

1. Take your 50 yarrow stalks and remove one of them (it will not be included in the casting process).
2. You have 49 stalks in your hand. Divide this group into two approximately equal bunches *without counting them.*
3. Put one bunch to your left, the other to your right.
4. *Take one stalk* from the bunch on the right, and put it between the little finger and ring finger of your left hand.

5. While holding this stalk, pick up, with your left hand, the bunch of stalks on the left.
6. With your right hand, take away 4 stalks at a time from the bunch in your left hand, and put them in front of you, without mixing them up with the other bunch, until you have four or less stalks.
7. Put these remaining stalks between the ring and middle fingers of your left hand.
8. Take the bunch of stalks on the right and do the same subtraction as in step 6 (taking away 4 stalks at a time until you have 4 or less remaining).
9. Put the stalks that are left between the middle and index fingers of your left hand.
10. On a piece of paper, write down the number of stalks that you have between your fingers (one number for each of the three piles). The possibilities are:

1 + 4 + 4
1 + 3 + 1
1 + 2 + 2
1 + 1 + 3

11. Add these numbers without *including the first number,* that is, the 1 representing the first stalk between your little finger and ring finger:

4 + 4 = 8
3 + 1 = 4
2 + 2 = 4
3 + 1 = 4

12. You are not going to use this result as is, you will give it a numeric value:

8 has a numeric value of 2
4 has a numeric value of 3

Write down the numeric value you have obtained and keep it for later.

13. Put aside the counted stalks that you have between your fingers in your left hand.
14. Regroup the stalks that you had pulled from your hand during the

last operation and divide these into two equal piles, without counting.
15. Repeat the subtraction process by following steps 3 through 9.
16. Write on your piece of paper the number of stalks that you have in your hand and add these *including*, this time, *the first stalk*. The possible results are:

$$1 + 4 + 3 = 8$$
$$1 + 3 + 4 = 8$$
$$1 + 1 + 2 = 4$$
$$1 + 2 + 1 = 4$$

17. Give the same numeric value as previously described in step 12 to your result, with 8 having a numeric value of 2 and 4 having a numeric value of 3.
18. Put aside the stalks you just counted and take up the stalks you subtracted during the last operation. Divide these into two equal piles without counting them and recommence the operation, following steps 3 through 9.
19. In order to calculate the result, the figures and their numeric values are the same as for the second deduction (steps 16 and 17).
20. You now have *three numeric values* on your paper. Add these and the number obtained will be that of the line for which you have made the cast, as follows:

7: Young Yang	——	non-mutable	
8: Young Yin	— —	non-mutable	
6: old yin	— —	mutable, becoming	——
9: old yang	——	mutable, becoming	— —

21. In order to obtain a complete hexagram, repeat the preceding steps 1-20 until you have six lines.

Each point of the casting process has a symbolic meaning. The *Da Zhuan* (The Great Treatise or The Great Commentary) explains that the two piles correspond to the two primary forces, that the stalks are counted into fours in order to reproduce the four seasons, etc. The scope of this book cannot examine this very complex symbolism in detail, but you can find some of its elements in *Richard Wilhelm's translation.*[26]

Casting with Coins

Purists use three ancient Chinese coins. They are round (like the symbol for Heaven) and pierced in the middle with a square hole (like the symbol for Earth). The side of the Chinese coin that has characters on it is Yang, and the blank side is yin. Pennies, although much less infused with mystical symbolism, are just as effective. "Heads" is Yang, "tails" is yin. You can use any coin, as long as you use three of the same coin. If there is no obvious "heads" side, designate the side that indicates the value of the coin as the yang side. Whatever you decide to do, be consistent!

1. Take your three coins in your cupped hands, give them a shake, and let them fall simultaneously onto a flat surface.
2. Heads equals a value of 2.
3. Tails equals a value of 3.

Add the numeric values of the tossed coins. The four possible results are:

7: Young Yang	——	non-mutable
8: Young Yin	— —	non-mutable
6: old yin	— —	mutable, becoming ——
9: old yang	——	mutable, becoming — —

4. Repeat this operation 5 more times to obtain the 6 lines of the hexagram.

Advice on Consulting the Oracle

Now we shall go over different aspects of consulting the oracle, keeping in mind that this information is a general guideline; nothing that follows here is "written in stone." I am proposing a simple basis for exploration and application, rather than pronouncing absolute truths. Like all apprenticeships, learning how to work with the *Yijing* requires trust and participation. It would be difficult for you to learn

[16] *The I Ching or Book of Changes* (Princeton, NJ: Princeton University Press, 1967) pp. 310-313.

to swim if you doubted the merits of your swimming instructor, but you can develop your confidence by observing those who went before you and by regularly evaluating your own progress. The same goes for the *Yijing*. An overly critical or skeptical attitude, or, on the other hand, an overly frivolous one, is a handicap.

Which Method to Choose?

Yarrow stalks or coins? The essential distinction between these two systems is the degree of ritual: amplified with the yarrow stalk method, minimized with the coin method.

Your choice should be guided by an honest assessment of your temperament. A ceremonial and symbolically charged process like casting the yarrow stalks might help some people become more focused, respectful, and attentive, while it might irritate others or make them very impatient. On the other hand, a bare-bones technique like throwing the coins might allow some to easily find the requisite concentration and spiritual state, while it might plunge others into indifference or negligence.

The mathematicians among you have probably noticed that the distribution of responses obtained from the yarrow stalk method is different from that obtained with the coin method. With yarrow stalks, the following probabilities are obtained:

9	———	changing to	— —	3/16 probability
8	— —	non-mutable		7/16 probability
7	———	non-mutable		5/16 probability
6	— —	changing to	———	1/16 probability

With coins, there is a:

6/16 probability of non-mutable lines (7 and 8);
2/16 probability of mutable lines (6 and 9).

The difference in probability between the methods is, for each type of line, plus or minus 1 in 16.

As I have already emphasized, these two systems have been tested throughout the centuries and found to be equally viable. However, if you would like to combine the simplicity of casting the coins with the probabilities of the yarrow stalks, Larry Schoenholtz recommends "The Method of Sixteen."[27] Get yourself sixteen poker chips of four different colors, which will represent the four different types of lines. You can also use coins with colored stickers.

- 7 of the 16 chips will correspond to 8.
- 5 of the 16 chips will correspond to 7.
- 3 of the 16 chips will correspond to 9.
- 1 of the 16 chips will correspond to 6.

Mix these 16 chips up in a bag, pick one, note the line to which it corresponds, then put it back it with the others and repeat this process until you obtain the six lines.

Whatever the method, note that the chances of obtaining a non-mutable line are higher than obtaining a mutable line.

Environment for the Consultation

Some books about the *Yijing* contain precise recommendations concerning the physical conditions surrounding the consultation, from the color of the table cloth, lighting in the room, to the type of incense to burn. It is difficult to distinguish which of these suggestions come from the personal preferences of the author and which come from a Chinese tradition (essentially Taoist). We do not find this kind of advice in the Ten Wings, although there are precise recommendations about the interior attitude of the questioner.

That said, the environment does have its importance because of the mental state that it can promote, so it should not be neglected. The ideal place is, above all, one where you will feel the most spontaneously self-possessed and serene. Using the same book, the same stalks, or the same coins reinforces a feeling of security and enhances concentration.

[27] See Larry Schoenholtz, *New Directions in the I Ching* (Seacaucus, NJ: University Books) 1975.

Do not forget that calmness is indispensable. So disconnect the telephone, turn off the television, the radio, in short, distance yourself from all possible sources of distraction.

Also, before you begin, make sure you have everything necessary on hand. Nothing is more aggravating than being settled down comfortably, concentrated, with you question in mind, only to have to get back up because you forgot a pencil or piece of paper!

It is also very useful to save your questions and answers. Get yourself a notebook or journal and write in it the date, the question, the answer, and, eventually, the commentaries that it will inspire you to write.

When to Cast the Yijing

Generally, you should not consult the oracle over futile questions, out of curiosity, to pass time, or to see if it will give you the same answer twice. Ordinarily, no one would act like that toward a respected person. You should have the same regard for the *Yijing* (on this subject, see the text of Hexagram 4).

Consulting the *Yijing* too often could lead to a kind of dependence—you would not dare take a step without the precious book—or great emotional vulnerability, by foundering in disproportionate joys or fears according to the oracle's answers. Multiple responses can also diminish the text's importance and effectiveness and create confusion, doubt, and lack of self-confidence. Finally, looking, at any cost, for THE best solution to each life problem can accentuate egocentric and manipulative tendencies, and prevents one's being completely "here and now," facing the totality of the situation. All of this is far from walking the path of the noble man.

On the other hand, used in the right measure, the oracle is an indisputable source of enlightenment and teaching. However, it does not offer facile solutions, escape, or small comfort for fear of the future, but a real opportunity for reflection and progress.

It is suitable to refer back to the *Yijing* when you feel the need to be spiritually guided, when you want to explore a situation and its repercussions, or when you need to determine a strategy; these are the three main types of interrogations. And sometimes you might need to consult the oracle for "reorientation" throughout the development of the action you have taken, especially if it extends over several months or years. Naturally, the frequency of this reorientation should be measured and justified. Hexagram 1, *Heaven*, speaks of the creative energy within the passing of time: the same seasons follow each other without looking the same because there is always a new element slipping into them. For certain problems, time has an essential role because it provides room for development and maturation. In these cases, it is preferable to stay silent for a while and put the *Yijing* aside. On the other hand, interrogations made during periods of transition are often beneficial.

Interior Disposition During the Consultation

The *Yijing* does not address the ordinary man, it speaks to the noble man, whose pure heart grants him access to the *Yijing*. In essence, the noble man is he or she who resonates with the Tao. He aspires to goodness, is not driven by any extreme, he works for the common good and meditates on the responses of the oracle in order to judge the correctness of his action. The noble man does not take refuge in the *Yijing* to escape his responsibilities or to reject the unpleasant aspects of his existence. His quest for wisdom is such that he does not repel unfortunate events, nor does he cling to happy events, but he looks, with equal interest, within each of them for the lessons they bring.

The fact that the *Yijing* is addressed to "the noble man" has an immediately practical value. It means that the oracle is useless for following narrow, petty, or futile goals, or for answering questions that would allow one to harm, second-guess, or manipulate others. That is why a good approach to the *Yijing* begins with a good motive for the consultation.

On the other hand, if you interrogate the *Yijing* with the intention of ignoring its answer (if it is not what you want to hear), you would be wasting your time, for such an attitude would make its advice inaccessible. One who thinks one knows, who does not listen to a bit of advice, or who lives only in one's own head cannot receive anything. Therefore, the extent to which you intend to heed the responses of the *Yijing* is important. Certainly, nothing obliges you to follow its recommendations but you should at least have the intention of sincerely examining them.

Interrogating the *Yijing* also encompasses a wish to embrace the movement of transformation, that is, to overcome the narrow boundaries of habit in order to truly enlarge your field of comprehension and action. This requires a very open spirit and a sincere dedication to self-analysis and self-criticism.

Naturally, it is difficult to consider oneself a "noble man" *par excellence,* but you can simply begin to do this with great sincerity, a positive attitude toward yourself and others, and the development of a calm mental state. When you first start using the *Yijing,* it will be hard to settle down because the uncertainty and excitement of a new approach, as well as hope or apprehension regarding a response, can make your heart beat faster and agitate your thoughts. With experience, quietude will settle into your mind more rapidly, and even the tendency to wish for or to discourage a certain type of response will vanish on its own. You will then be perfectly "in the here and now," open, without prejudice or preconception (or close to it!), ready to receive every response and every inspiration.

How to Formulate the Question

The Great Commentary indicates that the *Yijing* should be questioned with words. The choice of these words is important, for when a response is "inadequate" or impossible to interpret, it is generally because the question was inappropriate for the specific approach of the *Yijing,* or that it was incomplete or ambiguous.

When you formulate the question, take the *Yijing* into account, but also yourself, who you are. Here, three points are important:

• The first point to consider is the choice of words. A word can be significant for one person and mean nothing to another. Therefore, chose the words that "speak" to you. In the beginning you will have to try several types of formulations until a suitable one presents itself naturally. At this stage, you will also notice that you do not have to concentrate so hard.

• The second point to consider is the type of approach: intuitive or intellectual. It is, of course, a matter of personality. Here, also, it is best for you to express yourself within your own bounds, while taking into account certain precautions. Intuitive types will prefer to do away with verbalization, and mentally dive into the problem, interrogating the *Yijing* in this state. This approach has its good points; all the same, I would not recommend it for beginners. Basically, in complex situations, or if the answer is a hexagram that is difficult to grasp, the result will be confusing because of the vagueness of the question. The hexagram could give the impression of saying one thing and its opposite, and poorly define to whom or what it applies, or might seem to mix the past, present, and future. All of these pitfalls are the lot of questions with hazy outlines.

For those who prefer a more rigorous approach, the formulation of the question will naturally be more precise, but in doing so, you should try to avoid limiting your field of investigation. It is often preferable to ask several questions that go from the general to the particular. This method permits a broader, more complete analysis of the situation. We will study the practical techniques of this method in later examples (see page 103).

• Finally, the third point; each person approaches the *Yijing* with his or her own beliefs. According to the individual, the *Book of Changes* can be the tie with one or several gods, a teacher, a friend, a cherished parent, one's ancestors, cosmic forces, the unconscious, the "winds of change," and, of course, transformation. Naturally, one's beliefs play on the formulation of question and the interpretation of the response, and this makes adapting a question to bring to the *Yijing* a very personal matter.

Compared to astrology or the tarot, which are more widely known to Westerners, the *Yijing* is not solely comprised of symbols: it has a text. You should therefore familiarize yourself with its vocabulary and style. You will have to adapt yourself to its mode of expression, much in the same way you do in everyday life when you communicate with different people. If you do not adapt yourself to its symbolic language, the *Yijing* will seem bizarre or impenetrable, whereas you have simply not known how to approach it. This adaptation occurs, in the first place, with the formulation of the question; that is why we are going to define the principle criteria for working with the *Yijing*:

The Yijing addresses itself to the noble man. We have already said that to interrogate the *Yijing* is to wish to embrace the movement of transformations according to the way of "the noble man." This means renouncing stereotypical behavior, accenting the blossoming of luminous values, and abandoning negative reactions like anger, greed, egoism, etc. From a practical point of view, in order to stay on the path of the noble man, you could systematically add to your question the phrase "in order to be in accord with my Tao (or my Way)" or "in order to be in accord with the way of the noble man." Once this habit is anchored, you can do away with this formula because you will have made it an integral part of the consultation. By proceeding this way, your question will encompass the whole situation. As for its answer, the *Yijing* will indicate the best solution, not from a narrow viewpoint of immediate profit that might be regrettable in the long-term, but from a broad overview of the situation's evolution.

The Yijing is anchored in the present. If the objective of the *Yijing* was only to reveal the fortunate or unfortunate issue of a choice, where would be the opportunity for action and self-perfection? *The Book of Changes* takes into account your present circumstances and conditions, analyzes your possibilities for action, and frequently refers back to whatever, in the past, led you there.

Even though the *Yijing* is looked upon as an oracle of future possibilities, it is more effective for pinpointing the strong points of a situation, for helping you to envision it in a new light and for determining an optimal line of conduct. Therefore you will not get a "yes" or a "no" answer, for that would imply a kind of passiveness and would erase any trace of a learning experience. On the other hand, it always answers questions in which you implicate yourself in an active manner:

—"In the context of x, what should I do in order to be in accord with my Tao, my Way?"
—"What should be my attitude in the face of problem of y?"
—"How should I act in the circumstances of z?"

This strong connection between the *Yijing* and the present makes it hardly appropriate for delineating a hypothetical future and only validates answers for the given circumstances. Therefore, if a situation is unfolding over the years, a consultation of the *Yijing* at crucial stages of its development would be interesting. Or, if your motivation concerning a particular course of action changes, a new consultation will be necessary. For example, suppose that you envisioned a move in order to escape your family's control. You consult the *Yijing*, which gives you a favorable response. But even before setting about this project, the circumstances change, and you want to move in order to follow the love of your life. The important part is not so much the move as it is the motivation that instigated it; a change in motivation is one case in which a new interrogation of the *Yijing* could be justified.

The Yijing and the double formulation: On the Shang Dynasty oracular objects, we see, side by side on the same tortoise shell, two interrogations: "to do x" and "to not do x." The double interrogation often presents itself. Most of the time it greatly facilitates the approach to a problem. In certain cases, however, it can create some confusion. That is why it is preferable to proceed in stages by posing the first question and analyzing its answer before moving on to its negation.

With double interrogation, the question is not "should I do x or not?" but:

"What will be the situation if I do x?"
"What will be the situation if I do not do x?"

The best scenario will determine the choice.

In summary, you might need to take detours in order to obtain a lucid answer. Here are some examples:

Suppose that you would like to relocate but you are undecided between two cities—it would be useless to ask, "Which city should I chose?" Mentally project yourself into one of these chosen cities and ask "What advice can I get for my project to relocate to x?" You would do the same with the other city or cities. If you do not even know which city to choose, ask: "What should I do in order to find the city that will be good for me?" If you have doubts about the value of this move, do not hesitate to throw some light on it, and begin with interrogations like: "Relocate?" "Stay?" "What should my attitude be in the face of this relocation in order to be in accord with my Way?" Be careful! Above all, do not ask many similar questions for the same problem, for you will only confuse yourself.

On the other hand, you will never trick yourself by going from the general to the particular, even if you have the impression of being distracted from the problem. In fact, often you will resolve it more quickly and easily in this manner. In the example that we just looked at, going from the general to the particular, you would first ask about the value of moving before choosing a city. Once the first answer is at hand, take pains to study its words; they will enable you to better define the process in which you are engaged and will help you formulate the next question, if it is still necessary.

When you first start off, trying to pose the question in any way other than the way in which it first presents itself might be frustrating. Rest assured that this feeling will pass quickly and you will soon be able to adapt any question to the criteria of the *Yijing*.

If you have to ask some questions for a third party (and not about the third party!) nothing will prevent you from doing so. The essential part is to keep an inner attitude of impartiality. According to your preferences or according to the personality of the other person, either one of you can manipulate the yarrow stalks or cast the coins.

In any case, it is good to take the time to reflect upon the question. Writing it down forces you to be more precise, more concentrated, and to have better organized ideas. To neglect this stage is to take the risk of seeing, at the moment of the cast, a surge of related and destabilizing questions and the resulting answer will be surrounded by doubt, even if it is apparently satisfying.

Numerous other ways to interrogate the *Yijing* are imaginable. I have only included those that seem preferable for the beginner. Once familiarized with the *Cannon of Changes*, you will be able to understand its answers more quickly and more completely. You can then freely address the *Yijing*, which will only increase the scope of your investigations.

The Responses of the Yijing

You now know that a great part of the help that the *Yijing* gives resides in its capacity to reframe a problem in a dynamic set of circumstances. The past can truly allow you to comprehend the present situation. It also happens that the *Yijing* leaves behind what has been done and bluntly enlightens the present, emphasizing what you might be tempted to minimize or forget, and making you face the urgency of a decision, an action, or a readjustment. In any case, the

Yijing puts a very large range of resources at your disposition (do not forget, there is 4,096 possible answers). Of course, in theory, our creative power endows us with a vast array of options but most of the time each of us reacts in very predictable ways using the same strategies, even if they are poorly adapted. One of the main benefits of the *Yijing* is its capacity to present solutions that are outside of our usual way of thinking and functioning.

Consulting the *Yijing* can also give you valuable space to be objective. It offers advice that is more neutral than anyone else can give you. It also takes care of your sensitive points for it is easier to acknowledge your weakness, errors, or shortfalls with the *Yijing* than with any of your close relations.

Finally, not a single hexagram nor line gives the means for avoiding your situation. On the contrary, the *Yijing* permits you to fully live the situation by comprehending it as part of a totality. To pretend that it is Summer while in deep Winter is no help, but understanding the necessity of Winter permits you to take advantage of its potential.

The *Yijing* does not question free will. You always remain the master of your choices and your decisions. Often, we call freedom the possibility to let our desires and compulsions—whether or not they are good for ourselves or others—to take us over. The freedom conceived of in the *Yijing* is nothing like that. Freedom resides in positive action undertaken with complete understanding of the cause; it is based on a global point of view that takes into account all beings, the moment, and the natural order of things.

An understanding of the responses of the *Yijing* is equally inseparable from the greatest sincerity. We find an example of this in a divination disclosed by the *Zuo Zhuan* ("Commentaries on Spring and Autumn," circa 11th century). This divination was made at the request of Princess Mu Jiang who lived at the end of the Zhou dynasty. The seer predicted a favorable outcome for a pure heart. But the princess was conscious of her weaknesses; admitted having chosen wickedness, involving herself in all sorts of troublesome affairs, abusing her power over men, using her beauty to get what she wanted, losing her dignity, and not seeking peace for her people. She deduced that the outcome indicated by the hexagram could only be fatal, and it was.

Interpretation

In spite of its comprehensiveness, *The Book of Changes* is not a book of recipes to read and apply to the letter. Its symbolic language demands that one reflect and meditate upon it. What Marie Odile Hermand said about the tarot is also true for the *Yijing*:

Ce que j'écris ne vous suffira pas, vous pouvez en êtrer sur! Le nombre des symboles du Tarot est limité, mais le sens de chaque symbole est illimité, dans un sens vertical, celui de sa profondeur.

["What I have written will not be enough for you, you can be sure! The number of Tarot symbols is limited, but the meaning of each symbol is unlimited, in a vertical sense, in its depth."][28]

No one would dare say that he or she perfectly understood the *Yijing*, but that should not keep you from trying! The more you familiarize yourself with its style, the more it will speak to you. You may even be surprised by the difficulties you had when you first started to consult the *Yijing*. Right now, we will go over the main challenges of interpretation.

There are no strict rules concerning the interpretation of the cast. Nothing is systematic in the *Yijing*, even the logic behind the definition of the hexagrams and the lines. In the beginning, you might find this lamentable, but later, you will understand that this characteristic is necessary. It is a part of the flexibility of the *Changes*. Absence of fixed rules invites you to make use of your intuition in reaching an understanding of the oracle.

The first challenge to confront is the rapport between the first hexagram, the changing line or lines, and the second hexagram. Often the information for each can be contradictory. The general text of the first hexagram can call for action while the changing line or lines, or the second hexagram can discourage it.

The first hexagram is a representation of the terrain upon which you are situated. The lines are the "transformations." They are the salient points of the situation, and it is important to take them in particular into account. If the first hexagram urges action but the text for the changing line is against it, follow the advice of the latter.

[28] Marie Odile Hermand, *Le tarot divinatoire, guide et initiation* (Monaco: Editions du Rocher, 1995) p. 19.

The second hexagram is simultaneously a complement and a prolongation of the first. It colors the first with a positive, negative, or neutral aspect. It often reveals a hidden element that might come into play in the future. It can therefore indicate a future in gestation that is more or less close to the present.

You might notice that the ancient text gives a way to understand the relationship between the first and second hexagrams HEAVEN (Hexagram 1) and EARTH (Hexagram 2) when all of their lines are mutable. The qualities of the second hexagram add to those of the first, and enrich them:

Hexagram 1, when all lines are changing:

- Philastre: "Dans la troupe des dragons visibles, aucun ne précède les autres; Bonheur."[29]
- Wilhelm: "There appears a flight of dragons without heads. Good fortune."
- Centre Djohi: "Apparition d'un vol de dragons. Pas un n'est en tête. Ouverture."[30]

The flight of dragons (symbolizing the qualities of HEAVEN) is promising because not one of them places itself above another. This is due to the integration of the qualities of EARTH: letting go and flexibility.

Hexagram 2, when all lines are changing:

- Philastre: "Bien, perfection éternelle."[31]
- Wilhelm: "Lasting perseverance furthers."
- Centre Djohi: "Présage durablement favorable."[32]

Here, the qualities of EARTH are enriched by duration (one of the keywords of HEAVEN).

- The second challenge of interpretation comes up when one casts several changing lines. How do they communicate with each other? What do you do when they contradict each other? They generally represent the different stages of the dynamic in progress, going chrono-

[29] "In the troop of visible dragons, not one precedes the others; Happiness."

[30] "Appearance of a flight of dragons. Not one is ahead. Opening." Centre Djohi, *Le Yi King mot à mot* (Paris: Editions Albin-Michel, Collection Question de, 1994).

[31] "Good, eternal perfection."

[32] "Lastingly favorable presage."

logically from the first to the sixth line. An unfavorable line will warn you of a risk to avoid, a favorable one will indicate the way to follow. Sometimes their actions are somewhat simultaneous, that is why it is always interesting to make a synthetic, global evaluation of them, to determine the degrees of risk and success.

To these principles of interpretation can be added some others. For example, you could emphasize the lines as symbolic representations of the different personages implicated in the problem. For this kind of study, Philastre's translation is very useful.[33] As for the rapport between the two hexagrams, for Cyrille J. D. Javary, the second hexagram is not the future of the situation at all, but "the hexagram of Perspective," that is, the point of view from which the first hexagram should be read. He writes, "This hexagram 'to come' gives us information about the probable evolution of the situation that is described in the hexagram that has been cast. The Chinese call these two figures the rood hexagram and the bud hexagram. They are inter connected by a relationship that is less contingent than our idea of cause and effect, because the eventuality of the second figure depends neither on the mechanical laws of causality nor on the vague decree of fate...[it] depends entirely on the questioner's free will to follow the *I Ching's* advice or not."[34]

Whatever your choices, let yourself be guided by whatever experience teaches you.

• It happens that some people are disappointed by obtaining an answer without changing lines, because they think that they are at an impasse or in a static situation. By definition, everything is change. A hexagram always moves toward something. If your answer is a simple hexagram, it is because your action, your situation, is in correspondence with the full sense of the hexagram. It is a little like having cast the greatest changing line! Inside of this hexagram, hundreds of things remain to be done and by re-reading its text you will

[33] For readers who are not fluent in French, *The Complete I Ching: The Definitive Translation* by the Taoist Master Alfred Huang (Rochester, VT: Inner Traditions, 1998) describes personages symbolized by the lines.

[34] Cyrille Javary, *Understanding the I Ching*, translated by Kirk McElhearn (Boston: Shambhala Publications Inc., 1997) p. 98.

see the extent to which everything moves within it. It is not, in any case, a second-rate response and it often has the advantage of being easy to interpret.

• Do not forget that the language of the *Yijing* is symbolic. When it speaks of danger to the army or the retirement of the sage, these images simply need to be readjusted to the context of the question. Also, when you are faced with a weak, ordinary, or little man (according to whatever translation you consult), keep in mind that these qualifiers do not describe the fundamental nature of an individual but symbolize one of his or her aspects in a given situation. We are all "inferior men" to someone when a facet of our personality or our action thwarts his or her understanding, advancement, or expression. In the same manner, if the *Yijing* describes us as a sage, a little realism and modesty must make us suspect that we probably have not yet attained the ultimate realization of our existence.

• For the best comprehension of the general sense of a hexagram, do not hesitate to study its particularities. What is being emphasized as important? Is a line arriving? A line leaving? Another isolated? Others reassembled? Understanding the words of the text of the *Yijing* is the easiest way to tackle the mutations. However, a hexagram is, above all, a combination of yin and yang lines, and of trigrams. It is never a waste of time to reflect on this assemblage and delineate its implications. Look at the constituting trigrams: do they encompass one or several mutations? If not, which are changing? Which remain the same? The one on the outside? The inside? What does that mean? Also, take a look at the nuclear trigrams. You can also read the text of all the lines, knowing which among them that you have cast concerns you. Or, you can read the hexagram opposite of the one that you are analyzing (obtained by replacing each solid line with a broken line, and vice-versa). It will give you, in reverse, precious information.

Concerning the lines, if you want to examine them in more detail, ask yourself the following questions: "In which trigram is it found?" "What is the meaning and role of this trigram, and what can one deduce from it for the line?" "What position does it occupy in the trigram and in the hexagram?" If, when you have several changing lines, one of them escapes you, you can look at the hexagram resulting from the mutation of this single line.[15]

• All the same, keep in mind that many methods can lead more often to confusion than clarification. If confusion has overtaken you, forget everything. Put aside your *Yijing* and take it up again the next day, and the answer will be clear.

• Even experts sometimes cannot immediately grasp the significance or the relationship between a hexagram and the question posed. If this happens to you, wait, do not persist. Again, put aside your *Yijing* for a few hours or days and when you go back to it everything will seem easier.

• An answer can elude you because what you're looking for or see as something complicated is actually right under your nose. Some situations are heavy with consequences but their resolution demands an "humdrum" attitude, without great development (spiritual or otherwise). In this case, it is best to look at the summary or the image that condenses the meaning of the hexagram response. It is impossible to always rely on this condensation, for it depends on the context of the question, but you can take some inspiration for the "Predictions and Advice" and the "Notes on Interpretation" in Part II.

• Many beginners think they do not understand an answer if they are not able to discern the better choice. If the *Yijing* does not give distinction to one solution over another, it is because both are equivalent, good or bad. If they are all bad, ask the *Yijing*, once more, how to get through this impasse.

• If you cannot evaluate your answer, you can interrogate the *Yijing* again. For example, one of my clients asked what would be his situation if he reoriented his business. The answer indicated that things looked good, without great success, but without bankruptcy. But he felt that this answer could be applied to a previous experience, in which he had some success but he felt he had not the strength to go through such an experience again. He then interrogated the *Yijing* by asking how it would have qualified the previous situation. The response was: great difficulties from which one could learn a great

[15] Starting from the bottom of the hexagram up. For example, if you cast changing lines 1 and 2 in Hexagram 20, look at the resulting hexagram, 42, for insight into changing line 1, and read changing line 2 of Hexagram 42, and then go on to read the general text for Hexagram 61. Or you could just read Hexagram 59 if you do not understand changing line 2 of Hexagram 20.

deal. From this answer, he could establish a hierarchy between the two responses.

- Finally, keep a notebook in which you systematically note the date, the question, and the answer, and do this even for the "insignificant" questions (with time they can reveal themselves to be more important than you would have believed). Initially you might have no interest in keeping this notebook, but a day will come when you will be happy you did, for it is very instructive to review the hexagrams when you know the turn of events (sometimes after several years). You will also learn a lot by comparing situations in which you received the same hexagram.

PART II
INTERPRETATION OF THE 64 HEXAGRAMS OF THE ORACLE

THE 64 HEXAGRAMS

Compiling an interpretation of the hexagrams and the text for the lines is not an easy task, because of the many differences between the principle translations of the *Yijing*. My intent here has been to respect the Ancient Text while avoiding the enigmatic aspect of specialists' works and the excessive degeneration of facile vulgarization.

Those who are familiar with Wilhelm's translation will be surprised to discover that the "sublime success" of certain hexagrams (especially the first three) is transformed, according to the translators, "Fundamental Success" by Stephen Karcher, "Prime receipt" by Edward Shaugnessy, and "supremely blessed" by Gregory Whincup.[36] There are different levels of interpretation even for seemingly elementary mantic formulas. The archaic ideograms of these formulas originally referred to important sacrificial rites. Little by little, they were modified and gave way to the idea of expansion, of a fundamentally favorable period. However, to speak of "sublime success" is a step that few translators today will take. Choices in wording have to be made, and this explains the differences that you will find between the text proposed here and various other translations. My approach here has been to expound upon the general meaning of each hexagram, while remaining faithful to the Confucian commentaries, and to keep the interpretation of the lines close in symbolism and spirit to the Ancient Text.

In order to help you evaluate one or several changing lines cast within the hexagram, I added a "grade"—not be taken in a rigid manner—to each line, as follows:

+, ++, +++: good to very good
-, --, ---: delicate to very delicate
o: neutral

[36] Stephen Karcher, *How to Use the I Ching* (Rockport, MA: Element Books, 1997). Gregory Whincup, *Rediscovering the I Ching* (New York: St. Martin's Press, 1986). *I Ching: The Classic of Changes* translated with an introduction and commentary by Edward L. Shaughnessy (New York: Ballantine Books, 1997).

I have indicated the ruler or rulers for each hexagram. Where no differentiation is indicated between the constituting and governing rulers, it is because the constituting rulers are also governing.

Generally speaking, the mantic formulas that you will find in the *Yijing* can be classified in the following manner:

—At the summit you will find all the states of success: "great success," "success," "presage of success."

—Next are the periods of expansion: "very favorable period of great progress," "favorable," "profitable," "advantageous."

—Then come the risks of errors and faults, and the dissipation or avoidance of them: "absence of fault," "regrets disappear," "no fault is committed."

—The least bit of harm is signified by "disagreement," "setback," "trouble," "presage of danger," "presage of failure."

—When things are no longer favorable, you have: "error," "impasse," "danger," "wounding," and "failure."

Do not forget that each line is cast and read from the bottom to the top. The first line is therefore at the bottom of your hexagram, the sixth on top.

䷀

Constituting and Nuclear Trigrams: Heaven

Symbols and Images

—Six strong, luminous yang lines: all the great creative power of Heaven is there.
—Heaven in the upper and lower trigrams suggests movement. Movement needs time to develop, that is why this hexagram speaks of duration.
—This hexagram corresponds to the fourth month of the Chinese year (May-June), when the day attains its maximum length (Summer solstice).

General Situation

The situation described here is very favorable because it stimulates spiritual enlightenment, power, initiative, and activity.

This hexagram refers entirely to yang values, that is, luminous and dynamic. It indicates that you need to refer to the virtues of "the noble man" and adopt them in order to attain your goal. With these virtues, all potential will become manifest and operative. These virtues are: integrity, generosity, sincerity, the following of luminous goals for oneself and for others, confidence in oneself and others.

Your strength, your effectiveness, and the breadth of your action are going to depend on the scope and quality of your goal and your attitude. You must get to the root of things in order to envision the bigger picture, and to find the order and place of each element. It is important that you discern what is essential and has priority, and that you concentrate on this, for you will not be able to properly use your strength if you are scattered or spread too thin. Once the way is found, it is necessary to follow it without narrow or egotistical motives.

Whatever your action or situation, make good use of time. It is not necessary to hurry. Time is in your favor because it encompasses a creative function. The days, the seasons, the years follow each other but are never the same; something new is always sneaking into them. Therefore, in time, there is space for action, creation, and transformation. Time, which is also duration, invites you to advance from one stage to the next, to go through one creation to another. This progression should occur without tension, much in the way the sky contains the unhurried procession of the seasons. Working with times requires that, even if strength is on your side, you are constant, persevering, patient, and perfunctory.

Predictions and Advice

—Period of great and highly favorable progress.
—Perseverance is advantageous.

Notes on Interpretation

This hexagram can be double-edged. If you are tired or implicated in adverse circumstances, it is not always agreeable to learn that you must still prove your strength, courage, and patience. Furthermore, a hexagram that insists on time can sometimes leave the impression of some sort of delay.

Each line represents a stage of progress in realization. These stages are symbolized in the Ancient Text by the flight of a dragon. The dragon can live hidden in deep underwater caves, or in the entrails of the Earth, or it can fly off into the broad sky. It symbolizes the activity and perfected faculties of the noble man:

1st line: the dragon stays hidden in the waters and does not act;
2nd line: he appears in a field;
3rd line: he acts untiringly (the dragon is not mentioned here);
4th line: he hesitates from flying toward his resting place;
5th line: he flies into the sky;
6th line: he goes too far and regrets it.

When all the lines are mutable, this represents a flight of dragons without heads, or without a leader; that is to say that they are docile and full of abandon.

Hexagram 1/Interpretation of the Lines

Governing and Constituting Line: 5th

1st Line (9) +

You possess the qualities and capacities of the noble man, but you must keep them hidden. Do not act under the present circumstances.

2nd Line (9) ++

You possess the qualities and capacities of the noble man,and should render them manifest while looking for the support of someone superior.

3rd Line (9) +

You possess the qualities and capacities of the noble man, and should tirelessly put them to work. Even in moments of respite, you should remain extremely prudent and vigilant so that, in spite of danger, no fault is committed.

4th Line (9) ++

Whether you advance or retreat, act in broad daylight or cultivate your inner self, you commit no fault.

5th Line (9) +++

You possess the qualities and capacities of the noble man, and can manifest and fully expand them. It is advantageous for you to seek the support of a teacher or to support others.

6th Line (9) --

Pushing to the extremes of your strength and exceeding due measure can only lead to regrets.

All Lines Mutable (9 throughout) +++

You possess the qualities and capacities of the noble man, and express them fully with gentleness and open-mindedness. This promises success.

EARTH/HEXAGRAM 2

䷁

Constituting and Nuclear Trigrams: Earth

Symbols and Images

—Six dark, weak yin lines: all of the passive qualities of Earth's realization are there, with their virtues of suppleness and self-sacrifice.
—Earth in the upper and lower trigrams symbolizes expansiveness, understanding, the steadfastness and solidity that permits Earth, and equally the noble man, to sustain all beings.
—This hexagram corresponds to the tenth month of the Chinese year (November–December), when night attains its maximum length (Winter solstice).

General Situation

This hexagram describes a very favorable situation, distinguished by the singular values of yin. Yin values are flexibility, gentleness, self-sacrifice, and malleability. These are the qualities that you should adopt and develop if you want to attain your goal.

Abandon, suppleness, and docility mean that you allow yourself to be guided by events or to follow the guidance of those who are in possession of power and initiative, all while respecting conventions and hierarchies.

These receptive qualities are not a sign of weak character, but an appeasing strength that knows how to receive inspiration and adapt. If, contrary to this advice, you decide to take the lead and force things, you will lose your way and meet with failure. Your strength should manifest itself in determination, patience, courage, and benevolence. As for your action, it will orient itself toward blossoming and fruition. It is not for you to create or take initiatives, but it is up to you to accommodate, perfect, nourish, and enrich, for you dispose a great passive power of realization.

The submission of the Earth does not mean resignation, for it still takes joy and serenity to follow and be guided. Furthermore, this attitude will allow you to renew yourself, thanks to the teachings that it will bring you.

In order for your action to be complete, take into equal account the needs of others and seek to satisfy them, as exemplified by the Earth which nourishes all beings according to their needs, and sustains them impartially.

Finally, if others are a necessary an important part of the positive outcome of your action, solitude is indispensable to preserve your objectivity at the time of reckoning.

Predictions and Advice

—Period of great and highly favorable progress if your action is based on receptivity, perseverance, docility, and self-sacrifice.
—Follow, do not lead.

Notes on Interpretation

In the Ancient Text, the mare symbolizes the attitude that the noble man must adopt. The mare is gentle, obedient, regular, and persevering; she lets herself be guided by the forces around her.

This hexagram represents an overall situation with a wealth of possibilities but in which you lack independence and initiative. You will have to demonstrate your confidence, openness, and readiness to receive good and bad experiences with equanimity.

Letting yourself be guided by circumstances means that you adapt yourself to the present turn of events rather than strain toward an objective or occupy yourself with the future.

HEXAGRAM 2/INTERPRETATION OF THE LINES:

RULER OF THE HEXAGRAM: 2ND LINE.

1ST LINE (6) --

If your pliancy translates into repeated manifestations of laxity, carelessness, or negligence, it will lead to progressive signs of decay.

2ND LINE (6) +++

If your attitude is clear, simple, and just, spontaneously adopting the qualities of Earth, with no ulterior motive, will make everything favorable.

3RD LINE (6) ++

If you do not bring forth your qualities or competencies, you will remain perfectible and operative. If you work for a powerful person, you will attain your goal by remaining submissive and full of the values of Earth.

4TH LINE (6) o

In a blocked situation, you must have great reserve. Hiding your qualities and capacities will deprive you of praise, but you will guard against committing fault.

5TH LINE (6) +++

Adopting the qualities of Earth and remaining humble, even in a position of power, will lead you to very great success.

6TH LINE (6) ---

Taking initiatives instead of being flexible and directing instead of following will lead you into an open battle in which both sides will be wounded.

ALL LINES MUTABLE (6 THROUGHOUT) +++

When strength and duration are added to the qualities of Earth, the presage is favorable for a long time.

DIFFICULTIES OF BEGINNING/HEXAGRAM 3

Constituting Trigrams	*Nuclear Trigrams*
(No. 3 Difficulties of Beginning)	(No. 23 Usury)
Water ☵	☶ Mountain
Thunder ☳	☷ Earth

Symbols and Images

—The ideogram of this hexagram is a primitive representation of a shoot laboriously emerging from the earth.
—When Heaven and Earth meet (Hexagrams 1 and 2), beings and things come forth (Hexagram 3). They are affronted by the initial difficulties, the difficulties of every birth, of every first step.
—Thunder, in the lower trigram, has a naturally ascending movement. It tries to liberate itself from Water in the upper trigram, the natural movement of which is descending. This is the movement (Thunder) with which one escapes from danger (Water).
—Thunder and Water create the storm which encompasses a powerful germinating force.

General Situation

This hexagram indicates that you are facing the difficulties or troubles that are inherent in every birth.

Whatever you begin, it is normal for the first steps to be confused or laborious. It is not an alarming situation, for these obstacles will dissipate on their own, just as after the storm, everything calms down, lightens up, and regenerates. The overall scenario is, therefore, very favorable but in order to avoid nipping your project in the bud, you should be careful and keep a few things in mind:
—In the first place, there is too much disorder to act now. You must wait because any premature endeavor will incur a setback.
—Waiting does not mean standing about with your arms crossed. Overcome danger by leaving the confusion behind. You can do this by establishing a value system to sort through the surrounding profusion. This work will have to be done with clarity and without hurry. Even if everything seems to be upside-down, it has an inner order, which will reveal itself to you.

Finally, it is important for you to look for support and advice. You need to accept any help for the accomplishment of your task.

Predictions and Advice

A period of great and very favorable progress when respecting the following conditions:
—Do not hurry, be attentive, prudent, and do not become discouraged.
—Do not undertake anything before you're out of the confusion and danger.
—Look for advice and support.

Hexagram 3/Interpretation of the Lines

Rulers of the Hexagram: 1st and 5th Lines

1st Line (9) +

When you are both hesitant and frightened, undertaking nothing while remaining persevering and determined is favorable. It would be worth your while to look for help from others.

2nd Line (6) +

The Difficulties of Beginning have immobilized you and left you indecisive. An unexpected issue or event will present itself (the arrival of a friend, perhaps). Initially, this help will be fruitless because the circumstances are not favorable. Then, events will take a turn for the better and then you will be able to engage yourself. This is conveyed in the Ancient Text by the image of a young girl who rejects marriage proposals for ten years, and then finally consents.

3rd Line (6) -

If you rush ahead, blinded by your quest, without support or preparation, you will only mislead yourself. Signs already show it. Faced with a similar situation, the noble man prefers to renounce his intentions rather than encounter failure.

4th Line (6) +++

Immobilized by difficulties, you must commit yourself to alliances (seek marriage). Only then will you be able to advance successfully, and everything will be favorable.

5th Line (9) ++ or ---

When difficulties in the beginning intervene in your influence and effectiveness, actions of small scope, undertaken patiently and discretely, will lead to success. Putting forth ambition, force, or initiative will presage failure.

6th Line (6) o

When difficulties immobilize, discourage, and worry you, it is preferable for you to pull yourself together and mobilize your forces.

Constituting Trigrams (No. 4 Immaturity)		*Nuclear Trigrams* (No. 24 Return of the Light)	
Mountain Water	䷃	䷗	Earth Thunder

Symbols and Images

—Water springs forth impetuously and aimlessly at the foot of the Mountain. It is the image of youthful folly and inexperience.
—Water represents danger in the face of which youth finds itself paralyzed (Mountain).
—Water and Mountain symbolize the appropriate attitude when facing danger: inner perseverance (Water in the lower trigram) and outer calm (Mountain in the upper trigram).

General Situation

The situation described here is not without confusion and risk; whether or not it is favorable depends on your attitude. Your first tendency is to retreat like an adolescent paralyzed by lack of experience. This attitude is understandable but needs to be rectified by apprenticeship.

You must be receptive and attentive to everything that could be a source of instruction. Through learning, you will compensate for your immaturity, fill your own "gaps" and dissipate your impetuosity or lack of discernment. This is the way you will leave chaos behind you, escape trial and error, and discover the meaning of events. Learning will also permit you to acquire more independence, maturity, and depth.

It is essential to exchange your "immaturity" for perseverance. If you stop yourself, discouraged in the face of danger, you will be victimized by it. That is why it is necessary to be courageously conscious of your inexperience and to choose to transform yourself in order to be capable of assuming your present and future responsibilities.

In order to make good use of your apprenticeship, you must recognize the limits of your ability. Then, you must seek the advice of an experienced person with whom you can be open and modest, because no one can teach anything to someone who thinks he knows everything, and no one can help him, either.

Once this person, guide, or teacher is found, it is necessary to interrogate him or her with discernment. An initial question is legitimate, but if the following questions are inspired by mistrust, absence of reflection or seriousness, the teacher, like the oracle of the *Yijing*, will keep silent.

This hexagram advises the teacher who is responsible for dissolving the blindness of youth to wait for the student to come to him rather than approaching the student. His teaching will thus inspire respect and attention. Lastly, the teacher should not hesitate to repeat lessons again and again so that the student fully grasps the material and can collect the fruits of the teaching.

Predictions and Advice

—Favorable if you are aware of your confusion and inexperience, and you put yourself into apprenticeship.
—You need to adopt rules of conduct appropriate to your situation as either a student or a teacher, and to be persevering.

Notes on Interpretation

First of all, determine whether you are student and/or teacher. In any case, you need to know from whom you are learning or who you are teaching.

This response is also addressed to those who interrogate the oracle improperly or too often.

According to the Commentaries, the second line is the teacher. Even though its position is humble, it possesses the qualities of a true guide. The student is the fifth line; a prince who accepts instruction.

Hexagram 4/Interpretation of the Lines

Rulers of the Hexagram: 2nd and 5th Lines.

1st Line (6) o

The apprenticeship begins. In order to dispel the blindness of youth, it is important to be firm and to adopt just and clear rules of conduct. Recourse to punishment may even be taken. However, in order to keep progress from being restrained, one should not be too severe.

2nd Line (9) +++

Youthful blindness must be dispelled. A gentle, humble, and open attitude will lead to success. In the Ancient Text, it is said that to take a wife or to make inquiries to a woman brings success. It is added that the student is able to grasp responsibilities.

3rd Line (6) ---

It is not good to act when humble behavior and flexibility are too superficial. The image is of a young wife who only sees the husband's gold, without seeing the husband himself. In such circumstances, nothing is favorable.

4th Line (6) -

If the blindness of youth is unchecked, it will lead to disagreements.

5th Line (6) +++

When freshness and receptivity—auspicious for apprenticeship and progress—are present, this leads to success.

6th Line (9) o

When the blindness of youth must be punished, be neither too severe nor too conciliatory with the source of trouble.

Constituting Trigrams *Nuclear Trigrams*
(No. 5 Waiting) (No. 38 Opposition)

Water / Heaven

Fire / Lake

Symbols and Images

—There is danger without (upper trigram: Water), strength within (lower trigram, Heaven). Strength should be contained within because of the external danger.
—The clouds (Water), high in the sky, are gathering to bring beneficial, nourishing rain. It does not fall yet, but will come in due time.
—The second meaning attributed to this hexagram is "nourishment," for a person's nourishment depends upon Water and Heaven.

General Situation

In the situation represented here, the best course of action is to wait, because you are confronted with an obstacle or danger. Do not take it lightly; evaluate it lucidly in order to surmount it easily. If you are aware of the necessity of reflecting upon your actions beforehand, you will be more self-confident and will wait with joy and assurance, with no attachment to the outcome, instead becoming impatient or hopeless.

Events impose this time of pause, for none of your initiatives can modify the circumstances; they would only increase the danger. Wait for the situation to develop and mature in order to effectively intervene without risk.

The Wait is neither a renunciation nor a period of forced idleness. Put it to use to regenerate your physical and moral strengths by giving your body rest and nourishment and your spirit joy and understanding.

The Wait is only possible if you are strong. The weak person, in similar circumstances, gives up, charges blindly forward, or exhausts him- or herself in vain agitation. Generating this strength is only possible with perfect integrity, a clear vision of things, and an inner certitude, whatever the goal may be. Having a clear vision also means that you need to guard against being lulled by your illusions or being complacent about your deficiencies and limits.

Finally, the moment will come when it will be necessary to act. This moment will present itself clearly. You will then need to be determined, quick, and effective. In this way, success will be assured.

Predictions and Advice

Success under the following conditions:
—Waiting for the time to act while cultivating sincerity, calm, and determination.
—Taking advantage of the waiting time to restore your moral and physical strengths.
—When the moment to act comes, you can engage yourself in great enterprises.

Notes on Interpretation

For questions relative to health, this hexagram indicates overwork. In this case, rest and a healthy lifestyle are imperative.

Each line is more or less close to danger. The image of danger is represented by Water:

1st line: waiting in the meadow, far from the water;
2nd line: waiting in the sand, and where there is sand, water is not far away;
3rd line: waiting in mud (water has penetrated the earth);
4th line: waiting in blood, there is danger;
5th line: waiting with wine and nourishment;
6th line: one regains energy and the wait comes to an end.

Hexagram 5/Interpretation of the Lines

Ruler of the Hexagram: 5th Line

1st Line (9) +

Although you are far from danger, adopt a line of conduct based on perseverance and constancy. In this way you will commit no fault.

2nd Line (9) +++

Danger approaches. You confront some verbal criticism (rumors, gossip, disputes, etc.) but, finally, success will come.

3rd Line (9) -

If you rush ahead or advance prematurely, you will provoke the source of trouble ("raiders" in the Ancient Text).

4th Line (6) ---

When danger hits you head-on, staying calm, flexible, and patient will bring you out of the abyss.

5th Line (9) +++

Waiting in joyfulness and repose, perhaps even while enjoying some wine and nourishment, is a presage of success.

6th Line (6) +++

The Wait is at its apogee, you can reassemble your energy. Unexpected events or help will present themselves. Welcoming and respecting them will finally bring you success.

CONFLICT/HEXAGRAM 6

Constituting Trigram (No. 6 Conflict)	*Nuclear Trigram* (No. 37 Family)
Heaven / Water ䷅	䷤ Wind / Fire

Symbols and Images

—Heaven in the upper trigram has a naturally ascending movement. Water in the lower trigram has a naturally descending movement. Not only do the two elements move farther away from each other, but Water indicates the presence of an interior danger. This is the image of conflict.

—There is strength without (Heaven in the upper trigram), and danger within (Water in the lower trigram).

General Situation

The overall situation is favorable but it contains the seeds of disagreements or litigation, and you need to defuse them at any cost. In fact, as long as a disagreement persists, you will be blocked and you will not be able to undertake anything.

Whether or not the conflict has been declared, the attitude to adopt is, on the one hand, good faith and the desire for conciliation and, on the other hand, a sincere search for the source of the difficulty and its remedy.

You should proceed with a detailed analysis of the situation in order to discover where the roots of evil are hidden. Allowing misunderstandings, imprecision, or disharmony to stand will engender anxiety and then grievance. In order to defuse the crisis, you will have to clearly state a worthy objective, delineate the rights, duties, and functions of everyone involved, and inspire in them a common ideal or interest. In short, cover every detail and use diplomacy while searching for the support and advice from someone important.

If the conflict has exploded, you should not feed it and bring it to the point of no return; hold fast to serenity, prudence, and good will in order to dissipate it. You need to develop enough strength to make the first steps toward reconciliation and a sincere search for common ground.

If your actions are combative, you will enlist yourself in the conflict, it will go on interminably and harm everyone, whether you are right or wrong.

Finally, you cannot begin anything new during a time of Conflict, for it makes you vulnerable.

Predictions and Advice

—Success if you seek peace by defusing the conflict.
—Failure if you persist in the conflict.
—Examine things that are unfolding and call on someone impartial for advice.
—Do not undertake great things.

Notes on Interpretation

When searching for the possible sources of conflict, do not forget to examine yourself. Conflict can also come from friction brought on by an overly stubborn or energetic attitude on your part (Heaven, strength without).

The Commentaries note that this hexagram addresses civil proceedings while Hexagram 21 refers to criminal proceedings.

HEXAGRAM 6/INTERPRETATION OF THE LINES

RULER OF THE HEXAGRAM: 4TH LINE

1ST LINE (6) +++

If you put an end to the conflict, then gossip, rumors, and other verbal exchanges will subside and this will lead finally to success.

2ND LINE (9) +

When conflict pits you against an enemy that you cannot conquer, it is best for you to retreat and abandon the fight. Thus you will safeguard those who depend on you, and your humility will keep you from committing fault.

3RD LINE (6) +

You must rely on the experience of the Ancient Ones and wisely stand back, for the conflict is dangerous. In acting this way, you will finally come upon success. Do not seek honors or responsibilities, even if it is in the service of a superior.

4TH LINE (9) +

Refraining from defending your point of view, changing your attitude, and returning to the old order will bring you peace and will presage success.

5TH LINE (9) +++

Making your proper rights known, or assuming the role of an arbitrator or mediator will lead you to great success.

6TH LINE (9) ---

Pursuit of the conflict may momentarily bring you victory, but it will quickly be taken away in repeated defeat.

MOBILIZING THE ARMY/HEXAGRAM 7

Constituting Trigrams	*Nuclear Trigrams*
(No. 7 Mobilizing the Army)	(No. 24 Return of the Light)

Earth / Water 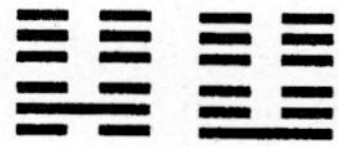 Earth / Thunder

Symbols and Images

—Water accumulated underground is similar to a nation's armed forces, which remain hidden while danger is not evident.
—The two constituting trigrams describe an army: danger within (in essence, an army is dangerous) and obedient without (it must submit to its general and strict discipline).
—The distribution of the lines also suggests an army; a single strong line (the general in the 2nd place) mobilizes all the other weak lines surrounding it.

General Situation

The situation described here is very delicate for it necessitates the implementation of rigorous discipline and mobilization of all your energy in order to confront danger or emergency.

Just as an army cannot become operational from one day to the next, but prepares itself in times of peace, you must develop, nourish, and gather together your physical and moral strengths. Even if combat is not imminent, you need to envision it and prepare yourself for it.

In order to make good your enterprise, you must above all have righteousness, discipline, and perseverance. Any power, left unguided, can lead to destructive violence. That is why it is imperative to channel and organize power while following just and balanced regulations that will prevent misunderstandings and promote the establishment of peace after the conflict.

Finally, an army needs a general who is competent and has integrity, who sustains enthusiasm and galvanizes the troops with legitimate and brilliant objectives, because leading an army by force or with unworthy motives never brings long-lasting results.
This general must also be able to count on the liberty of movement granted to him by the support of a sovereign. All of these images indi-

cate that you should develop your inner attitude and support circumstances that will make you an effective leader.

Predictions and Advice

—Presage to success if you are developing the qualities and capacities of a good general.
—Nourish, discipline, and mobilize your combative strength, and only use it as a last resort when a clear and just goal has been defined.

Notes on Interpretation

This hexagram can sometimes simply indicate that you need to gte yourself together or discipline yourself. It can also warn you about a delicate situation that demands a strategy or exceptional measures. If you have a leading role, or you are responsible for others, Mobilizing the Army gives all the necessary indications for correct action.

Finally, if you have a fiery temperament, this hexagram underscores the need to channel your energy and make sure that its use is justified.

HEXAGRAM 7/INTERPRETATION OF THE LINES

RULERS OF THE HEXAGRAM: 2ND AND 5TH LINES

1ST LINE (6) o

If, when mobilizing the army, the objective is not justified or if order and discipline are deficient, there will be failure.

2ND LINE (9) +++

Being at the center of the army and mobilizing it promises success and the absence of fault. Furthermore, your superiors recognize your merit and will expand your field of action.

3RD LINE (6) ---

If the army is not directed by someone appropriate or in an appropriate manner, this is a presage of failure.

4TH LINE (6) +

An army that retreats in order to abandon an impossible fight is not to blame.

5TH LINE (6) ++ OR ---

With a justifiable reason you can mobilize the army and capture the perpetrators of trouble. This way, no fault is committed. It is imperative that the army be directed by a competent and experienced leader. If the army has a leader with no authority, knowledge, and legitimacy, it will know defeat.

6TH LINE (6) +++

Once the army's task has been accomplished, it is time to dispense new functions and acknowledge those who have supported you. Each person should be rewarded according to his or her value and merits. To give authority or responsibilities to those who do not have breadth of scope will cause trouble.

Constituting Trigrams (No. 8 Solidarity)	*Nuclear Trigrams* (No. 23 Usury)
Water ䷇	䷖ Mountain
Earth	Earth

Symbols and Images

—Water over Earth: the waters of the earth unite whenever the occasion presents itself in order to follow the same course. This is the image of mutual helpfulness, of gathering and solidarity.
—The gathering takes place with the help of the single yang line (the sovereign), which unites all the yin lines around it.
—Water adheres to the surface of the Earth; it flows into each crevasse and follows each slope. This is the image of the profound adhesion necessary in any union.

General Situation

This hexagram indicates that this is not the time for solitary action, but for rallying together. You should approach others and create alliances with and between people who hold ideas or interests in common. This alliance is the requirement for success and growth. In fact, nothing in nature prospers without union, association, or cooperation. However, this unification, in order to be profitable, should meet several criteria.

In the first place, there has to be a point of convergence for the union. Whether it is an idea or a person, this element should be strong and brilliant. The oracle advises re-interrogating the *Yijing* in order to find out if this center has the necessary qualities. The worthiness of this center of convergence is important because if your enterprise fails, the consequences will be heavier than if nothing had been undertaken.

Secondly, each member of the group should benefit from this alliance and find within it his or her function. The organization and inner unity that this implies are symbolized by the waters of the earth, which respond to the same laws.

Thirdly, at the heart of this alliance, each member needs to preserve a sincere spirit of solidarity and mutual helpfulness. Supervisors need helpers to accomplish their tasks, toward whom they should be supportive and magnanimous. As for the helpers, they should respect their supervisors and follow their directives, so that the helpers will be assured of protection and will be able to progress.

Lastly, the time during which you will be able to join with others is limited. If you are too hesitant or too uneasy, you will arrive too late and find the door closed.

Predictions and Advice

—Success with the help of a solid alliance.
—Ask the oracle a second time if the center of the alliance has the required qualities. This way, not a single fault will be committed.
—If you are too hesitant, you will arrive too late, and that would be a failure.

Notes on Interpretation

If you are alone, this hexagram clearly indicates that you need to get out of this isolation. Success and joy will come from exchange and mutual helpfulness.

The delicate point in this response is often determining what or who is the point of union. Once this is determined, ask the oracle if this center has the requisite qualities.

Hexagram 8/Interpretation of the Lines

Ruler of the Hexagram: 5th Line

1st Line (6) ++

Everything favors union; you can ally yourself with others without committing fault. External events conspire to support you if you are confident and sincere. All of this will lead to success.

2nd Line (6) +++

An alliance born of true inner affinity is presage of success.

3rd Line (6) -

The alliance is made with those who are unsuitable.

4th Line (6) +++

Creating an alliance with the center of the group will bring you success.

5th Line (9) +++

When you possess a luminous point to rally around, allowing those who approach complete liberty to come and go as they please is essential. This way, everyone will be confident and serene. All of this is a presage of success.

6th Line ---

Alliance is impossible if there is not a point of communion or if you arrive too late at the center of the group. This would be failure.

Constituting Trigrams	*Nuclear Trigrams*
(No. 9 Small Tames)	(No. 38 Opposition)

Wind / Heaven  Fire / Lake

Symbols and Images

—This hexagram has only one weak, small yin line, in the position of the minister. This minister is able, because of his qualities, to momentarily contain all the other strong yang lines. The small (yin) has the power to tame.
—The Wind, high in the sky, gathers together the clouds. This is a modest and temporary action. One expects a storm which has not yet come.
—Gentleness without (upper trigram: Wind) and strength within (lower trigram: Heaven) are the qualities that the noble man should develop.

General Situation

This hexagram represents situations where an action of forcefulness or great scope is neither favorable nor possible. The necessary force, initiative, or power is not at your disposal. On the other hand, you can master the situation by demonstrating your flexibility, gentleness, and adaptability. With moderation, diplomacy, and modesty, you will succeed.

You can contain, tame, or pacify hostile forces with gentle and benevolent action, as well as with a progressive and constant amelioration of your qualities and capacities. You should also refine the expression of your character by adopting a more flexible and subtle behavior, state of mind, and way of speaking.

Although the influence that you can exercise as the weak over the strong can only be temporary, it can prepare the groundwork for other more important actions. Although you cannot directly intervene, it is possible for you to influence. Therefore, even if your will and your action are limited by powerful or hostile circumstances or people, these will not remain insensitive to the appeasement that you can bring them.

Predictions and Advice

—Favorable for showing gentleness, moderation, and flexibility.
—Limit yourself to small actions.
—Refine your outward expression.

Hexagram 9/Interpretation of the Lines

1ST LINE (9) +++

Forcing nothing, containing yourself, and returning to your path is without fault and will lead you to success.

2ND LINE (9) +++

Even if you are tempted to rush ahead forcefully, returning to your original position because of the pressure of events or people will lead you to success.

3RD LINE (9) ---

When circumstances prevent you from rushing ahead, you are like a chariot without an axle. In this position, the weak and the strong elements disassociate; they are estranged, like a husband and wife scowling at each other in a stand-off.

4TH LINE (6) +

When the situation calms down, elements that could have been a harmful source of worry dissipate. If you regain your confidence while remaining vigilant, you will commit no fault.

5TH LINE (9) +++

The weak and the strong need to find equilibrium, to complement and benefit each other. If both are loyal to each other, this relationship will be mutually enriching.

6TH LINE (9) o

The storm arrives and relaxes the atmosphere. An equilibrium is attained and should be preserved very prudently. You must no longer influence but follow and satisfy yourself with what has been acquired. Taking on more or going forward can only attract trouble and lead you to failure.

Constituting Trigrams: (No. 10 Treading Carefully)

Nuclear Trigrams (No. 37 The Family)

Heaven / Lake

Wind / Fire

Symbols and Images

—The weakest of the trigrams, Lake, is in direct contact with the strongest, Heaven. The highest, Heaven, is with the lowest, Lake.
—The youngest daughter walks behind the father (Heaven).
—Joy (Lake) is associated with strength (Heaven). Since this proximity of Heaven and Lake is prudent and absent of rivalry and impertinence, all goes well.

General Situation

The situation is delicate because you are in direct contact with strength, rudeness, or hostility, while you yourself are weak, accommodating, or gentle. You will prevail without damaging your chances for success only by advancing openly, without arrogance.

You need to act with precaution for, contrary to protocol, here the weak—that is to say, you— approaches and solicits the strong. This situation is naturally dangerous. That is why you must adopt a line of conduct based on conciliation and good humor, for nothing can resist a cheerful, confident, and sincere character.

Follow the order imposed by convention and hierarchies. Be joyful without carelessness, solicitous without importunity, and approach without encroachment.

Finally, try to establish a justifiable value system that applies to your inner self as well as to external elements and events. The positive should be encouraged and followed, and the negative should be rectified or abandoned. Then, the role of each person or element will be clearly defined and peace and liberty will be established.

Predictions and Advice

—Favorable if your conduct is founded on benevolence, good humor, and respect.
—A clear hierarchy of things and people must be respected.

Notes on Interpretation

In the Ancient Text, direct contact with the strong element is symbolized by the act of stepping on a tiger's tail. When the approach of the weak is made under good conditions, the tiger does not bite. But if, as in the third position, the step is uncontrolled, the tiger bites.

The treading in the lines follows a progression:

1st line: simple treading;
2nd line: treading on a flat path;
3rd line: a lame, one-eyed man treads on the tiger's tail and the man is bitten;
4th line: treading prudently on the tiger's tail;
5th line: treading dangerously with resolve;
6th line: reflecting upon the treading.

Hexagram 10/Interpretation of the Lines

Constituting Ruler: 3rd Line.

Governing Ruler: 5th Line.

1st Line (6) ++

Advancing in a simple and sincere manner will allow you to progress without committing fault.

2nd Line (9) ++

Treading with righteousness, clarity, and determination, and remaining aloof and solitary presages success.

3rd Line (6) ---

A lack of clarity and overestimating your capacities will entail perilous detours that can only hurt you and lead you to failure. This would be acting like a soldier pretending to be a general.

4th Line (9) +++

The fear instilled by advancing on perilous terrain will force you to redouble your vigilance and prudence. This will lead you to success in the end.

5th Line (9) -

Even great determination in advancing will not shelter you from danger.

6th Line (9) +++

When everything that needs to be accomplished is done, it is time to make an assessment. Examine your actions and their results. In so doing, you will recognize your value and know what to expect in the future. Carrying out this investigation properly and bearing the consequences will lead to great success.

Constituting Trigrams	*Nuclear Trigrams*
(No. 11 Prosperity)	(No. 54 Erroneous Engagement)
Earth ☷	☳ Thunder
Heaven ☰	☱ Lake

Symbols and Images

—Earth, in the upper trigram, has a naturally descending movement; Heaven, in the lower trigram, has a naturally rising movement. The two elements meet and unite their forces, bringing prosperity to all.
—The luminous yang lines arrive. The dark yin lines leave.
—This hexagram corresponds to the first month of the Chinese year (February–March).

General Situation

The times are favorable. Harmony can begin and with it, cooperation and understanding. These circumstances allow each person to find a place to express his or her nature, for the influence of the luminous element is so powerful that everyone benefits and prospers.

The strong and the weak are sincere toward each other: the strong in its benevolence, the weak in its enthusiastic compliance. In this way, they can unite for mutual benefit in a common effort.

It is important to take advantage of such good conditions so they can be truly fruitful. In order to do this you should:
—Harmonize your activity with the course of events. That means determining what needs to be done and acting in the right place, at the right moment. Neither procrastinating nor hurrying.
—Balance everything by increasing whatever is deficient and reducing whatever is in excess.

Predictions and Advice

—A naturally very favorable time, because the luminous principle arrives and dissolves obscurity.
—Because of the union and cooperation of the superior and the inferior, there is success.

Hexagram 11 /Interpretation of the Lines

1ST LINE (9) +++

You can and should make sure your peers follow you and stand by you. Then, you will be able to undertake great things with success.

2ND LINE (9) ++

Even a period of prosperity has its dry spots. You should resolutely continue your advance. If you pay attention to every single detail, however insignificant or remote, and do not limit your attention to those close to you, you will find the middle path and progress.

3RD LINE (9) ++

Life is made of ups and downs. Even though difficulties appear, your integrity, inner strength, and lucidity will prevent you from committing fault. You should remain confident, for the times are favorable. You will then benefit from a prosperous windfall.

4TH LINE (6) ++

Detachment from power and riches allows you to simply and sincerely unite with the weak. There is no need to worry, the times are favorable.

5TH LINE (6) +++

If, strong and forceful, you unite yourself with the weak in a humble and sincere manner, it will result in great success and happiness.

6TH LINE (6) --

When times are unfavorable, you should not force anything. Although you may limit your power and activities to your immediate environment, there is a presage of a predicament.

Constituting Trigram (No. 12 Decline) *Nuclear Trigram* (No. 53 Gradual Progress)

Heaven ☰ ☴ Wind
Earth ☷ ☶ Mountain

Symbols and Images

—Heaven, in the upper trigram, naturally rises; Earth, in the lower trigram, naturally descends; the two elements become increasingly separate. They no longer relate, bringing decline.
—The luminous yang lines leave. The dark yin lines arrive.
—This hexagram corresponds to the seventh month of the Chinese year (August–September).

General Situation

This hexagram describes a period in which darkness is too strong and nothing can grow or prosper. Not a single outward action is possible, for in times of obstruction everything is frozen. You must withdraw from all engagements, retreat, and hide your value, for these is a risk of discord or rivalry.

In such an environment, it is also preferable to turn down enticing propositions that might entail compromises that you will later regret. In this way you would spare yourself worries and difficulties because nothing can further your enterprise.

Lastly, the obstacles only pertain to the outside world. Your integrity is safeguarded within your self. You can be confident because this period of decline will not last.

Predictions and Advice

—Circumstances are adverse or hostile.
—Best not to act and retreat than to struggle in vain.

Notes on Interpretation

Decline can indicate that you are going toward an impasse or that you are already there. But the fact that none of the lines in this hexagram are negative shows that this period of obstruction will come to an end.

HEXAGRAM 12 /INTERPRETATION OF THE LINES

RULERS OF THE HEXAGRAM: 2ND AND 5TH LINES.

1ST LINE (6) ++

Retreating, followed by your peers, is presage of success, and can only be favorable.

2ND LINE (6) ++

Patiently bearing constraints will bring success to the weak. As for the strong, even adversity cannot wear down its inner value.

3RD LINE (6) o

You bear worries, embarrassment or shame.

4TH LINE (9) ++

If you keep your engagements and assume your responsibilities, you will commit no fault and benefit from support which will illuminate your action.

5TH LINE (9) +++

When the period of adversity reaches its end, remaining firm with integrity promises success. It is, however, important to remain extremely prudent and vigilant, while firmly adhering to fundamental values.

6TH LINE (9) +++

Adversity comes to an end, but you must still show perseverance and courage in order to eliminate the last obstacles; only then will you be able to rejoice.

Constituting Trigram (No. 13 Concord among People)	*Nuclear Trigram* (No. 44 Approach of the Malleable)
Heaven ☰	☰ Heaven
Fire ☲	☴ Wind

Symbols and Images

—Inner clarity (lower trigram: Fire) and outer strength (upper trigram: Heaven) are indispensable for creating a true concord among people.
—Fire and Heaven rise up in the same direction, symbolizing concord among people.
—The single weak yin line, in the place of the high functionary (2nd line), unites around it five strong yang lines. This means that this community rests upon inner qualities (the high functionary) rather than upon power (the role of the sovereign).
—The idea of community is reinforced by the presence of the nuclear hexagram, which is also known as "Coming to Meet," Hexagram 44.

General Situation

This hexagram indicates a time in which concord and community between people are necessary and favorable. Because of this fact, you will be able to undertake something ambitious and inspire those around you to assemble and unite their forces. Then you will be able to surmount obstacles and put your efforts into a good outcome.

In order to mobilize others and find the necessary support, you should be sincere, firm, and persevering. Furthermore, the group should not be based on private and short-sighted interests but on the greater matters of heart and mind. In fact, for a true concord among people, all the members must be tolerant and capable of welcoming everyone involved, whatever their differences, so that each one can freely and serenely develop. Completely opening up your heart and mind will give your actions unlimited horizons.

Finally, in order for concord to emerge from a viable community, the members should firmly and unanimously follow a worthy goal or guide. Everyone's place and role should be defined so that not a single misunderstanding arises.

Predictions and Advice

—Favorable for bringing yourself into accord with everyone.
—Clarity regarding the goal and organization is necessary.
—It is advantageous to undertake and persevere in great efforts.

Notes on Interpretation

When examining the text of the lines, you can see the extent to which a great clarity of spirit is necessary to establish harmony between people even though their differences may be numerous.

Hexagram 13/Interpretation of the Lines

Rulers of the Hexagram: 2nd and 5th Lines.

1st Line (9) ++

Bringing yourself into accord with everyone, without being limited by private or partisan interests, is without fault.

2nd Line (6) -

If communal bonds are made only with those who are related to you by blood or ideals, it will lead to regret.

3rd Line (9) --

When hidden agendas oppose agreement, there is a great risk of rising tension. The more the mistrust grows, the more the union is delayed.

4th Line (9) ++

If, unable to conquer, you embark upon the path of reconciliation, success will be assured.

5th Line (9) ++

After many tears and sighs, concord is at last joyfully attained, permitting reconciliation between even the strongest or most redoubtable persons.

6th Line (9) o

Either by personal choice or because of circumstances, you cannot agree with everyone. However, there is no regret in this.

GREAT POWER OF ACHIEVEMENT/HEXAGRAM 14

Constituting Trigram	*Nuclear Trigram*
(No. 14 Great Power of Achievement)	(No. 43 Resolution)

Fire   Lake

Heaven Heaven

Symbols and Images

—The single yin line occupies the place of the sovereign, the 5th line. It is the humility and benevolence (yin) of the sovereign that causes all the other lines to rally around him.
—Fire above, Heaven below: this is a Fire that shines high in the sky. This Fire is clearly visible, and enlightens everything.
—Outwardly there is the clarity of intelligence and order (Fire), inwardly there is strength (Heaven). Additionally, Heaven and Fire each have a naturally ascending movement. All of these signify recall a great power of achievement.

General Situation

The situation described here is naturally very favorable because it is inscribed in a time of fruition and progress in which you are accorded free reign and great achievement. Furthermore, you will benefit from the support of your entourage.

The association between the clarity of your spirit and intentions and the strength of your value and position attracts and promises great things. If you also cultivate modesty and generosity, your strength will manifest in an enlightened and refined way. You should take advantage of this wealth and opportunity to act in the right place, at the right moment, and in the right manner.

Great strength that is given to an inwardly weak person will produce poor results. That is why the great power of achievement needs to be accompanied by great inner worth. In this way, you will be like a fire that burns high in the sky, clearly discerning the good from the bad. Nourishing the good and correcting the bad, whether it is of an interior or exterior nature, should be a major aspect of your activity.

Predictions and Advice

—A period of great and very favorable progress due to humility, benevolence, nourishment of the good, and repression of evil.

Notes on Interpretation

The overall hexagram is so favorable that not one of the lines really falls into excess. The lines describe how to use the great power of achievement to escape the dangers associated with its use: self-importance, pride, vanity, jealousy, avarice, or excessive prodigality.

Hexagram 14/Interpretation of the Lines

Ruler of the Hexagram: 5th Line.

1st Line (9) +

By avoiding the dangers inherent in the great power of achievement, you commit no fault, in spite of difficulties.

2nd Line (9) ++

If you bear the weight of the great power of achievement without losing your firmness and integrity, you will be able to pursue your goal without committing any fault.

3rd Line (9) ++ or -

A person of quality, who disposes great power of achievement, acts to benefit all. A small person is incapable of this.

4th Line (9) +

By refraining from extreme measures or abusing the power of great achievement, you will commit no fault.

5th Line (6) +++

When the great power of achievement is associated with great responsibilities, it is necessary to excahnge, to share, and to unite while commanding respect and authority. Success is then assured.

6th Line (9) +++

When the great power of achievement is associated with true moral and spiritual qualities, everything is favorable.

Constituting Trigram	*Nuclear Trigram*
(No. 15 Restraint)	(No. 40 Deliverance)

Earth ☷ ☳ Thunder
Mountain ☶ ☵ Water

Symbols and Images

—The Mountain is hidden in the Earth. This is height which is balanced by depth. In this way excess gives way to equilibrium and restraint.
—The Earth (submission) is above the Mountain because the humble is superior to all. Humility elevates people.

General Situation

The situation described here indicates that restraint, flexibility, and simplicity should be your guides in leading you to a good outcome in your affairs. By seeking the most humble positions and keeping great restraint regarding your qualities and successes, you will attain your goal.

Humility and restraint allow the weak to distinguish and elevate him- or herself, and the strong to shine without self-glorification or expectation of honor. Humility and restraint are truly active forces that shape destiny and lead to great freedom of spirit and action, so powerful are the changes that affect inner attitude.

This hexagram also invites you to erase—on the outside as well as the inside—whatever is in excess and to make up for whatever is wanting:
—Outwardly, restraint eliminates arrogance which estranges people and generates conflicts, and it augments modesty which engenders love and mutual helpfulness.
—Inwardly, restraint imparts an even mood, the recognition of others' qualities, and patience that makes all things flow easily.

Predictions and Advice

—Your goal will be obtained with the help of restraint and true humbleness.
—Restraint balances and appeases all things.

Notes on Interpretation

Humility and restraint are such powerfully positive inner attitudes that none of the lines is truly unfavorable. This hexagram can also indicate that your field of intervention is limited and that it is preferable to remain modest in your objectives and the methods for carrying them out.

HEXAGRAM 15/INTERPRETATION OF THE LINES

RULER OF THE HEXAGRAM: 3RD LINE.
1ST LINE (6) +++
Great modesty and restraint will permit you to undertake great things with success.
2ND LINE (6) +++
Truly sincere restraint will generate tangible results. To continue in this way presages success.
3RD LINE (9) +++
Even if it requires great effort, restraint should be persevered in until the end. It alone will permit the successful accomplishment of what needs to be done.
4TH LINE (6) ++
All circumstances will be favorable if you cultivate sincere and effective restraint and modesty.
5TH LINE (6) +++
Sincere restraint, even in the absence of riches, will cause others to follow you. Thus you will be able to lead an energetic initiative and everything will be favorable.
6TH LINE (6) ++
Even though your restraint is manifest for all to see, it should not keep you from acting vigorously and firmly in taking the necessary sanctions.

Constituting Trigram (No. 16 Joyful Enthusiasm)			*Nuclear Trigram* (No. 39 Obstacle)
Thunder	☳	☵	Water
Earth	☷	☶	Mountain

Symbols and Images

—The single yang line, in the place of the minister, attracts the yin lines. Because the yin lines are by nature submissive and full of abandon, the attraction happens without resistance and with liveliness. This is joyful enthusiasm.

—Thunder above, Earth below: this is the movement (Thunder) that gives birth to flexibility and self-sacrifice (Earth).

—Thunder in the upper trigram accentuates its naturally ascending movement. Earth, in the lower trigram, accentuates its naturally descending movement. However, the two nuclear trigrams restrain and balance the whole situation: Water in the upper nuclear trigram descends, and Mountain in the lower nuclear trigram is immobile.

General Situation

You should make sure that you arouse the enthusiasm of others so that they follow and support you. The minority of yang lines signifies that you are not up to the task, and that you need to find and mobilize the support that you lack. That is why the notion of enthusiasm is important. It will make it possible to resolve differences of opinion and conduct, for the strengthening of will, and the creation of cohesion and harmony favorable for action. If this mobilization is done with flexibility and submission, it will make the whole situation dynamic and will lead to joy and satisfaction.

The majority of yin lines signifies that truly active force is lacking. It should be compensated for by action lead with determination, according to the path of least resistance. That is why you should make sure that there is a spontaneous "coming together," and that things are not forced.

If your goal is brilliant and serves everyone involved, if those who follow you are lead by joy, then everyone will advance with enthusiasm and devotion.

Finally, Thunder above Earth is the image of movement which comes out of the ground to be united with divine and ancestral forces. Sacred music, offerings, and dance elevate all beings and express this communion of rejoicing souls.

Predictions and Advice

—Enthusiasm, gathering, and unity around a common objective are profitable.
—Once the gathering is operative, it is favorable to conduct energetic and determined action.

Notes on Interpretation

This hexagram can pertain to the enthusiasm that you need to generate within yourself, that impels you to follow someone, or the enthusiasm that makes others rally around you. It is very difficult to ensure that enthusiasm is rational and measured, as joy and satisfaction can easily cause lucidity and restraint to fly out the window. The mistakes to avoid are essentially excessive or premature outbursts, as well as indifference or negligence. This is what is emphasized in the text of most of the lines.

HEXAGRAM 16/INTERPRETATION OF THE LINES

RULER OF THE HEXAGRAM: 4TH LINE.

1ST LINE (6) ---

If satisfaction and enthusiasm are too buoyantly or prematurely expressed, they will lead to failure.

2ND LINE (6) +++

If you are inwardly firm and stable, enthusiasm will not lead you astray and you will not wait until the last minute to act. This will presage success.

3RD LINE (6) o

Goals that are too elevated for your enthusiasm will bring deception. Being slowed down by doubts and hesitations will bring regrets.

4TH LINE (9) +++

When the motives of satisfaction or enthusiasm reside within you, you possess greatness. You will then be unanimously and unreservedly followed by your companions.

5TH LINE (6) o

Your situation hints of a persistent agitation or illness (a fever in the Ancient Text) which, fortunately, is not serious.

6TH LINE (6) o

If enthusiasm and satisfaction are tied up in confusion and blindness and at the height of this state you regain your composure and modify your attitude, you will commit no fault.

Constituting Trigram (No. 17 Following)	*Nuclear Trigram* (No. 53 Gradual Progress)
Lake ䷐ Thunder	䷴ Wind Mountain

Symbols and Images

—The strong yang lines of the two trigrams are below the weak yin lines and put themselves at their service. In gratefulness, the weak lines follow the strong lines.
—The association of joy (Lake) and movement (Thunder) makes one follow cheerfully.

General Situation

The overall situation is very favorable. This period of fruitfulness and progress should rest on the cohesion between people, for "following" and "being followed" are the two primary ideas of this hexagram.

Following does not depend on your position, for even if you are an eminent person, you must at least follow an ideal, let yourself be guided by it. Following also means espousing the movement of time. During the day it is appropriate to work and at night, to rest. In order to obtain joy and serenity, you should balance activity and rest, strength and flexibility, companionship and solitude.

In order to be followed, you should foster understanding and harmony because force is never effective in motivating others over a long period of time. Be open-minded in order to listen to the most humble and respond to their needs.

"Following" and "being followed" demand enthusiasm and joy; however, these feelings should not degenerate into carelessness or inconstancy. That is why perseverance and firmness of character are indispensable for avoiding any outbursts.

Predictions and Advice

—Period of great and highly favorable progress if you follow and/or are followed.
—Do not let your enthusiasm and joy lead you astray.

Notes on Interpretation

In the Ancient Text for the 2nd and 3rd lines, he who is worthy of a following is symbolized by a strong or older man of experience, while he who is unworthy is symbolized by a small child.

HEXAGRAM 17/INTERPRETATION OF THE LINES

RULERS OF THE HEXAGRAM: 1ST AND 5TH LINES.

1ST LINE (9) ++

Invested with certain responsibilities, you firmly follow the correct path. This presages success. Furthermore, welcoming and listening to others, without clannishness, will be fruitful.

2ND LINE (6) -

Attaching yourself to persons of little experience or mediocre penchants and values will distance you from luminous qualities and people who can really help you.

3RD LINE (6) ++

Following worthy persons or ideals will distance you from unworthy ones. In this way you will obtain what you are looking for; but it is good to remain firm and determined.

4TH LINE (9) --

While following, you overtake what you were following because you have gone too far or have lacked humility; this is a presage of failure. The revaluation that these circumstances instigate can enlighten you and save you from committing fault.

5TH LINE (9) ++

By sincerely following the good, success is assured.

6TH LINE (6) +++

It is favorable to attach yourself to the just with proven sincerity and fidelity. You can proceed with rituals and present precious offerings.

Constituting Trigram (No. 18 Restoring What Has Deteriorated)	*Nuclear Trigram* (No. 54 Erroneous Engagement)

Mountain / Wind  Thunder / Lake

Symbols and Images

—Wind blows at the foot of the Mountain, wreaking havoc with everything it encounters.
—The Mountain is like an overturned container inside of which something sweet (Wind) is rotting. The Chinese ideogram for this hexagram represents a plate of swarming maggots.
—External inertia (upper trigram: Mountain) and internal weakness of character (lower trigram: Wind) have caused the situation to deteriorate.

General Situation

This hexagram describes a period of very favorable growth because you have the chance to repair whatever has sunken into decline brought about by negligence, indifference, laziness, or inertia. You must transform and renew the situation represented here so as to reestablish an order that has deteriorated. Great progress is assured if you attend to this work without rushing, with flexibility, determination, and courage.

In spite of the urgency, you should not act rashly. First of all, try to understand what led to the degeneration because it did not happen by accident, but by previous inadequate activities. By finding the cause you will know where to apply yourself. If this research is done correctly and if the remedies are appropriately applied, the results will be enduringly favorable.

It is also important to closely evaluate your possibilities and your limitations and to refrain from throwing yourself into action until you are certain of what you can accomplish. If a lack of preparation arrests your calm progress, you will fall back into the errors of the past and lose your strength and confidence.

Finally, in order to keep the corruption from reinstating itself, you will need to regenerate, refresh, or stir up spirits and institutions. This will also require an inner examination. It would be illusory to try to re-establish order around you if you are incapable of doing so within yourself. With an inner examination, you will find a new departure, when a reviving and joyful force will be born, which will be the antidote to future causes of degeneration.

Predictions and Advice

—Period of great and highly favorable progress if you whatever has fallen into decline.
—You can undertake great things but you should maturely reflect upon all your actions; before acting in order to be perfectly prepared, and after acting in order to avoid a relapse.

Notes on Interpretation

In the Ancient Text, deterioration linked to inertia and rigidity (Mountain) is attributed to the father; that which is engendered by weak character or negligence (Wind) is attributed to the mother. The questioner of the oracle is the guardian succeeding the father and mother in taking charge of their affairs. These are symbols that are only rarely taken literally.

1st line: restoring what has been spoiled by the father. The deceased father is exempt of blame.
2nd line: restoring what has been spoiled by the mother.
3rd line: restoring what has been spoiled by the father.
4th line: restoring what has been spoiled by the father.
5th line: restoring what has been spoiled by the father.
6th line: here is the sage who is no longer implicated in the situation.

Hexagram 18/Interpretation of the Lines

Rulers of the Hexagram: 1st and 5th Lines

1st Line (6) +++

Capable of restoring what has deteriorated because of inertia, rigidity, or overwhelming forces, you must intervene with determination so that the damage is not allowed to recur. By being extremely vigilant and prudent, you will surmount the danger and finally know success.

2nd Line (9) o

When deterioration is due to carelessness and weakness of character, in order to stabilize the situation, you must be flexible, conciliatory, and without rigor. In spite of everything, the results of your action remain uncertain.

3rd Line (9) +

If, while restoring what has deteriorated because of inertia, rigidity, or overwhelming forces, you use too much energy or rigor, it will bring some regrets but will not be a great fault.

4th Line (6) -

If, while restoring what has deteriorated because of inertia, rigidity, or overwhelming forces, you are too indulgent or weak in character, you put yourself in a predicament.

5th Line (6) +++

Being capable of restoring what has deteriorated because of inertia, rigidity, or overwhelming forces, and associating yourself with companions, will allow you to bring this work to a good conclusion and you will be praised for it.

6th Line (9) +++

You are no longer directly implicated in the re-establishment of order, but can work on what has deteriorated by ameliorating and purify your own self.

Constituting Trigram (No. 19 Benevolent Attention)	*Nuclear Trigram* (No. 24 Return of the Light)
Earth ䷒	䷗ Earth
Lake	Thunder

Symbols and Images

—Two strong, luminous yang lines arrive. This is the increase of light.
—Earth above in the upper trigram and Lake below in the lower trigram: The Earth prospers around the Lake and contains it.
—Self-sacrifice is without (upper trigram: Earth) and joy is within (lower trigram: Lake).
—This hexagram corresponds to the twelfth month of the Chinese year (January–February).

General Situation

You are in a period of great and highly favorable progress that inspires growth and prosperity. The mood is joyous and optimistic. In order to take advantage of these beneficial circumstances, you should go forward with determination and uprightness. There is a danger of allowing yourself to dwell in negative emotions—carelessness, pride, jealousy—which can thwart success and growth.

This hexagram also speaks of the sage's role toward the people. The sage is as deep as the Lake and as vast as the Earth. His depth is that of his inexhaustible teaching, which penetrates all beings the way water penetrates the earth and stimulates growth. His expansiveness stems from his compassion, which neither excludes nor favors anyone. Thus, if you must teach and help others, you should look to this example so that everyone benefits from your activity.

Finally, no period of development and expansion is eternal. Keeping this in mind, you will be able to take the necessary measures so that the period of prosperity can prevail.

Predictions and Advice

—Period of great and highly favorable progress.
—Times of prosperity are not without limits. That is why you should be prudent and take measures to avoid a reversal of the situation.

Notes on Interpretation

This hexagram is favorable to the extent that not one of its lines falls into excess, even though the third place encompasses some difficulties. The three first lines arouse development and prosperity, the last three master it.

HEXAGRAM 19/INTERPRETATION OF THE LINES

RULERS OF THE HEXAGRAM: 1ST AND 2ND LINES.

1ST LINE (9) ++

If you stimulate growth with your positive qualities, this will presage success.

2ND LINE (9) +++

If you stimulate growth with your positive qualities, this will lead to success and all circumstances will be favorable.

3RD LINE (6) o

If development is distorted by egoism or negligence, a general degradation will ensue. If you regain your self-control, you will commit no fault.

4TH LINE (6) +

If you are careful to put growth to the service of all, not a single fault will be committed.

5TH LINE (6) +++

If development is mastered competently and you fulfill the duties and responsibilities of a sovereign, you will know success.

6TH LINE (6) +++

When growth is aligned with generosity and wisdom, it leads to success and the absence of fault.

Constituting Trigram (No. 20 Contemplation)	*Nuclear Trigram* (No. 23 Usury)
Wind ☴	☶ Mountain
Earth ☷	☷ Earth

Symbols and Images

—Two yang lines are atop four yin lines. This shape recalls a tower from which one can contemplate the surroundings and which can itself be contemplated from afar.

—The Wind makes itself felt throughout the Earth, its breath curves the grasses. This is how the gentle influence of the superior being is manifested.

—This hexagram corresponds to the eighth month of the Chinese year (September–October).

General Situation

The situation represented here demands that you be an example upon which others can depend to help them progress. Because of your position, your role, or your personality, you are like a beacon upon which all eyes converge. It is therefore imperative that your inner attitude and conduct is worthy of such a responsibility and that these rest upon sincerity as well as respect for others and essential values.

It is also imperative that you elevate your point of view while examining the situation and people involved in an unbiased or detached manner. In so doing, your understanding will have depth and will be founded upon reflection, meditation, and introspection.

In the Ancient Text, it is said that this hexagram corresponds to the moment when, in a religious ceremony, "the ablution has been made, but not yet the offering."[37] The accent is therefore placed on the moment of reflection and devotion which accompanies the beginning of ceremonies during the ablutions. This means that it is not yet time for action, but for preparation. This is a moment of pause, of reflec-

[37] Wilhelm, p. 82.

tion, of seriousness, where not a single detail is neglected.

This hexagram also speaks of learning and of the religious sentiment that allows one to be receptive to inspiration. By contemplating Heaven, your actions will conform to it, you will cultivate yourself, and be capable of elevating others through your example as well as through your teachings.

Predictions and Advice

—Not the time for action, but for preparation.

—The period is favorable if contemplation, research, and reflection are present with a view to elevate your conduct and have it serve as an example.

Hexagram 20/Interpretation of the Lines

Rulers of the Hexagram: 5th and 6th Lines.

1st Line (6) o or -

A puerile, superficial, or confused vision of things and people will bring no blame if you have no responsibilities, but if others depend upon you, this would be a source of disagreement.

2nd Line (6) o

A narrow or limited vision can eventually be profitable if it is compensated by a flexible, gentle, and virtuous attitude.

3rd Line (6) +

By focusing your attention on what has been accomplished in your life, you will be able to understand why it is sometimes necessary to advance or retreat, and how you should adapt yourself so as not to lose touch with the tao.

4th Line (6) ++

If your vision is broad and comprises the possibilities and needs of entire kingdoms, it is profitable to put yourself in the service of someone powerful.

5th Line (9) +++

You must focus your attention on your life so that it can be a perfect example. In this way, you will act like the noble man and commit no fault.

6th Line (9) +++

You must contemplate the results of your actions and your life so that it is a perfect example. In this way, you will be like the noble man and commit no fault.

Constituting Trigram	*Nuclear Trigram*
(No. 21 Cutting Through Separation)	(No. 39 Obstacle)

Fire
Thunder

Water
Mountain

Symbols and Images

—The general shape of this hexagram evokes a biting mouth that cannot close because an obstacle, the solid line in the 4th position, prevents it from doing so. In order to freely articulate itself, it must energetically bite through the obstacle.
—The association of Fire and Thunder suggests a prompt, firm, and energetic action.
—The action (Thunder) should be founded on the clarity of intelligence (Fire).

General Situation

An obstacle blocks your advance and prevents any union or reconciliation. Whatever it is, you must act promptly and energetically to eliminate it, because the longer you wait, the larger it will get, and it will settle in for a long time.

In nature, all things blossom and fructify with the help of union. Union and conciliation engender peace and equilibrium while conflicts and disruptions generate stagnation and then decline. That is why there is no worse disaster than disunion and there is no more urgent activity than restoring understanding.

In order to cut through the obstacle that created the separation, one must even go as far as using punishment. Even if a litigation is easy to evaluate and judge, you will need determination to bring it to an end.

Your intervention should be based upon the clarity of intelligence, upon discernment of justice and injustice, good and evil, serious errors and slight errors. You must find an equilibrium between hardness and flexibility. To be too cutting would be inappropriate and unjust. Being too conciliatory would belie a weak character or capitulation. The ideal is to keep a gentle attitude along with a decisive position in order to inspire respect.

Finally, it is important, in order to keep such a situation from cropping up again, to clearly define the limits of transgression and to enumerate the applicable sanctions.

Predictions and Advice

—Favorable if you act quickly and firmly to eliminate the obstacle preventing unity.
—Intervene with justice and clarity.

Notes on Interpretation

The Commentaries consider the obstacle to be a crime and the remedy a punishment. They also state that this hexagram alludes to criminal proceedings while Hexagram 6 speaks of civil proceedings.
The Commentaries add that the first and sixth lines suppress the punishment that one inflicts upon the "thieves" while the intermediary lines sanction it.

Inflicted or suppressed punishment, obstacle or crime are imaged in the following manner:

1st line: fetters around the feet, the feet disappear;
2nd line: biting into skin or tender meat so that one's nose disappears;
3rd line: biting into dried meat and coming upon poison;
4th line: biting into dried, hard, or bony meat and finding a metal arrow;
5th line: biting into dried meat and finding yellow gold;
6th line: a yoke of wood around the neck, the ears disappear.

HEXAGRAM 21/INTERPRETATION OF THE LINES

RULER OF THE HEXAGRAM: 5TH LINE.
1ST LINE (9) +

If a minor obstacle hampers you and dissuades you from advancing, this keeps you from committing a fault.
2ND LINE (6) +

Even if it is easy to cut through the obstacle, a certain amount of severity is necessary so that the punishment is felt. Thus there is no fault.
3RD LINE (6) +

Cutting through a very resistant obstacle brings about disagreements. In spite of the discomfort that this causes you, there is no fault.
4TH LINE (9) +++

Cutting through an extremely resistant obstacle necessitates penetration, swiftness, and determination. Although these difficulties should not be underestimated, they will be profitable. Success.
5TH LINE (6) ++

Biting through a very resistant obstacle necessitates justice, uprightness, and energy. Taking the risk of danger seriously will save you from committing fault.
6TH LINE (9) ---

If the obstacle or fault is great and the consequences heavy, remaining deaf to all warnings will lead to a failure.

Constituting Trigram (No. 22 Refinement)		*Nuclear Trigram* (No. 40 Deliverance)
Mountain / Fire		Thunder / Water

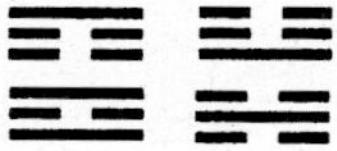

Symbols and Images

—Fire is at the foot of the Mountain. It illuminates and embellishes it, but this brilliance does not shine far.
—The weak line of the lower trigram beautifies the strong lines.
—Refinement flows from clarity within (lower trigram: Fire) and calm without (upper trigram: Mountain).

General Situation

This hexagram speaks of the need to have recourse to the refinement brought by beauty and grace in particular. You should carry gentleness, peace, and harmony, within yourself as well as outwardly. In this way you will be able to smooth out the rough spots, soften the bumps, making personal and formal relationships more flexible and easier to deal with. This refinement also allows things to be presented in their best light by giving them more brilliance. It is, however, necessary to use refinement with moderation and to grasp its limits, for refinement attaches to appearance and not essence. That is why it should not be given undue importance and, above all, you should not limit yourself to appearances when regulating important affairs; this would lead to a superficial or ephemeral approach to things.

The overall indications of this hexagram are of positive circumstances because they are infused with calm and clarity, but your influence and range of activity are restrained. It is a favorable period for clarifying current matters and giving them form, but you should limit yourself to modest actions.

Lastly, let refinement reflect your intrinsic value, the result of your inner development.

Predictions and Advice

—Favorable for introducing refinement, peace, and gentleness and for recognizing their limits.
—Favorable for clarifying things, for defining a brilliant goal and undertaking actions of small consequence.

Notes on Interpretation

This response can sometimes indicate that your attitude is too superficial or frivolous. You need to attach yourself a little less to the form and a little more to the intrinsic value or adjust the former through a greater understanding of the latter.

It can also give evidence of an overly brusque or uncompromising attitude which needs to be corrected with flexibility and civility. On the other hand, if you tend to take things too much to heart, this hexagram invites you to relax and lighten up.

Hexagram 22/Interpretation of the Lines

Rulers of the Hexagram: 2nd and 6th Lines.

1st Line (9) +

Refinement touches the feet: you regulate and coordinate your steps and your conduct, even abandoning advantage and prestige in order to continue on your way in total simplicity.

2nd Line (6) o

Refinement touches the beard: whether something is good or bad does not depend on the ornament that you add to it but on its intrinsic value.

3rd Line (9) +++

Refinement deeply penetrates what it touches. This is a presage of long-lasting success.

4th Line (6) ++

A refinement that brings you more simplicity will allow you to rise above a separation and will lead you to union or marriage.

5th Line (6) +++

Refinement touches upon both your immediate surroundings and the world outside. Even if what you have to offer is modest, the embarrassment that results from this will pass. In the end you will come upon success.

6th Line (9) +

If the refinement does not mask what is essential, there will be no fault.

Constituting Trigram (No. 23 Usury)			*Nuclear Trigram* (No. 2 Earth)
Mountain	☶	☷	Earth
Earth	☷	☷	Earth

Symbols and Images

—The single, strong, yang line is at the summit, chased by the yin lines. The position of the superior man falls under the pressure of his adversaries.
—There is friction between Earth and Mountain to the point where the Mountain is worn down. The adversaries have gained supremacy through usury.
—The defeat of the yang line is indicated by the general shape of the hexagram: a house with thin walls and a roof on the verge of collapse.
—In order to face the situation, one must be outwardly firm and calm (Mountain) and inwardly submissive (Earth).
—Firmness (Mountain) can be assured by a great and stable foundation of generosity (Earth).
—This hexagram corresponds to the ninth month of the Chinese year (October–November).

General Situation

This hexagram indicates that you cannot undertake anything right now because your foundations are threatened by usury or collapse. Before you do anything else, you must remedy this state of things by consolidating your support. This is done by understanding the overall situation.

When a person is strong, which is your case here, his adversaries do not risk an all-out frontal attack. They approach via detours and take their time to insinuate themselves into the situation—the effect of usury—to wear a strong person down. But as a rotten fruit reveals its seed, your defeat is the prelude to a new beginning.

Periods of darkness like this one are, in nature, a normal and transitory phenomenon. The light hides in order to regenerate, but when darkness is present, strength and wisdom should impel you to stay calm and serene, refrain from undertaking anything, and keep safely to the background.

In order to face usury, you must make sure your foundations are solid. What is above depends on what is below it. The base of the Mountain is Earth, as the base of the superior is the inferior. The superior should therefore show attentiveness and benevolence to the inferior. Inwardly, he or she will develop a true generosity of heart and spirit—the qualities of Earth which nourishes and sustains all things—for the adversaries designated here can also have negative emotions such as egoism, anger, lack of compassion or clarity of spirit.

Predictions and Advice

—Develop calm and flexibility in order to face the danger.
—You should not undertake anything; consolidate your supports.

Notes on Interpretation

The lines approach and then distance themselves progressively from danger: the fourth line submits to the full effect of it. The breakdown is sometimes symbolized by a bed—a resting place—breaking into pieces:

1st line: the feet of the bed split into pieces;
2nd line: the frame of the bed splits into pieces;
4th line: the entire bed splits into pieces.

Hexagram 23 /Interpretation of the Lines

Ruler of the Hexagram: 6th Line.

1st Line (6) --

Darkness has lightly touched you. If you are obstinate, this will be a fault that will presage failure.

2nd Line (6) --

Darkness has touched you. Persisting will be an error that presages a setback.

3rd Line (6) +

Darkness touches you. In spite of everything, you commit no fault.

4th Line (6) ---

Darkness fully penetrates you. Failure.

5th Line (6) ++

By mastering and directing the dark elements, you will be able to benefit from the support of those in high places, and everything will be favorable.

6th Line (9) +++

Darkness cannot last long. The remaining light is like a good fruit, intact and promising. You regain your full capacities. The dark principle can only hurt itself in the end.

Constituting Trigram			*Nuclear Trigram*
(No. 24 Return of the Light)			(No. 2 Earth)
Earth	☷	☷	Earth
Thunder	☳	☷	Earth

Symbols and Images

—A strong yang line arrives. This is the return of the light after a period of darkness.
—Movement is within (lower trigram: Thunder), self-sacrifice and submission is without (upper trigram: Earth).
—This hexagram corresponds to the eleventh month of the Chinese year (December–January).

General Situation

This hexagram indicates a period of renewal and change where the old, outworn, or inadequate is replaced by the new. This transformation is progressive, beginning on the inside, in order to gradually manifest on the outside. It is a natural, effortless process, for it is written in the course of time. All attempts to accelerate the process will be in vain, but not taking advantage of it would be a shame.

The Return of the Light happens by leaving behind distractions and confusion in order to hold to a superior goal. For this, it is important to adopt a positive attitude, and to reject anything that could lead to troubles or mistakes. This way, the foundation of your action and your character will be sane.

It is equally important to realize that you are only at the beginning of the renewal and that it could even take some time to truly manifest (seven days, according to the Ancient Text); it is therefore still extremely fragile. Because of this, you must act with caution, like a person who is recuperating from an illness: do not hurry anything, respect the time of convalescence, follow the rhythm of nature, do not overestimate your strengths and capacities. In so doing, you will increasingly nurture the positive values of this time.

Finally, the single yang line in the hexagram attracts the others: spontaneously, your peers come to join and support you.

Predictions and Advice

—Do not hurry anything, and do whatever is necessary whenever it is necessary, in order to leave behind confusion and past mistakes.
—The return of the light is just beginning. You must be prudent for the danger is still not far enough way.
—Determinedly follow a luminous goal.

Notes on Interpretation

The Return of the Light implies that it had been, at one time, chased away. That is why this hexagram often comes after a mistake or a fault has been committed; you must in the first place recognize this, for it can go unseen. Then, it is necessary to return to the correct path for this hexagram indicates the return to the light as well as the return of the light. The sooner this return is encouraged, the easier it will be; this is indicated by the different lines.

This hexagram can also simply indicate that the confusion and obscurity that surrounds you are on the point of disappearing.

HEXAGRAM 24/INTERPRETATION OF THE LINES

RULER OF THE HEXAGRAM: 1ST LINE.

1ST LINE (9) +++

The return of the light is easy when the mistake is slight and it only brings a few regrets. This return to the correct path will lead you to great success.

2ND LINE (6) +++

The return of the light will happen if you are flexible and humble. Success.

3RD LINE (6) o

Constantly going back over your errors and dwelling on them is dangerous, but protects you from fault.

4TH LINE (6) +

If, in the middle of obscurity, your activity remains luminous, even alone you can encourage the return of the light.

5TH LINE (6) ++

When the return of the light is accomplished masterfully, you have nothing to regret.

6TH LINE (6) ---

If you do not go back over your mistakes, your confusion will lead to failure and complications of every order. Persevering forcefully or stubbornly will only aggravate and amplify problems. This will lead to an impasse. It would be best, for the moment, not to undertake anything.

Constituting Trigram	*Nuclear Trigram*
(No. 25 Innocence)	(No. 53 Gradual Progress)

Heaven
Thunder

Wind
Mountain

Symbols and Images

—Thunder grumbles under Heaven. It is Spring, the image of innocence.
—The two nuclear trigrams—Wind (dispersion) and Mountain (immobilization)—temper the rising movement of the constituting trigrams.

General Situation

The period described here is very favorable; it is a period of blossoming and progress. Even if you have to face a difficult situation, you need not worry because it will disappear on its own. What is demanded of you here is essentially to remain in a state of receptivity, innocence, and sincerity.

Innocence is a state of simplicity and total openness that is free of anything preconceived, calculated, fearful, or any mental ruminations that do nothing more than confuse your vision of the world. Carry out your action without seeking profit, recompense, or recognition, for rediscovering innocence is also rediscovering a state of fundamental confidence—in yourself and others—where there is no room for doubt and expectation.

Innocence is neither ignorance nor reflexive instinct. It is an enlightened state, a spontaneous adhesion to that which is just, balanced, and harmonious. By cultivating this attitude, your inner wealth will be manifested by naturally responding to the necessities of the moment and people around you.

On the other hand, if you are not sincere and correct toward others as well as toward yourself, if your attitude is calculated, if your action is manipulative, then your enterprise will fail. Under such conditions, it is clearly preferable to undertake nothing.

The notion of the unexpected is equally linked to Innocence for, in second-guessing nothing, you are ready to receive even that which you did not anticipate.

Predictions and Advice

—Period of great and highly favorable progress by staying on the path of innocence, sincerity, and openness.
—Unfavorable if you are not what you should be or if you act in a calculated, instinctive, or puerile manner.

Notes on Interpretation

Everything—the general text for the hexagram as well as the text for the lines—leads us to believe that if you are in a state of innocence, it is good to undertake something; leaving this state will lead to failure.

Hexagram 25/Interpretation of the Lines

Rulers of the Hexagram: 1st and 5th Lines.

1st Line (9) +++

Advancing, if you are innocent and sincere, will lead to success.

2nd Line (6) ++

If you respond to the requirements of the situation, without ulterior motive, and with no other motive than to do what is needed, as needed, and when needed, then you will be able to undertake something.

3rd Line (6) --

If you confound innocence and negligence, a fortuitous or undeserved acquisition will, in reality, be a loss.

4th Line (9) +

Resting firmly in innocence and sincerity will save you from fault.

5th Line (9) +++

Even if you are sincere, there may still exist some points of confusion. Without doing anything to remedy them, they will disappear on their own. What a blessing!

6th Line (9) ---

When sincerity is transformed into excessive confidence, it becomes credulous, naïve, or indiscriminate. Acting this way will bring fault and nothing will be to your advantage.

Constituting Trigram	*Nuclear Trigram*
(No. 26 The Great Tames)	(No. 54 Erroneous Engagement)

Mountain ☶ ☳ Thunder
Heaven ☰ ☱ Lake

Symbols and Images

—Mountain is above Heaven, that is, it surrounds it. It is the taming or mastery (Mountain) of the creative forces (Heaven). This is done through the assertion (Mountain) of character (Heaven).
—The idea of accumulation or the gathering of force is encountered in two ways: Mountain gathers Heaven (the latter, in the lower trigram, rises and is restrained by the Mountain), and the two weak yin lines in the places of the minister and the sovereign gather and tame all the yang lines.

General Situation

You are in circumstances where your creative strength and resources have grown considerably; leaving your cocoon so that they may be expressed for all to see will bring you success.

The time in which you can dispense the creative power will depend on your determination and your interior attitude. As with any extreme, this situation is a little dangerous and demands that your inner strength be proportionate to your outer strength. For this you should maintain inner determination and integrity and meditate on the words and experience of the Ancients. The fruit of the inner work is a part of the accumulation to which the hexagram refers. It permits you to overcome your habits and past experiences. You are therefore better able to master and utilize the accumulation of new forces and can preserve them more effectively.

The accumulation of greatness should also encourage you to act publicly and accept official duties. In this fashion, that which you possess of greatness (or in greatness) will not be for your benefit alone, but to everyone's advantage; this is what will lead you to success, even if your endeavor is difficult.

Predictions and Advice

—Success in cultivating, educating, and affirming your character.
—Persevering and taking on official responsibilities will allow you to successfully engage yourself in difficult enterprises.

Notes on Interpretation

Being in a phase of expansion and possessing greatness is not devoid of danger, for any accumulation is a source of trouble.
The first lines are confronted with a lack of power, the last face the danger that surrounds the use of this power.

HEXAGRAM 25/INTERPRETATION OF THE LINES

RULERS OF THE HEXAGRAM: 5TH AND 6TH LINES.
1ST LINE (9) --
When danger is present, it is profitable to not advance.
2ND LINE (9) -
You are like a chariot without an axle, which cannot advance.
3RD LINE (9) ++
Even if your qualities allow you to advance, danger imposes prudence and vigilance. Carefully examining and regulating your forces and methods of action, and keeping sight of your goal will be favorable.
4TH LINE (6) +++
To ward off danger even before it appears will lead to great success.
5TH LINE (6) +++
Disarming the danger and rendering it nearly inoffensive will lead to success.
6TH Line (9) +++
A great freedom of action is attained. Success.

NOURISHMENT/HEXAGRAM 27

Constituting Trigram (No. 27 Nourishment)			*Nuclear Trigram* (No. 2 Earth)
Mountain	☶	☷	Earth
Thunder	☳	☷	Earth

Symbols and Images

Several symbols justify the name of this hexagram:
—Its appearance recalls a wide-opened mouth.
—The upper trigram, Mountain, is immobile, while the lower trigram, Thunder, moves upward, which is akin to the workings of the upper and lower mandibles of the face.
—The nuclear trigrams are Earth, which represents nourishment; the Earth nourishes all beings. This hexagram touches upon all that gravitates around the administration of nourishment because the mouth is open, that is to say, it is active. This action should find equilibrium between movement (Thunder) and calm (Mountain).

General Situation

You situation contains a presage of success but demands some attention so that you can be satisfied or provide for your needs and those of others.

On the outset, you need to properly determine the vital necessities. This hexagram talks about what enters and leaves the mouth, but the nourishment can very well be what feeds both the mind and the body. Nourishment should contribute to developing as well as preserving the vital energy of the body and mind.

In order to discern the needs of others you have to examine how and on what each person nourishes him- or herself: where do their interests, desires, priorities lie? What is valued? What is rejected? What is neglected? What is appreciated and sought? Make this investigation non-judgmentally, without rivalry or jealousy. It should render you capable of giving each person what he or she needs, for your action will be in vain if it is not adapted to its recipient; it would be the equivalent of giving solid food to a newborn.

You should not, above all, favor or reject anyone or anything, and distribute nourishment in a manner that is most profitable for everyone without neglecting the essentials. Earth gives to all beings what is vital to them, without preference or exclusion.

Finally, this hexagram indicates that beyond nourishment, it is necessary to respect the just and to reject injustice in everything that enters and leaves your mouth, including words. Neither too much nor too little; a correct equilibrium is desirable.

Predictions and Advice

Success under the following conditions:
—Knowing the nature of good nourishment, and knowing the nature of who is nourished by it;
—Observing a balance between what enters and leaves your own mouth.

Notes on Interpretation

Try to understand what you can give or receive, that is, what stands for "nourishment" in your situation.

Because of an unsound attitude, the first three lines indicate a personality that is in a position to provide for itself yet does not. The persona of the last three lines is more balanced in conduct and more successful.

Hexagram 27/Interpretation of the Lines

Rulers of the Hexagram: 5th and 6th Lines.

1st Line (9) ---

If you do not make use of the wealth represented by your qualities and possibilities, and choose to depend on others, this will lead to failure.

2nd Line (6) --

If you stray, not acceding properly to nourishment, and if you set your sights still higher, you will not be able to undertake anything.

3rd Line (6) ---

Distancing yourself from nourishment is presage of failure. Under these conditions, you will not be able to act for a long time because nothing will be favorable.

4th Line (6) ++

If, in refusing proper nourishment, you become humble and re-examine yourself, you will know success. You must preserve your dignity and show consistency and determination. Then you will commit no fault.

5th Line (6) ++

If your attitude is unconventional, remaining correct and persevering will lead you to success, but you will not be able to undertake any great things.

6th Line (9) +++

You have the qualities and power to nourish others. Remaining conscious of the difficulties and responsibilities that this entails will lead to success. Thus will you be able to undertake great things.

Constituting Trigram	*Nuclear Trigram*
(No. 28 The Great in Excess)	(No. 1 Heaven)

Lake  Heaven
Wind/Wood Heaven

Symbols and Images

—The strong yang lines are surrounded by weak yin lines. This is the image of a great beam, too weak at its extremities. There is an excess of that which is great, strong, heavy.
—The idea of excess is also found in the internal structure of the hexagram: two strong nuclear trigrams—Heaven—and two light constituting trigrams at the extremities: the joyful Lake and the gentle Wind.
—Lake above Wood imparts the idea of inundation. The water rises above the trees.

General Situation

Even though the situation is, on the whole, favorable, it demands extreme prudence and circumspection. The principle image of this hexagram is of a central supporting beam that threatens to give way because it is too heavy for its weight-bearing extremities.

This excess weight can, in some cases, indicate that you have embarked upon an exceptional path with goals that go well beyond the limits of convention. More often, it signifies that you are facing a threat capable of leading to collapse. If such is the case, an urgent solution must be found to quickly modify the situation so as to avoid rupture and re-establish equilibrium. Carry out this solution with determination and perseverance, but without violence or suddenness. The lower trigram symbolizes the gentleness that you have to develop internally, while outwardly displaying your confidence and good humor. During this time of great excess, it is paramount that you follow a clear and brilliant goal.

This hexagram also reminds us that the sage prefers to retreat rather than founder in excess. He lives harmoniously in this way because he is not affected by any estrangement or renunciation.

Predictions and Advice

—Favorable if you avoid crumbling under an excessive charge and if you follow a luminous goal.

Notes on Interpretation

In the first place, you must determine if you are someone great doing something great; in this case the prediction is favorable. On the other hand, if there is an excess, it is urgent to find out where or in what way you are exceeding the limit.

Do not forget that the overall situation is favorable. Therefore, if your project exceeds your possibilities and threatens to be too heavy for your shoulders, reducing it to more reasonable proportions will allow you to persevere.

Hexagram 28/Interpretation of the Lines

Rulers of the Hexagram: 2nd and 4th Lines.

1st Line (6) +

By taking the exceptional measures of gentleness and prudence, you will commit no fault. The image of this line is the load that one carefully places on a bed of reeds in order to keep it from breaking up.

2nd Line (9) ++

You can bring to fruition a situation that would have otherwise seemed hopeless. The image is a marriage between an old man and a young woman that is finally fruitful. Everything is profitable.

3rd Line (9) ---

If the load is too heavy, if you are too stubborn, the beam is going to give way, and this would be a failure.

4th Line (9) +++ or -

You have the required qualities to successfully redress the situation. But a lack of sincerity, or a desire to push for more will bring about disagreements.

5th Line (9) -

The situation can flourish for a while but will not bear fruit. This is without blame, but it is also without merit. One of the images of this line is an older woman marrying a young man.

6th Line (6) ---

If the task is too heavy, it will bury you, you will bring fault upon yourself and experience failure.

Constituting Trigram (No. 29 Danger)   *Nuclear Trigram* (No. 27 Nourishment)

Water ☵ ☶ Mountain
Water ☵ ☷ Earth

Symbols and Images

—The single, strong yang line of the Water trigram is stuck between two yin lines like a stream between the sides of a ravine. In order to get out of it, one must be like Water: persevering, determined, and patient.
—The repetition of the trigram Water is sometimes the repetition of danger, sometimes the untiring activity of the sage who teaches constantly while his student repeats his lessons.

General Situation

The situation represented here is favorable on the whole, even though you may face some kind of danger. You will be able to conquer it by adopting the qualities of Water.

Water takes the necessary time to overcome obstacles. If it encounters a hollow space, it fills it up, if it is a projection, it wears it down. It acts without hurry or hesitation, always with the same force, the same determination, and without ever losing the qualities of its nature. Following this example, confident in your resources, you should remain faithful to yourself and act incessantly. This way, the danger will only be exterior; inwardly, you will remain free and serene.

Like Water, flowing eternally, passing over the same path again and again, do not be afraid to repeat yourself in exercising correctness in order to move from a superficial attitude and understanding to a profound and durable integration. From this, you will enlarge yourself, learn, and teach.

It is also important to cultivate a peaceful and sincere heart. If you are clear like fresh water, your comprehension and your actions will be profound and just, and your influence will be effective.

The danger represented by this hexagram can also arise from sinking into or becoming accustomed to negative feelings (covetousness, pride, anger, et cetera). Your inner purity (yang line) in this case is in the grips of less noble impulses (yin lines), which must be overcome.

Predictions and Advice

—Favorable for working primarily on your inner attitude: try to be limpid sincere, patient and persevering.

Notes on Interpretation

Danger is sufficiently present so that not one of the lines comes upon success. However, it is possible to avoid fault.

Hexagram 29/Interpretation of the Lines

Rulers of the Hexagram: 2nd and 5th Lines.

1st Line (6) ---

If you accustom yourself to evil to the point of sinking further into it, failure is lying in wait.

2nd Line (9) +

Surrounded by danger, you can clear up an issue through actions of small scope.

3rd Line (6) o

No matter where you go, there is danger. Only faultless uprightness will give you some respite. Otherwise, it is best to not move.

4th Line (6) +

In an emergency, it would be better to give preference to sincerity and simple offerings than to grand ceremonies. With an open heart, you will be able to unite with and benefit from needed support. In the end, you commit no fault.

5th Line (9) +

As long as the danger has not yet been surmounted, you should follow the line of least resistance. In this way you will avoid fault.

6th Line (6) ---

If you are fettered and powerless in the midst of danger, you cannot obtain anything. This will be a failure.

Constituting Trigram (No. 30 Clarity) — *Nuclear Trigram* (No. 28 The Great in Excess)

Fire
Fire

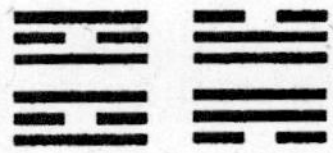

Lake
Wind

Symbols and Images

—Fire in the upper and lower trigrams: inner clarity creates outer clarity. This is the redoubling of clarity.
—In order to shine everlastingly, the Fire should attach itself to good fuel, as should the noble man attach himself to superior values.

General Situation

The overall meaning of this hexagram indicates a favorable situation where the accent is on the ties of dependence that unite all beings and things. In fact, in order to grow and prosper, each person should cling to someone or something that enlightens and leads, following the example of the Fire that clings to a good combustible in order to shine for a long time.

Thus, the weak should cling to the strong, and the strong should cling to a luminous ideal. This hexagram indicates that you are at once linked to and nourished by whatever or whoever you espouse. Certainly, the notion of exchange is not totally absent but dependence has priority. The dependence implies that you need to be flexible, humble, and persevering. Understanding the necessities and desires that create this dependence, and accepting them freely will lead to success.

Finally, you should not burn like a straw fire but diffuse a light deprived of excess. Thus, your enlightenment will extend far, favorably and durably influencing everyone.

Predictions and Advice

—Success by recognizing your dependence and by adopting an open-minded and docile attitude.
—Be persevering in following luminous principles.

Notes on Interpretation

Fire also symbolizes intelligence in as much as inner clarity casts light upon and understands the world. Therefore the lines of this hexagram can highlight the way, whether good or bad, in which you apprehend and understand the entire situation.

HEXAGRAM 30/INTERPRETATION OF THE LINES

RULERS OF THE HEXAGRAM: 2ND AND 5TH LINES.

1ST LINE (9) +

Being dependent and wishing to move or advance is not correct. In demonstrating your self-mastery, you will commit no fault.

2ND LINE (6) +++

Following that which is just and correct is like following a "golden light," which promises great success.

3RD LINE (9) --

Before shining anew, the sun sets. Keep yourself from falling into useless pleasures but regret what there is to regret; otherwise there will be failure.

4TH LINE (9) ---

Without flexibility or submission, your light is lively and sudden. It burns like a straw fire and is extinguished. In acting this way, you will be quickly forgotten.

5TH LINE (6) +++

Preoccupying yourself with others to the point of experiencing sadness and regret gives material for meditation, and depth to reflection. This leads to success.

6TH LINE (9) +

In order to fight inner or outer darkness, it is necessary to grasp them at their roots and master their minor effects. In this way, you will commit no fault.

INFLUENCE OF ATTRACTION/HEXAGRAM 31

Constituting Trigram	*Nuclear Trigram*
(No. 31 Influence of Attraction)	(No. 44 Approach of the Malleable)

Lake / Mountain  Heaven / Wind

Symbols and Images

—The summit of the Mountain forms a basin that receives the Lake. The Mountain is enlivened by the Lake and the Lake is nourished by the clouds that the Mountain draws around it. This is the image of the noble man who receives all persons and accepts their advice.
—Attractions are more intense among the young: Lake is the youngest daughter, Mountain is the youngest son.
—The weak (Lake) is above the strong (Mountain). The two elements attract and influence each other spontaneously. Mountain is stimulated by Lake, and Lake is stabilized by Mountain.

General Situation

You situation promises success if the influence that you exercise or to which you submit yourself is sincere and spontaneous.

Fiancés are a representation of this hexagram because one of the most intense influences is at work within their hearts. Of course, the game of attraction ensuing from influence is not limited to amorous exchanges, but touches upon all domains of life. It is found in all unions between a weak, yin element—submissive and joyful—and a strong, stable yang element. The two complete and enrich each other while they enrich others.

If that which influences kneels and abases itself before the weak element, and that which is influenced is joyful and docile, the relationship will be stimulating and full of sweetness, peace, and openness. An influence founded on sincere communion is naturally favorable for long-lasting unions. It is said that "To bring a maiden to wife brings good fortune." [38]

[38] Wilhelm, p. 122

In order for a reciprocal influence to exist between two people, each one needs to be attentive to the other; but in order for this attraction to keep from degenerating into an emotional tempest, uprightness and maturity are necessary. Therefore, joy should be united with self-restraint, openness toward others, and humility. These qualities ensure that, even at the summit of power, you will allow yourself to influence and welcome people and listen to their advice.

Predictions and Advice

—Influence and union based on mutual attraction, humility, and inner openness will lead you to success.

Notes on Interpretation

This hexagram symbolizes fiancés and places the accent on attraction, while Hexagram 32 represents marriage and emphasizes duty. It can indicate that you are too self-reliant and do not allow yourself to be penetrated by the influence of others. By the same token, a personality that is too arrogant, egocentric, or dominating will not benefit from the influence of others, and will therefore lose the possibility of renewal and self-improvement.

Being under an influence or exercising influence is difficult because attraction easily leads to premature, unreflective decisions or decisions lacking in depth and self-restraint.

The influence is imaged, except for the fourth line, by its action on different parts of the human body. The three first lines are under influence, the last three exercise it:

1st line: the influence is in the big toe;
2nd line: it is in the calf;
3rd line: it is in the thighs;
5th line: it is in the back;
6th line: it is in the lower part of the face.

HEXAGRAM 31/INTERPRETATION OF THE LINES

RULERS OF THE HEXAGRAM: 4TH AND 5TH LINES.

1ST LINE (6) o

A newly-born or superficial influence has no effect.

2ND LINE (6) --- OR +++

An influence that results in premature movement will lead to failure. On the other hand, not moving promises success.

3RD LINE (9) -

When the influence is too strong, you should slow down, restrict movement, otherwise it will bring regrets.

4TH LINE (9) ++

The influence here is a presage of success and disperses your regrets. However, if your influence is indecisive or inconstant, it will only motivate those who you have already won over.

5TH LINE (9) +++

The influence is correct and central. Thus, no fault is committed.

6TH LINE (6) -

The influence only manifests in words or lacks sincerity.

CONSTANCY/HEXAGRAM 32

Constituting Trigram (No. 32 Constancy)		*Nuclear Trigram* (No. 43 Resolution)	
Thunder	☳	☱	Lake
Wind	☴	☰	Heaven

Symbols and Images

—Thunder, masculine movement and impulse, is outside. Wind, feminine gentleness and self-sacrifice, is inside. These are the positions and qualities of married couples.
—Thunder above, Wind below: each element reinforces the other.
—Each yin line in one trigram corresponds to a yang line in the other trigram.

These three complementary elements symbolize marriage, the constancy of what is meant to endure.

General Situation

This hexagram describes a situation where you need to develop the qualities of endurance, permanence, and constancy with the help of a gentle and penetrating action. It symbolizes marriage, as well as the virtues and duties of the spouses.

Being constant does not mean being heavy, rigid, or static. That is why this hexagram unites two movements: the impulse of Thunder and the penetration of Wind.

The impulse of Thunder should incite you to follow a goal and to act outwardly. This movement should respond to the necessities of the moment to keep from sinking into hard-headed and narrow-minded obstinacy. The penetration of the Wind signifies that your action should be conducted with calm, serenity, and perseverance. Then, the flexibility and mobility of the Wind will not degenerate into frivolity and puerile agitation. Furthermore, if you have depth and constancy in your actions as well as your thoughts, you will not allow yourself to be distracted by the diversity of appearances.

Finally, possessing the constancy that gives firmness to your character will prevent you from committing errors and will make your conduct an example for those around you. They will be able to trust and count on you and then will find their place and function on their own.

Predictions and Advice

Favorable under the following conditions:
—demonstrating constancy through an open-ended action that corresponds to the demands of the moment;
—keeping your goal in sight and persevering.

Notes on Interpretation

This hexagram symbolizes marriage and emphasizes the duties of the married couple, while Hexagram 31 represents the fiancés and accentuates mutual attraction.

As is indicated by the majority of the lines, it is very difficult to attain a supple constancy for perseverance and attachment can easily become stubbornness and obsession.

Hexagram 32/Interpretation of the Lines

Ruler of the Hexagram: 2nd Line.

1st Line (6) ---

If you insist on your own way, you will be incapable of embracing the necessities of the moment. This will presage failure. Nothing will be favorable

2nd Line (9) +

Regrets disappear.

3rd Line (9) --

If you lack constancy and endurance, you will not be able to assume your responsibilities and this would be shameful. It will lead to difficulties.

4th Line (9) ---

If you persist upon a path that leads nowhere, you cannot hope to find what you are looking for.

5th Line (6) +++ or ---

You are full of determination and endurance. This brings success to the woman, through determination balanced with gentleness, and failure to the man, through rigid and excessive determination.[39]

6th Line (6) ---

If determination and endurance give way to impatience and agitation, this will lead to failure.

[39] "Woman" and "man" should be understood as yin and yang, respectively. Therefore, you should determine whether your role is yin or yang.

Constituting Trigram	*Nuclear Trigram*
(No. 33 Retreat)	(No. 44 Approach of the Malleable)

Heaven / Mountain

Heaven / Wind

Symbols and Images

—The dark yin lines are ascending and push the luminous yang lines into hiding.
—Mountain can rise high into Heaven, but its thrust is limited by its own nature. Heaven, itself, can retreat indefinitely before the Mountain in order to stay out of the fray. Thus does the noble man withdraw from danger, remain inaccessible (Heaven) and entice his adversaries into immobility (the Mountain).
—This hexagram corresponds to the sixth month of the Chinese year (July–August).

General Situation

You are in a period where adversity is gaining strength. Trying to fight it will be ineffective and will end in failure. Stepping back in order to take refuge, preserve your strength, and prepare for victory in the future is the wisest move.

The retreat is a voluntary action that is born of an understanding of the overall situation; it is not a debacle or a desperate escape. Therefore, you should proceed to retreat while you still have strength and initiative.

Retiring does not mean leaving the field open to the enemy. Your motivation should not be to harm the him, but to halt his progress, without forcing anything, by limiting yourself to small actions and offering him no compromise. It is not a question of seeking conflict or provocation, for the retreat should be done without hatred, rancor, or vengeance. In victory as in adversity, one must be upright, reasonable, and sincere. Furthermore, this attitude will certainly help you favorably influence your adversaries.

Predictions and Advice

—Favorable if you retreat while preserving your determination.
—Actions of small scope are favorable.

Hexagram 33/Interpretation of the Lines

Rulers of the Hexagram: 1st and 2nd Lines.

1st Line (6) --

It is best for you to make yourself totally inconspicuous and promptly retreat when there is danger; you cannot undertake anything whatsoever.

2nd Line (6) o

Even during the retreat, it happens that underlings are legitimately and firmly united to their superiors. Exceptionally strong links will then be created.

3rd Line (9) ++

If your retreat is hampered by attachments, it will give rise to tension and agitation, which will provoke danger. Gathering those who are close to you and concerning yourself with their safety will lead to success.

4th Line (9) +++ or ---

When the retreat is completed in an adequate manner, it is a success for the noble man but a loss for the ordinary man for he cannot resign himself to estrangement.

5th Line (9) +++

A perfect retreat is a presage of success.

6th Line (9) +++

Your retreat is fruitful. Everything is profitable.

GREAT STRENGTH/HEXAGRAM 34

Constituting Trigram	*Nuclear Trigram*
(No. 34 Great Strength)	(No. 43 Resolution)

Thunder  Lake
Heaven Heaven

Symbols and Images

—The strong, luminous yang lines are gaining in number.
—Thunder is above Heaven, which is the power of movement that is deployed and fully manifested.
—Movement without (upper trigram: Thunder), strength within (lower trigram: Heaven): strength is fully externalized.
—This hexagram corresponds to the second month of the Chinese year (March–April).

General Situation

You have at your disposal a great liberty of action and real capacities for fulfillment. Strength is on your side and permits you to triumph over difficulties. However, the danger will be in taking control of it as indicated by the yang lines, which have surpassed the middle of the hexagram.

If you allow yourself to be led by this strength, it will push you into acting too soon, too energetically, or without uprightness. Therefore, you need self-mastery and reasonableness and you need to pause for an evaluation of the situation.

A great force always generates proportionate reactions. Great prudence and vigilance are therefore indispensable. Furthermore, you should not rest on your laurels, for it is up to you to make good use of your strength so that it brings forth the fruit that it promises.

Ordinary strength can be gauged by the amount of energy that is deployed or by its temporal superiority but superior strength depends on one's inner values; that is one's capacity to respectfully and consistently follow objectives devoid of egocentric interests. You should make it your priority to cultivate this superior strength; do not neglect it.

Predictions and Advice

—Favorable for developing vigilance in order to use your strength properly and for persevering in order not to lose the right path.

Notes on Interpretation

Do not underestimate the dangers of misused or controlling strength. In the text of the lines, strength is sometimes represented by a ram who endangers himself through his own impetuousness.

HEXAGRAM 34/INTERPRETATION OF THE LINES

RULER OF THE HEXAGRAM: 4TH LINE.

1ST LINE (9) ---

You are strong, but your position or your means are weak and do not allow you to undertake anything. This can be verified.

2ND LINE (9) ++

The situation is a presage of success.

3RD LINE (9) – OR +

The ordinary man uses force, but not the noble man. These is a presage of danger. If, like a young ram, you butt your lowered head into everything you face, you will end up exhausted and hampered.

4TH LINE (9) +++

Everything indicates a presage of success. Regret over past faults have vanished. Nothing hampers your progress. The strength here is compared to the axle of a great chariot: it goes unnoticed, but all the power of the chariot rests upon it.

5TH LINE (6) o

When strength transforms into something gentle, there is nothing to regret.

6TH LINE (6) ++

If you are like a young ram whose horns are caught in an obstacle and find yourself unable to advance or retreat, you must not persist. In spite of difficulties, success will come.

ADVANCEMENT/HEXAGRAM 35

Constituting Trigram	*Nuclear Trigram*
(No. 35 Advancement)	(No. 39 Obstacle)

Fire — Water
Earth — Mountain

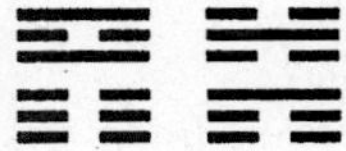

Symbols and Images

—Fire above Earth represents the rapid and natural ascension of the sun above the earth. Everything is brought to light. This is a period of advancement.

—Advancement is also a person's innate clarity (Fire), which appears after the dispersion of elements that had obscured (Earth) it.

General Situation

The situation described here is set within a period of rapid advancement and expansion; the expansion is progress that is being accomplished on all sides.

This hexagram speaks of the qualities and responsibilities that you must take on, which are those of a good sovereign. In fact, like a king, you should take part in these favorable circumstances by demonstrating purity of heart and spirit in order to pacify the people, re-establish virtue, and prevent anything that could lead to fault or error. Also, you should not take umbrage over the qualities of others, but recompense them generously and delegate some of your responsibilities and power. In this way, everyone will follow you and advance.

You should advance the light by destroying anything that might obscure intelligence and a true understanding of things. You will have to refine your knowledge and qualities, for true progress consists of developing a luminous interior attitude from which an influential outer conduct can issue.

Finally, it is desirable to set aside personal gain from this expansion of the light. You should take advantage of it for the good of all. Then, all circumstances will unite in easy and rapid progress.

Predictions and Advice

—Period of progress and expansion in which you should show generosity of heart and spirit.
—True progress rests upon inner clarity that brightens outer conduct and makes it influential.

Notes on Interpretation

The lines insist on the fact that the period of progress is only truly put to use by cultivating a limpid and generous interior attitude.

HEXAGRAM 35/INTERPRETATION OF THE LINES

RULER OF THE HEXAGRAM: 5TH LINE.

1ST LINE (6) ++

Whether you advance or retreat, a perfect inner attitude will presage success. In spite of the obstacles, by being generous and open, you will commit no error.

2ND LINE (6) +++

Even if your progress has seen its ups and downs, a perfect inner attitude will presage success; you can even receive great satisfaction or recognition from higher authorities.

3RD LINE (6) +

If you are approved of and supported by others, your regrets will disappear.

4TH LINE (9) --

Looking for personal profit during a period of progress is a presage of danger.

5TH LINE (6) +++

Regrets will disappear when you no longer worry about what you have lost or gained. Continuing on this path will lead you to success and will render all circumstances favorable.

6TH LINE (9) ++

You must not progress by force, except when controlling yourself. In this case, in spite of danger and presage of difficulties, you will know success and will commit no fault.

Constituting Trigram (No. 36 Darkening of the Light)	*Nuclear Trigram* (No. 40 Deliverance)
Earth ☷	☳ Thunder
Fire ☲	☵ Water

Symbols and Images

—The sun (lower trigram: Fire) sinks below the earth (upper trigram). The light is obscured, wounded.
—Facing the darkening of the light, one should be inwardly luminous (lower trigram: Fire) and outwardly carefree (upper trigram: Earth).

General Situation

Even though circumstances are hostile, the difficulties will reveal themselves to be profitable, for you will gain strength and clarity from them. This will be beneficial for you as well as others, for your influence will spread out to dissipate the surrounding darkness.

In such moments, it is preferable to be prudent and persevering while hiding your light and your qualities. This will allow you to keep your strength intact.

By the same token, if the wrong-doings and failings of people and circumstances do not escape you, it is not good to unveil them and bring them to light. It would be better for you to tone down the brilliance of a vivacious spirit that could be wounding to others and for you to demonstrate humility and tolerance.

You should also be open-minded and bow to the demands of the times by avoiding bellicose attitudes. If you keep your distance with your adversaries while remaining agreeable, the difficulties will, little by little, be erased.

By respecting all of these points, you will have developed, due to your perfect uprightness, an inner clarity that will radiate until the external obscurity dissipates.

Predictions and Advice

—Inner determination, prudence, and flexibility in the face of the circumstances will allow the light to dissipate the darkness.
—Difficulties are profitable.

Notes on Interpretation

Fire also symbolizes intelligence. That is why the Darkening of the Light can sometimes indicate confusion that disturbs your perception of the situation.

The archaic Chinese image for Darkening of the Light is a wounded bird:

1st line: bird wounded in the wing;
2nd line: bird wounded in the left thigh;
3rd line: bird wounded during the chase toward the South;
4th line: bird wounded in the left flank.

Hexagram 36/Interpretation of the Lines

Constituting Ruler: 6th Line.

Governing Rulers: 2nd and 5th Lines.

1st Line (9) o

When darkness arrests your momentum and handicaps your action, you must, in spite of privations and gossip, preserve your integrity and your goals

2nd Line (6) ++∴

When darkness touches you and only disrupts your advance, remedying the problem or rapidly and vigorously distancing yourself from it will lead to success.

3rd Line (9) + or -

It is possible for you to repel the dark elements or to control them at the source. But you will have to be vigilant, for you are tempted to act precipitously and impatiently, which would be ineffective.

4th Line (6) o

When obscurity touches you deeply, apprehending the reasons for it will allow you to distance yourself from it.

5th Line (6) ++

Hiding and preserving your inner light—your intelligence, value, and capacities—is favorable.

6th Line (6) ---

If you let darkness prevail over the light by not developing your virtues and qualities, initially you can rise up high into the sky, but you will then fall back into darkenss.

FAMILY/HEXAGRAM 37

Constituting Trigram	*Nuclear Trigram*
(No. 37 Family)	(No. 64 Before Order)

Wind
Fire

Fire
Water

Symbols and Images

—Inner clarity (lower trigram: Fire) manifests itself outwardly through a gentle influence (upper trigram: Wind).
—Wind above Fire evokes the energy of Fire and its effect: clarity.
—Each line of the hexagram represents a member of the family, possessing the nature suitable to his or her function. When order is respected in the family, it is also respected in society.

General Situation

This hexagram accents the necessity of an inner development of your qualities and capacities while remaining in your place in order to perfectly assume your role and functions. In so doing, you will cultivate a serenity that will generate outer positive effects.

The situation represented here is favorable, according to the Ancient Text, for the woman featured in her role of wife and mother. This can be interpreted as men and women who adopt the functions and qualities of yin: nourishing, assisting, taking a self-effacing secondary position, open-mindedness, and modesty.

The value of a wife or a mother is discreet but has immediate repercussions on the entire family. Therefore, if you cultivate your inner qualities, the first beneficiaries of this will be your next of kin, then your community, then your country.

A person who develops the strength and endurance of inner qualities and reveals his or her intrinsic value through his or her words is naturally hard to ignore. Discussions that do not correspond to a true realization will not be taken seriously for very long, nor have influence.

In the family, clarity comes when each person accomplishes his or her task: when the father is a father, the son is a son, the wife is a wife. Try to carry out what your position requires.

Predictions and Advice

—Favorable for the woman or for whoever has yin functions.
—Develop inner virtues that radiate outwardly.
—Accomplish what your functions demand.

HEXAGRAM 37/INTERPRETATION OF THE LINES

RULERS OF THE HEXAGRAM: 2ND AND 5TH LINES.

1ST LINE (9) +

If you define and respect strict rules in order to preserve the cohesion of your community, your regrets will disappear.

2ND LINE (6) +++

Refraining from selfish whims while remaining in a central position in order to assume your responsibilities and distribute to everyone what he or she needs will presage success.

3RD LINE (9) ++ OR -

If recriminations appear because of excessive discipline or rigors, regretting this in time will make it possible to surmount danger and attain success. If, because of a lack of discipline, even the most submissive members of the community (signified by wives and children in the Ancient Text) become unrestrained, this will lead to disagreements.

4TH LINE (6) +++

Bringing prosperity to your community will lead to a big success.

5TH LINE (9) +++

If your position as well as your virtues and qualities directly benefit your community, you will have nothing to fear and will meet with success.

6TH LINE (9) +++

Dignity and integrity will allow you to lead others and to finally attain success.

Constituting Trigram	*Nuclear Trigram*
(No. 38 Opposition)	(No. 63 After Order)

Fire Water
Lake Fire

Symbols and Images

—Fire on high increasingly rises (upper trigram, with a naturally ascending movement), Lake below descends more and more (lower trigram, with a naturally sinking movement). The two elements distance themselves from each other and cannot reach an understanding. That is opposition.
—The nature of a flame is to rise, the nature of water is to flow to the bottom. In this natural opposition, Fire and Water preserve their proper natures; in the same way, the noble man preserves his nature and integrity regardless of the quality of his entourage.

General Situation

This hexagram describes a situation where your initiative and your field of action are limited by a lack of cohesion and communion.

When oppositions exist, it is impossible to engage yourself in grand enterprises. On the other hand, you can undertake small things with success, especially those that attempt to re-establish understanding.

Opposition has important positive aspects. It is polarity: shadow and light, man and woman, heaven and earth. These are complementary elements that create a whole. Furthermore, opposition highlights differences and permits the establishment of distinctions in species, nature, and function. Because of opposition you will be able to delineate the common as well as the contradictory points between people and you will be able to act while knowing what needs to be adapted or rejected. Then you can avoid being influenced or corrupted by an unfavorable environment, even when a common objective necessitates otherwise undesirable associations.

Predictions and Advice

—Success in small actions.
—You must look at what unites people, what separates them, and keep your integrity intact, no matter who you are with.

Notes on Interpretation

In order to remedy opposition, one must aim for union. This is what most of the lines are concerned with.

Hexagram 38/Interpretation of the Lines

Rulers of the Hexagram: 2nd and 5th Lines.

1st Line (9) +

Regrets will disappear if you give up worrying and stop tyring at all cost to regain union; it will happen on its own if sincere affinities exist. The image here is of a horse that runs farther away when one pursues it, but which returns on its own if it is truly yours. By refraining from repelling contrary or hostile people, you will commit no fault.

2nd Line (9) +

When opposition reigns, one must, while remaining upright and sincere, take some torturous roads in order to meet one's teacher or guide. This is without fault.

3rd Line (6) +

If youı every attempt at union is thwarted until it grieves you deeply, keeping your integrity intact even if everything has started badly will enable you to attain your goal.

4th Line (9) +

Isolated in the opposition, you encounter someone who is your complementary. Circumstances favoring union will see that, in spite of the danger, you will commit no fault.

5th Line (6) +

Regrets will disappear if you act energetically, guided by a wise one, to triumph over obstacles. Putting yourself in motion will bring no fault.

6th Line (9) +++

Opposition isolates you and falsifies your perception of things, making you believe in dangers that are not there. If, ready to fight your enemies, you realize that these are friends, you will unite with them and this will bring appeasement and success.

OBSTACLE/HEXAGRAM 39

Constituting Trigram (No. 39 Obstacle)			*Nuclear Trigram* (No. 64 Before Order)
Water	☵	☲	Fire
Mountain	☶	☵	Water

Symbols and Images

—Danger without (upper trigram: Water), calm within (lower trigram: Mountain).
—Water is blocked by the rocks at the summit of the Mountain. The only way it can flow again is by accumulating and submerging the obstacle.

General Situation

This hexagram describes a situation in which there is an obstacle or a danger into which you risk throwing yourself. It is necessary to reconsider the facts of the problem, to remain steadfast and honest, and to resort to the advice of a wise person. In this way, it will be possible for you to find an opening.

The obstacle is powerful and confronting it will lead to failure. In order to conquer it, you must find a place of refuge, where you can stop and conduct an attentive inner examination.

In the face of difficulties and failure, the ordinary person looks for something external to blame. Once he thinks it has been found, he is powerless to change people and things, and submits to what he calls "fate." The noble man looks at his own deficiencies and weaknesses, fixes them, and then applies himself to keeping his integrity intact. Then he can progress as well as effectively change the entire situation, such is the depth and power of the inner transformation. This is what is signified by Water which accumulates at the summit of the Mountain until it overcomes and submerges the obstacle. The accumulation of Water is the positive development of personality, which allows the cultivation of the capacities appropriate for dissolving obstacles.

Predictions and Advice

Success under the following conditions:
—do not meet danger head-on; stop yourself and find refuge.
—Examine your deficiencies, find remedies for them, and develop your positive qualities.
—Seek the support of an enlightened guide.

Hexagram 39/Interpretation of the Lines

Ruler of the Hexagram: 5th Line.

1st Line (6) -- or ++

Advancing will throw you into difficulties. Going back will bring felicitations.

2nd Line (6) o

When obstacles accumulate, if you tend to your obligations and responsibilities, you will not be blamed.

3rd Line (9) ++

Advancing will throw you into difficulties. Turning back will put you on the right path.

4th Line (6) ++

Advancing will throw you into difficulties. Turning back will allow you to create alliances.

5th Line (9) ++

The obstacles are great, but friends will come to your aid.

6th Line (6) +++

Advancing will throw you into difficulties. By turning back, you will meet with greatness and success. It is preferable to seek the advice and support of someone with a broad overview.

Constituting Trigram	*Nuclear Trigram*
(No. 40 Deliverance)	(No. 63 After Order)

Thunder 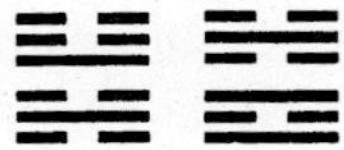 Water

Water Fire

Symbols and Images

—Thunder and Water bring on a storm, a deliverance that follows long-accumulated tension.

—Thunder, which has a naturally ascending movement, is above, and disengages itself from Water, or danger, in the lower trigram, which has a naturally descending movement.

General Situation

The overall situation indicates that the horizon has appeared after a long accumulation of worries and problems. It is only a beginning, but this upturn will give you the necessary courage and calm to successfully attain complete liberation.

The best way to disengage yourself from past difficulties is to pinpoint the different aspects of the situation and adapt yourself to the necessities of the moment. If you have not anymore reasons or motives upon which to act, you should wait for the situation to calm down and become clear before recommencing normal activity. You should calm down and allow tension to unwind. On the other hand, if you still have some problems to resolve, take care of them without delay so that they will not increase. When you are newly delivered of your troubles, you should adopt a fully attentive attitude, like that of a convalescent.

Finally, when confronting faults or errors, you must show clemency and heart-felt generosity. It is useless to harbor a grudge. In this way, your spirit will be delivered of ruminations linked to what has been done or what should have been done, and you will be open to the renewal that is beginning.

Predictions and Advice

—Success by quickly returning to a free and serene state of mind, and by making sure you did everything that was in your power to do. It is not necessary to hold any grudges.

Notes on Interpretation

You must keep in mind that this hexagram indicates that deliverance has just begun, that is why the changing lines warn of the proximity of danger.

HEXAGRAM 40/INTERPRETATION OF THE LINES

RULERS OF THE HEXAGRAM: 2ND AND 5TH LINES.

1ST LINE (6) +

You commit no fault.

2ND LINE (9) +++

You will succeed in removing or disarming the danger by being correct, just, and swift. Such an outlook is a presage of success.

3RD LINE (6) -

If you do not adopt an attitude and conduct fitting of your position, this will be a source of danger and presage of apprehension.

4TH LINE (9) ++

If you withdraw from sources of danger and forge ahead, reliable companions will join you.

5TH LINE (6) +++

Acting with strength, integrity, and sincerity will deliver you from danger and lead to success. Sources of trouble will then fade away.

6TH LINE (6) +++

Your elevated position and your great qualities allow you to apprehend the source of trouble and master it. Everything is profitable.

Constituting Trigram (No. 41 Reduction)			*Nuclear Trigram* (No. 24 Return of the Light)	
Mountain Lake	䷨	䷗	Earth Thunder	

Symbols and Images

Reduction for one is always augmentation for another:
—A strong line in the lower trigram has passed to the summit of the upper trigram. This diminution of the lower trigram benefits the upper trigram.
—Lake evaporates at the foot of the Mountain: the Lake becomes diminished but the Mountain is vivified.

General Situation

The situation is very favorable and promises great success on the condition that excesses are reduced and defects are corrected.

Reduction demands that you turn away from the superfluous and appearances to concentrate on the essential: materially or financially, this means economy and simplicity; in terms of power it means slowing down your expansion and learning to be humble and flexible; inwardly, it means getting rid of your excesses and defects, and nourishing your virtues and qualities. The two constituting trigrams give an example of this by reminding us that anger rises like a Mountain and is mastered by the immobility of the Mountain; passions have the depth of a Lake but can be limited and contained, like the waters of the Lake.

This hexagram also indicates that you must be sincere, determined, and persevering. If your efforts are inconstant, your results will be inconsistent, hardly viable, and without great effect.

Finally, this hexagram does not encourage action because you lack the necessary strength. On the other hand, you can and should define a worthy objective and prepare yourself for it by proceeding with the necessary gifts and offerings.

Predictions and Advice

—Diminishing darkness favors the augmentation of the luminous and creates circumstances leading to a great success.
—Following your goal with determination and proceeding with offerings and the appropriate rites is profitable.

Notes on Interpretation

Remember that the spirit of diminution in question here does not touch upon the essential but is concerned with the superfluous and anything that would violate sincerity. When you have cast this hexagram, it is important to locate what is in excess, what is lacking in correctness, or what merits being ameliorated; concentrate your energy on this task.

Hexagram 41/Interpretation of the Lines

Rulers of the Hexagram: 3rd and 6th Lines.

1st Line (9) +

If, once your task is accomplished, you quickly withdraw without expecting anything in return, you will commit no fault. You should know how far you can go or not go in Reduction.

2nd Line (9) o

Remaining fair and upright is profitable, but undertaking something will lead to an impasse. If you lose your inner worth, no one will be increased.

3rd Line (6) o

Diminish excess and augment whatever is insufficient. Three voyagers cannot travel together for long, for tensions will drive one away. A single traveler is assured of meeting a companion on the way.

4th Line (6) +

Diminishing what is excessive or incorrect will bring joy and allow no fault to be committed.

5th Line (6) +++

Augmentation engendered by the diminution is so precious that no higher authority can contradict it. Great success.

6th Line (9) +++

If, without reduction, you are able to enrich others, no fault will be committed and it will be a presage to success. You should follow your goal with determination and occupy yourself with all beings in a non-partisan spirit.

Constituting Trigram (No. 42 Augmentation) — *Nuclear Trigram* (No. 23 Usury)

Wind / Thunder

Mountain / Earth

Symbols and Images

—Wind and Thunder amplify one another; this is the time of augmentation.
—The fourth line has been diminished in favor of the first. This means that a luminous personage leaves an advantageous position in order to help the weak lines. This is an augmentation for the latter.
—Movement is within (lower trigram: Thunder) and humility, without (upper trigram: Wind).

General Situation

This hexagram describes a very favorable period of expansion, growth, and accumulation.

On an inner level, each of your experiences is a possibility for opening, for development, and enrichment. On an outer level, your action can attain such scope that everyone can draw great comfort from it. If, carried in this way by events, you wish to increase the well-being of the weak, you will be able to pursue worthy goals and undertake great things.

It is also important to use your power to favor the good and reprimand the bad, whether it be of an external or internal nature. In doing this, you should try to discover your deficiencies and get rid of them, and when you recognize quality in someone else, you should make it yours by emulating and cultivating it. This is the most remarkable way to augment your inner value and increase your outer influence.

Predictions and Advice

It is profitable to:
—put yourself in the service of those who have less;
—diminish your faults and augment your qualities;
—pursue your goal and undertake great endeavors.

Hexagram 42/Interpretation of the Lines

Constituting Rulers: 1st and 4th Lines.
Governing Rulers: 2nd and 5th Lines.

1st Line (9) +++

Being employed in great initiatives will lead you to great success. In this you will commit no fault.

2nd Line (6) +++

Being open-minded and receptive creates such a sincere and valuable augmentation that not a single higher authority can contradict it. Great and lasting success. It is important to respect propriety and rites and to show gratitude to those who support you.

3rd Line (6) ++

Even unfortunate experiences augment you. No fault will be committed if your attitude is sincere and your activity just. It is important to announce your intentions to those who are your superiors.

4th Line (6) ++

If your activity is just and balanced, it is preferable to put yourself in the service of a superior who will grant you support and confidence. Thus, you will be able to change the capital, to find a new place for the augmentation.

5th Line (9) +++

If you have a confident and sincere heart, it is useless to interrogate the oracle, so great is the success it promises. This is the fruit of one whose benevolence profits all.

6th Line (9) ---

If you look only toward your personal interest, you will be a target for your adversaries. If your attitude is rigid and inconstant, it will lead you to failure.

RESOLUTION/HEXAGRAM 43

Constituting Trigram	*Nuclear Trigram*
(No. 43 Resolution)	(No. 1 Heaven)

Lake   Heaven
Heaven Heaven

Symbols and Images

—The single, weak, dark, yin line is on the point of departure. It is the announcement of a resolute breakthrough of the luminous lines.
—The water of the Lake evaporates and rises toward Heaven. The cloud thus formed threatens to break open at any moment.
—This hexagram corresponds to the third month of the Chinese year (April–May).

General Situation

This hexagram indicates that you have one last obstacle to overcome and you need to act energetically with resolve to vanquish it.

You can assure your victory over the last dark elements by clearly proclaiming your intentions and resolutions. Thus, the good or the bad should be frankly defined so that everyone is aware of the vigilance that the lingering danger demands.

You must also be firm in your decisions by establishing no compromise with evil and by sincerely and clearly examining your own wrongs before pointing out those of others. This work should be carried out without delay for a single negative emotion or bad habit would be enough to distort your mood, judgment, and the actions that follow.

In order for your progress to be effective, you should maintain a justifiable and benevolent attitude. In this way, you will avoid excesses and argument, for defensiveness or aggression will give something for your adversaries to hang onto.

Finally, the great number of yang lines should inspire you to be wary of too much accumulation, for a breakdown could follow. That which has been acquired (strength, good fortune, or power) should be used or distributed in such a way that everyone benefits. In this way, you will be assured of a solid foundation and a path with integrity.

Predictions and Advice

—It is advantageous to take a decisive step toward good so that evil will dissipate on its own.
—Avoid combative and belligerent attitudes and find a luminous goal to follow.

Notes on Interpretation

As the text for most of the lines shows, one should not underestimate the last difficulties of conquering darkness.

Hexagram 43/Interpretation of the Lines

Governing Ruler: 5th Line.

1st Line (9) --

If the struggle against darkness is premature or rests upon a weak resolution, you will not come out of it victorious. Advancing without vanquishing is a fault.

2nd Line (9) o

You should show extreme vigilance toward the last dark elements and relentlessly fight them day and night. In this way, you will have nothing to fear.

3rd Line (9) o

An overly energetic or ego-motivated struggle against darkness will lead to failure. You should be steadfast in remaining upright. By acting alone, you can, by accident, be isolated amid the dark elements and be unhappy there, but you will commit no fault.

4th Line (9) -

Your progress is hesitant, sometimes fraught with disagreement, sometimes interrupted. If you had been more flexible and had let yourself be guided by what is luminous, all would have been well, but you do not want to hear about it.

5th Line (9) ++

You will be able to resolutely vanquish darkness only by acting in a perfectly correct, just, and determined manner. In this way, you will commit no fault.

6th Line (6) ---

Ignoring the call to act against the darkness will, in the end, lead to failure.

Constituting Trigram (No. 44 Approach of the Malleable)		*Nuclear Trigram* (No. 1 Heaven)
Heaven Wind	䷫ ䷀	Heaven Heaven

Symbols and Images

—It is not in the order of things for a woman (the weak, malleable yin line) to approach men (the strong yang lines). It is preferable to not act.
—Heaven above Wind: Wind carries the message of Heaven.
—This hexagram corresponds to the fifth month of the Chinese year (June–July).

General Situation

This hexagram describes a time in which a weak, malleable, obscure element advances to confront a majority of strong and luminous elements. The situation is dangerous because the obscure element seems amiable and inoffensive to you. You do not see the danger and allow it to approach. However, it is important to arrest its progress before it reaches fullness and becomes difficult to fight. This dark principle is represented, in the Ancient Text, by a young woman coming to meet five men. She is impetuous, strong, and should not be married.

Meetings between the weak and the strong can sometimes be fruitful: Heaven and Earth make all things prosper, a minister and his sovereign regulate affairs of state. These are exceptional circumstances involving extraordinary objectives. But even in these instances the weak element should imperatively be advanced with discretion, submission, and diplomacy. It should act with the yin qualities of gentleness, flexibility, and self-sacrifice.

This hexagram also symbolizes the action of the sovereign who, even when far away from his people, affects them by his actions and decisions.

Predictions and Advice

—You must not welcome and embrace the dark principle, for it is strong even though it seems inoffensive.
—It is advantageous to refrain from action and to adopt a flexible, docile attitude devoid of arrogance or demonstration of force.

Notes on Interpretation

The dark principle can be a person, an emotion, or an event toward which you are too compliant and which, more or less in the long run, will disturb your peace or be contrary to your path. Whatever its nature, you must localize it and pay attention to it.

When the dark element approaches, it is not good to welcome it. If you are the weak one who is approaching, you should only do so with extreme prudence and under exceptional circumstances.

If your question regards a partnership, this hexagram is rarely favorable.

Hexagram 44/Interpretation of the Lines

Constituting Ruler: 1st Line.
Governing Ruler: 2nd and 5th Lines.

1st Line (6) +++ or ---

Firmly stopping the obscure principle is presage to success and allows you to pursue your goal. Failure is evident if you allow the obscure principle to come to you because you think it is harmless, but it can paralyze you.

2nd Line (9) +

If you restrain the dark principle, you will commit no fault. The urgency is to be relentlessly vigilant so that it comes no further.

3rd Line (9) o

If, when faced with the dark principle, you are hesitant or indecisive, observing a time of pause in order to get yourself together and become aware of the danger will keep you from fault.

4th Line (9) ---

If you do not contain the dark principle, your chances of failure will increase.

5th Line (9) +++

Showing sincerity and gentleness toward inferiors and hiding your values and distinctions will bring you recompense for your efforts.

6th Line (9) o

Being hard or arrogant toward others will generate apprehension, although no fault is committed.

GATHERING/HEXAGRAM 45

Constituting Trigram (No. 45 Gathering)	*Nuclear Trigram* (No. 53 Gradual Progress)
Lake ☱	☴ Wind
Earth ☷	☶ Mountain

Symbols and Images

—Two strong yang lines (the sovereign and the minister) gather together the other weak lines.
—Lake is above Earth: the Lake has gathered a great deal of water and threatens to overflow.
—Joy is without (upper trigram: Lake) and self-sacrifice is within (lower trigram: Earth).

General Situation

This hexagram indicates that the overall situation is favorable if you proceed to a gathering in order to attain your goal.

The gathering should be conducted according to certain rules. In the first place, it should be motivated by a luminous goal that inspires unanimous support. It should also be called together by an experienced and integral leader. He or she should be highly responsible in order to inspire confidence and respect. This leader will then be followed by everyone in the gathering and each person will be able to use the leader's advice and benefit from the leader's support.

Once the conditions for the gathering are in place, you should put everything, such as rituals and special offerings, toward expressing the intentions and aspirations that will be at the foundation of this gathering.

Lastly, it is important to know that while there is a gathering or accumulation of good or powerful forces, the is also a risk of trouble (conflicts, controversy, et cetera). You should therefore develop great vigilance and take preventive measures to avoid misfortune.

Predictions and Advice

—Advantageous for enterprises started by gathering.
—The group should be conducted by a confident leader who is worthy of gathering around.
—The gathering should be motivated by a luminous goal expressed by adequate offerings.

Notes on Interpretation

As shown by the lines' text, joining a group or being part of one is not an easy task. The first lines seek union, the last three lines participate in it.

Hexagram 45/Interpretation of the Lines

Rulers of the Hexagram: 4th and 5th Lines.

1st Line (6) – or +

Wishing for union with those who are not worthy will lead to an impasse and create confusion, hesitation, and disorder. Placing your appeal for union with a noble man might not be taken seriously, but you should persevere. Then, your regrets will disappear and you will be able to advance without fault.

2nd Line (6) ++

Joining the group will lead you to success and prevent you from committing fault. It is important to be confident and sincere, and to proceed to the necessary offerings.

3rd Line (6) - or +

Wishing to join with those who are unworthy can only bring suffering and end up at an impasse. On the other hand, approaching a noble man is without fault, in spite of your apprehension.

4th Line (9) +++

If the gathering is led without seeking personal profit, it will bring great success and no fault will be committed.

5th Line (9) +++

A righteous gathering will bring no fault. Even if some persons are a little unconfident, your perseverance and integrity will presage lasting success. Not a single regret will prevail.

6th Line (6) -

Having the wrong attitude or being in the wrong place will bring regret and sadness, although you commit no fault.

GROWTH/HEXAGRAM 46

Constituting Trigram (No. 46 Growth)			Nuclear Trigram (No. 54 Erroneous Engagement)
Earth Wind/Wood	䷭	䷵	Thunder Lake

Symbols and Images

—Wood, beneath the Earth, grows and pushes upward.
—Suppleness and abandon are without (upper trigram: Earth), growth and expansion are within (lower trigram: Wood)

General Situation

It is time for expansion and elevation. The situation is full of promise, although it may not yet be apparent and that is why you must be persevering and confident.

The growth linked to this hexagram is not without effort and tenacity. This is indicated by the image of wood which pushes discretely under the earth with patience and determination, although its efforts cannot be seen.

In order to make way for growth, keep an open-minded, conciliatory, and carefree attitude. Wood does not directly confront the obstacles that it encounters. It follows its contours and continues gently and discretely on its path. This image indicates that you must act according to the path of least resistance and advance progressively in small steps, by accumulating small actions.

Lastly, in order to take advantage of the period of growth and to accomplish great things, be courageous and go forward. It would also be good to seek the aid and advice of persons in authority who have the competencies that you need. Meet these persons without hesitation, for success is foreseeable.

Predictions and Advice

—A period of great and highly favorable progress, due to constant and adaptable growth.
—You must courageously seek someone of great stature.
—The accumulation of small actions will allow you to realize great things.

HEXAGRAM 46/INTERPRETATION OF THE LINES

GOVERNING RULER: 5TH LINE.
CONSTITUTING RULER: 1ST LINE.
1ST LINE (6) +++
Growth which is affected with modesty, submission, and loyalty will lead to a great success.
2ND LINE (9) +
Because you are sincere, it is profitable to make offerings, even if they are modest. Thus not one fault will be committed.
3RD LINE (9) ++
Growth encounters no obstacle.
4TH LINE (6) +++
Demonstrating openness, tolerance, and strength and proceeding with offerings will lead you to success. In this way no fault will be committed.
5TH LINE (6) +++
Everything leads you to success if your progress is measured, step-by-step.
6TH LINE (6) +
Growth that cannot be stopped or is accomplished blindly is only profitable if it is in the service of a luminous goal.

Constituting Trigram (No. 47 Exhaustion)	*Nuclear Trigram* (No. 37 Family)
Lake ☱	☴ Wind
Water ☵	☲ Fire

Symbols and Images

—Lake is in the upper trigram and Water is in the lower trigram: the Lake is emptied of its substance; exhaustion.
—In the upper trigram, the weak line is above and keeps the strong lines in its grip. In the lower trigram, the strong line is surrounded by weak lines. In these two cases, the yang lines are incapacitated by the yin lines.

General Situation

This hexagram indicates that you are going to submit to the pressure of adverse circumstances. The situation seems difficult, but nothing is lost, for although you cannot act upon the exterior world, you possess an inner liberty that will be determining in future events.

The ordinary person in similar circumstances exhausts his resources, gives himself over to despondency, and draws nothing positive from this situation. The noble man, however, knows that once the darkness has passed, success is possible. While waiting, the essential point is to cultivate good humor, strength, and determination.

In periods such as this, it is very important to be true to your deepest self and to be faithful to your principles and values.

Lastly, in a time of despondency, nothing you can say or undertake is heard or followed. It is therefore useless to expose yourself by vainly trying to justify yourself or to change things. The wisest thing to do is to retreat and keep your thoughts and intentions to yourself. In this way you will escape danger as well as preserve your strength.

Predictions and Advice

—Presage of success by adopting a humble and noble attitude and by keeping silent about your projects and reflections.

HEXAGRAM 47/INTERPRETATION OF THE LINES

RULERS OF THE HEXAGRAM: 2ND AND 5TH LINES.

1ST LINE (6) --

If you give yourself over to despondency or discouragement, you will find no rest and will sink to such a point that no one will be able to help you.

2ND LINE (9) o

You have been overtaken by too much satisfaction or desire. Take hold of opportunities that present themselves and respond to them with appropriate offerings. Then, even if you still cannot act, you will commit no fault.

3RD LINE (6) ---

Confronting obstacles that are too heavy will prevent you from acting and make your situation very uncomfortable. You will then be without rest, isolated, seemingly abandoned, even by your own spouse, and that will be a setback.

4TH LINE (9) ++

If you cannot act energetically or promptly, you will know the despondency of one who cannot go to the aid of others. This will bring sorrow but will not keep you from attaining your goal.

5TH LINE (9) ++

When your capacities and forces are inhibited on all fronts, even the power or prestige that you possess will not help you get out of this despondency. Only uprightness and determination, along with prayer and appropriate offerings, will gently make the situation evolve.

6TH LINE (6) +++

When you are incapacitated by adverse circumstances that bind and fetter you, any movement is risky. However, if regrets and apprehensions allow you to reassess and escape the dangers, you will be able to undertake something.

THE WELL/HEXAGRAM 48

Constituting Trigram (No. 48 The Well)		*Nuclear Trigram* (No. 38 Opposition)	
Water Wind/Wood	䷯	䷥	Fire Lake

Symbols and Images

—Wood under Earth conveys the image of a well, because water is pulled up with the help of a wooden pole.

General Situation

This hexagram speaks of the necessity of using your qualities, your capacities, and your resources. If you abandon them or use them inadequately, they will become useless to others as they degenerate.

The image of this hexagram is the well, the role and action of which are just and constant. In fact, whether or not it is drawn from, the well does not dry up nor overflow. Furthermore, each person has access to it without infringing upon his or her neighbor. Likewise, you should render yourself inexhaustible by keeping your integrity and developing a generous heart and soul that will enliven your action and make it infinite and equitable.

Having resources at your disposal is valuable. Overlooking them or using them incorrectly is like breaking the jug that allows the water to be drawn from the well; it is a failure. By the same token, if you are negligent or egocentric, you will exhaust yourself, which would be a shame to yourself as well as others.

The Well also symbolizes permanence and renewal. A city can be moved, but not its well; wherever it is, it stays. In antiquity, rural life revolved around the well. That is why this hexagram dwells on your social role and responsibility toward others. You should put yourself in the service of others and act according to the values of stability and social permanence founded on solidarity, cooperation, and interdependence, for drinking without sharing with others quenches none of the senses. With justice and generosity, you will be, like the well, deep, stable, and accessible to all for the good of all, without necessarily having to act directly.

To keep the water of the well fresh, it must be renewed. Your renewal comes through a supple adaptation to the necessities of the moment and of the people around you.

Lastly, the well represents our vital needs; without water, life is impossible. People can seem to be very different from one another, but their fundamental needs are the same. Let the example of the well inspire you to examine the roots of your problem without being limited by the apparent diversity of phenomena.

Predictions and Advice

—You must be stable and reliable, like a well.
—If your foundations, your values, or the use of your resources are incorrect, you will meet with failure.
—Permanence and continuity of action rest upon interdependence.

Notes on Interpretation

From the first to the sixth line, the water of the well is purified:

1st line: muddy water;
2nd line: stagnant water;
3rd line: fresh water;
4th line: relining the well;
5th line: invigorating water;
6th line: pure and abundant water.

Hexagram 48/Interpretation of the Lines

Ruler of the Hexagram: 5th Line.

1st Line (6) ---

If you neglect your resources to the point where they have disintegrated and are useful to no one, you will be like an old well, full of mud, abandoned even by the birds.

2nd Line (9) --

Having the resources to help others and not doing so is like letting water run wastefully.

3rd Line (9) ++

It is a great pity that your fine resources benefit no one. If the sadness that this brings inspires you to look for the support of someone important, it will bring a happy outcome.

4th Line (6) ++

By purifying and ameliorating your resources you will commit no fault.

5th Line (9) +++

You possess excellent resources and allow everyone to benefit from them.

6th Line (6) +++

If your resources are like perfectly pure water, accessible to all, this will be a great success.

Constituting Trigram	*Nuclear Trigram*
(No. 49 Revolution)	(No. 44 Approach of the Malleable)

Lake
Fire

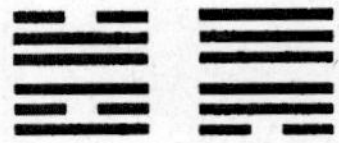

Heaven
Wind

Symbols and Images

—Lake in the upper trigram has a naturally descending movement, while Fire in the lower trigram rises. The two elements confront and seek to destroy each other.
—Fire evaporates Lake; Lake extinguishes Fire.

General Situation

In order to progress successfully, you must proceed with profound and radical changes in order to transform whatever is outdated or inadequate. It is important work that should be carried out at the right moment and with the right methods, otherwise the change will bring about more evil instead of good.

The right moment is when all the evidence indicates that deteriorated, inoperative, or corrupted elements can no longer remain in place without causing further damage. The right methods reside in equilibrium and justice. It is important to avoid any excess, whether in your motivations—which should be exempt of egocentric views—or in the dispositions you take, which should be luminous and supple.

If you operate in the right manner, your results will inspire confidence and this will increase your freedom of mind and action; if your action is incorrect, there will be mistrust, annoyance, and regret. Your determination is also an important element for success; use it to act with regularity and constancy.

This hexagram urges you to be very attentive to the changing times. Each period and each season entails different demands and modifications. By trying to comprehend the laws of change, you will be able to use foresight in order to effectively respond to the needs of all things.

Predictions and Advice

—A period of great and highly favorable progress through a transformation or revolution that espouses the necessities of the times.
—You must have altruism and integrity in order to avoid excess.

Notes on Interpretation

The first three lines prepare for action, the last three bring about change.

HEXAGRAM 49/INTERPRETATION OF THE LINES

RULER OF THE HEXAGRAM: 5TH LINE.

1ST LINE (9) o

You must control yourself, for action undertaken now will be awkward and premature. Balance and fairness should stop any temptation toward movement.

2ND LINE (6) +++

The time for change is now, and you can undertake something with great success. In doing this, you will commit no fault.

3RD LINE (9) -- OR ++

Acting without circumspection will end up at an impasse and will be presage to danger. Wait for the moment when revolution announces itself with vigor (three times in the Ancient Text). Then circumstances will be favorable.

4TH LINE (9) +++

There is nothing to regret when a time of revolution has begun. Positive transformations are already visible. Success is at hand.

5TH LINE (9) +++

A transformation operated within yourself will have favorable repercussions on others. The circumstances are so favorable there is no need to interrogate the oracle.

6TH LINE (6) +++

The results of the transformation are profound for the profound being, superficial for the ordinary being. It is no longer time to act. Resting with integrity is presage to success.

Constituting Trigram (No. 50 The Cauldron)			*Nuclear Trigram* (No. 43 Resolution)
Fire	☲	☱	Lake
Wind/Wood	☴	☰	Heaven

Symbols and Images

—The general shape of this hexagram suggests a cauldron: the two segments of the broken line in the fifth place are the two handles; the two segments of the broken line in the first place are the feet. The solid central lines make up the belly of the cauldron.
—Yu the Great, one of the Five Sovereigns, forged magic cauldrons that contained the virtue of Kings. In antiquity, bronze cauldrons were used in major religious ceremonies Taoists visualize a cauldron as the energetic center of the human body. Mythology, religion, and yoga refer to the cauldron as a place for alchemical mutations.
—Wood nourishes Fire, which symbolizes the nourishment of the principles of life.

General Situation

This hexagram indicates that you can blossom and elevate yourself with the help of the changes that are stirring. It is a favorable time for transformations which promise great success and favors spiritual development.

Cooking in the cauldron transforms the raw into the cooked, it tenderizes the tough and renders edible the inedible. Thus, the cauldron allows the welcoming of the new and enlarges human possibilities and nourishes liberty. This hexagram indicates that the present circumstances are favorable because they allow you to transform everything into something nourishing for yourself and others. This is done by developing gentleness inside and the clarity of your intelligence outside. This gentleness and intelligence will renew you and awaken you to whatever is misguided, narrow, and stagnant; these qualities will allow you to carry out the adjustments that circumstances demand while preserving and nourishing your strength.

The cauldron is also characterized by its massive and solid aspect; you will assure your destiny by being solid in your determination and massive in your correctness and virtues. If you must act within or upon a social organization, do so by establishing fixed and well-defined rules upon which the stability of your enterprises can depend.

Predictions and Advice

—Great success. A very favorable period.
—You can act on your destiny and renew yourself by turning toward the superior.

Hexagram 50/Interpretation of the Lines

Rulers of the Hexagram: 5th and 6th Lines.

1st Line (6) +

Turning the situation upside-down is profitable if it allows for a purification and elimination of whatever is obstructive, paralyzing, or corruptive. Extraordinary alliances are possible if they yield results that would be impossible to obtain otherwise ("taking a concubine I order to have a son," according to the Ancient Text). In this way, no fault is committed.

2nd Line (9) ++

The fact that you possess qualities and capacities can disturb or worry your partner. Without approaching or forcing anything you will obtain success.

3rd Line (9) ++

You possess quality and capability but a renewal is necessary in order to free up your activity. In this way, even if your possibilities are not realized, tensions and regrets will disappear and success will finally come.

4th Line (9) ---

If you are not up to the task required of you, you will experience loss and waste. Confusion will lead to failure.

5th Line (6) +++

When you possess that which is just and precious, it is favorable to persevere.

6th Line (9) +++

Possessing, calmly and with balance, whatever is precious promises a great success. Everything is favorable.

Constituting Trigram (No. 51 Shock of Thunder)	*Nuclear Trigram* (No. 39 Obstacle)
Thunder Thunder ䷲	䷦ Water Mountain

Symbols and Images

—The doubling of Thunder in the upper and lower trigrams evokes its constant rumbling, which inspires fear.
—The nuclear trigrams Water and Mountain remind us of the presence of danger (Water) and the necessity of facing it firmly (Mountain).

General Situation

This hexagram depicts a situation where an impulse takes place, a sudden and energetic movement that shakes you up and inspires fear. This fear is positive and should not be ignored, for it is an important element of reformation and growth. In fact, far from paralyzing you, it should galvanize you and lead you to a personal examination that will allow you to rectify your defects and nourish your qualities.

Because you have experienced this fear, you will be vigilant and circumspect. Then, you will neglect nothing, postpone nothing, and will remain, in spite of the tempest, calm and serene. In this state of mind will be able to develop the necessary qualities to guide people and undertake something.

Repose has not yet occurred because the shock that the Thunder aroused is far-reaching. In order to face the shock, you must be calm and concentrate on what needs to be accomplished, like a leader of a religious ceremony who is not disturbed nor distracted from his faith and the procession of the ritual. By working this way, you will be fully able to assume your responsibilities and your action will have great scope.

The fear referred to by this hexagram could be that which arouses your own activity. The presage is not bad if your foundations are good, your determination firm, and your motivations altruistic.

Predictions and Advice

—Profitable if fear inspires you to carefully examine yourself and the overall circumstances.
—Remain calm, serene, and concentrated upon the task to be accomplished.

HEXAGRAM 51/INTERPRETATION OF THE LINES

RULER OF THE HEXAGRAM: 1ST LINE.
1ST LINE (9) +++

If, shaken by the rolling of thunder, your fear makes you examine yourself and act prudently and vigilantly, you will be assured of your security. Then you will relax and be cheerful. Success.

2ND LINE (6) +

If the shaking caused by thunder reminds you there is danger and makes you afraid of losing everything, you will be able to retire to an isolated place that favors contemplation. If you do not advance and wait for things to calm down, you will attain your goal.

3RD LINE (6) o

The shaking caused by the thunder is intense and destabilizes you. If the fear that it inspires in you allows you to reassess and return to the correct path, you will commit no fault.

4TH LINE (9) --

You allow yourself to be overwhelmed by the shock caused by thunder.

5TH LINE (6) +

When the shaking of thunder is present, any movement is inherently dangerous. Remaining confident, fair, and persevering will allow you to pursue your endeavor.

6TH LINE (6) o

The shaking caused by thunder tends to strip you of your courage, your will, and to led you astray. You should not act. Reforming yourself and being circumspect when the shaking comes, but has not quite touched you, will allow you to commit no fault. Only a few differences or words of gossip concerning alliances will remain.

Constituting Trigram (No. 52 Stillness)		*Nuclear Trigram* (No. 40 Deliverance)	
Mountain Mountain	䷳	䷧	Thunder Water

Symbols and Images

—In the trigram Mountain, the strong yang line is above the weak yin lines. It is stopped because there is no reason to move.
—The doubling of this trigram recalls the image of a mountain range. The body's repose (upper trigram) should be accompanied by the repose of the heart and spirit (lower trigram).

General Situation

This hexagram indicates a time of stopping, immobilization, and repose.

The stillness to which you should resort is not a rigid, sterile, or imposed one. It is in harmony with the necessities of the moment. It would be in vain and even harmful to try to take one more step. The other aspect of stillness consists of not projecting yourself into the future, calming overly self-involved thoughts and desires that can agitate you.

Stopping yourself, limiting yourself to your duties, and facing facts will prevent you from committing mistakes and allow you to clearly determine the outlook of events. This work toward repose demands much firmness—one of the qualities of Mountain—and determination.

It is said that this hexagram represents the end and the beginning of all movement. When action is no longer called for, both stoppage and inner stillness takes place. This allows for reflection, the fruit of which will be the next stage: external, justifiable action.

Predictions and Advice

—Still yourself and limit yourself—outwardly and well as inwardly—to the present. In so doing you will commit no fault.

Notes on Interpretation

This hexagram can be an indication of overwork. Stillness therefore signifies rest.

In the Ancient Text, the first five lines are associated with different parts of the body:

1th line: the feet;
2th line: the calves;
3th line: the hips and the waist;
4th line: the entire body;
5th line: the mouth.

Hexagram 52/Interpretation of the Lines

Ruler of the Hexagram: 6th Line.

1st Line (6) ++

By stilling yourself at the beginning of any movement, you will commit no fault. Continuing in this way is a favorable presage.

2nd Line (6) -

If stillness is delayed or incomplete, it will not be enough to ameliorate or stabilize the situation, which will sadden you.

3rd Line (9) ---

If stillness is accomplished in a contrite and forced manner, it will lead to rigidity in your entire being; this is dangerous because your heart and mind will be troubled and stifled.

4th Line (6) +

Keeping your entire body still will prevent you from committing faults.

5th Line (6) ++

By stilling your words, you will give order and balance to your speech. In this way, regrets will disappear.

6th Line (9) +++

Stillness that is perfectly accomplished with perseverance will lead to success.

Constituting Trigram (No. 53 Gradual Development)

Nuclear Trigram (No. 64 Before Order)

Wind/Wood — Fire

Mountain — Water

Symbols and Images

—Wood grows on the Mountain, slowly, surely, and acquires solidity and scope.
—Outward penetration (upper trigram: Wood) assures development. Calm within (lower trigram: Mountain) allows progress without haste.
—A tree (Wood) on the Mountain can be seen from afar and changes the entire landscape. This is the image of the influence that development exerts.

General Situation

The situation demands that you progress gradually, with measure, without cutting corners or acting impulsively. A regulated advance, made with consistency and determination, will allow you to follow each stage of the project at hand and will lead you to success.

This hexagram is a fortunate presage for union. The fiancé progresses gently by obeying the rules of courtesy and propriety, and can therefore approach his beloved and lead her to marriage. You should do the same and progress with correctness, sincerity, and respect.

In order to progress gradually and correctly, you should be very attentive and vigilant, and use every occasion to take a step forward in order to arrive at each stage in the correct sequence. Impatience and agitation will distance you from the goal; but patience, perseverance and careful effort will lead you to success. Finally, this hexagram emphasizes the need to gradually improve your character by examining yourself daily. In this way, you will obtain results deep inside you and will be able to have a lasting and favorable influence.

Predictions and Advice

Success through:
—a step-by-step progression;
—the marriage of the woman;
—progressively softening your character.

Notes on Interpretation

Gradual Progress is represented by a wild goose—the symbol of conjugal fidelity—whose migratory flight is accomplished in successive and programmed steps:

1st line: the goose is vulnerable near a river bank;
2nd line: it is secure on the cliff;
3rd line: it loses its way on a mountain plateau;
4th line: it finds a precarious refuge in a tree;
5th line: it takes flight again and rises up;
6th line: it reaches the clouds.

Hexagram 53/Interpretation of the Lines

RULERS OF THE HEXAGRAM: 2ND AND 5TH LINES.

1ST LINE (6) o

Your progress leads you to an inhospitable river bank. The danger resides in the fact that you are still small and subject to remonstrance. If you are aware of this, you will commit no fault.

2ND LINE (6) +++

Your steadfast progress leads you to a safe place and brings you comfort, well-being, and various forms of satisfaction. Success.

3RD LINE (9) ---

If your progress takes you too high, you will lose your uprightness and your moderation. You will advance without being able to return, or conceive without being able to give birth. This will be a failure. You must firmly oppose harmful elements.

4TH LINE (6) +

Your progress leads you to a place where it is impossible for you to establish yourself. At the most, you can take provisional refuge there. No fault is committed.

5TH LINE (9) +++

Your progress leads you to an elevated goal. At first, union is thwarted (the wife is not pregnant, according to the Ancient Text), but finally nothing will oppose it any longer. Success.

6TH LINE (9) +++

Your progress leads you to your highest goal. The qualities that you have developed on this path make you a guide or example for others. Success.

Constituting Trigram (No. 54 Erroneous Engagement)		*Nuclear Trigram* (No. 63 After Order)	
Thunder	☳	☵	Water
Lake/Cloud	☱	☲	Fire

Symbols and Images

—Movement (upper trigram: Thunder) is motivated by satisfaction and pleasure (lower trigram: Lake, Cloud). This union based on desire and passion is not favorable.
—The young woman takes the first step and demands marriage. This does not auger well for her character.
—The constituting and nuclear trigrams of this hexagram are those of the four cardinal points of the King Wen Arrangement of the trigrams (see page oo). This hexagram therefore symbolizes a complete cycle, encompassing its beginning and its end.

General Situation

This hexagram describes a situation in which movement and initiative are not based on correct motive. You are tempted by engagements aroused primarily by pleasure or the search for immediate or egocentric forms of satisfaction, which can only lead to an impasse. Therefore it is necessary to establish more legitimate foundations for your action.

The principle image of this hexagram is the marriage of the youngest daughter. The presage in it is unfavorable because when only passion guides the union, the smallest change of heart will bring about outbursts, hurt feelings, or instability. Furthermore, the solidifying elements of the relationship between spouses—reciprocal obligations, sincerity, correctness, and justice—are quickly forgotten.

This hexagram also indicates that you are not independent. You must be submissive, supple, and modest. Advancing yourself or taking initiative will be really unwise because you must be discrete and prudent. The situation, in itself, is not bad; it is the loss of correctness that brings danger and leads to an impasse. It is therefore essential that you do not overstep your boundaries and that you respect hierarchies and conventions.

For the sage, the overall situation places in evidence what should reside and what should be removed and replaced by something durable. Generations perpetuate themselves because of marriage, which transforms a woman into a wife and mother. You should examine, in your situation, what is enduring, what constitutes a finality, and what disappears. In so doing, you may find new foundations—respect and reciprocal duty—for a union motivated by attraction, which will result in something lasting such as marriage.

Predictions and Advice

—Prudence and submission are your safeguards.
—Undertakings in the present circumstances will lead to an impasse.

Notes on Interpretation

This hexagram can also warn you against immature, impulsive, or inconsequential behavior.
In the principle text of the hexagram, it is said that the situation is not bad in itself. This is confirmed by the fact that the lines—except the sixth—are favorable as long as correctness and wisdom are safeguarded.

Hexagram 54/Interpretation of the Lines

Constituting Rulers: 3rd and 6th Lines.

1st Line (9) ++

Within the union you are dependent or occupy a subordinate role (that of second wife, in the Ancient Text), even without great liberty you can advance, thanks to perseverance and humility. In this way, you can undertake something with success.

2nd Line (9) ++

When the union becomes an obstacle to the development of your wisdom and clarity, withdrawing and remaining solitary is a favorable presage.

3rd Line (6) +

If too much passion or too many demands delay the alliance that you desire, returning to a flexible, gentle attitude will make union as the second wife possible.

4th Line (9) ++

It is preferable to remain solitary rather than engage yourself without real affinity or at the wrong time. Delaying union will allow a timely conclusion.

5th Line (6) +++

In the union, you are able to demonstrate humility and modesty. Furthermore, if you choose sincerity and uprightness rather than appearances and pleasures, this wise and flexible attitude will lead to success.

6th Line (6) ---

In a union, if neither of the spouses can assume their responsibilities, nothing is favorable.

Constituting Trigram	*Nuclear Trigram*
(No. 55 Abundance)	(No. 28 The Great in Excess)

Thunder / Fire  Lake / Wind

Symbols and Images

—When movement without (upper trigram: Thunder) is guided by inner light (lower trigram: Fire), there is perfect abundance and strength.
—Movement (Thunder) is prompt and just (clarity, Fire).

General Situation

This hexagram indicates the summit of abundance, success, and plenitude. This great radiance is the fruit of your capacities and qualities, which allow you to continue your work. The responsibilities that are incumbent upon you are important and, above everything else, you should understand that the time of abundance cannot last indefinitely. Once at the summit, it is impossible to go any higher, but you can plan to maintain your position if you know how to renew yourself and avoid the pitfalls of excess. In abundance, not overdoing it is essential.

This warning should motivate you to do everything so that the clarity of intelligence lights up and supports the whole universe. You should nourish your vigilance and prepare yourself to act, should signs of decline appear. Understanding that a summit is followed by a decline should render you more strong, effective, and keep you from being excessive or proud. In short, the qualities that have led you to an elevated position should be cultivated so that you can always be like "the sun that shines at noon." This will be beneficial for those around you and those who depend on you.

Lastly, this hexagram advises acting promptly and reasonably if conflicts appear.

Predictions and Advice

—Favorable if you apprehend the signs of decline by being measured and vigilant.
—Do not let disagreements linger; restrain them promptly and justly.

Notes on Interpretation

At the peak of abundance, it is easy to lose one's head and sink into confusion. That is the danger that the majority of the lines advise you to avoid.

HEXAGRAM 55/INTERPRETATION OF THE LINES

RULER OF THE HEXAGRAM: 5TH LINE.

1 LINE (9) ++

It is possible that you will meet a valuable supporter (or a teacher) who is your exact complement. This unexpected meeting will last for a while. Thus, no fault will be committed and undertaking something will inspire praise.

2ND LINE (6) -- OR ++

When the clarity of intelligence is covered by a thick veil, you see no more at noon than in the middle of the night. Advancing will bring only doubt, confusion, and agitation. Remaining confident and secure to the point where it shows outwardly will bring you success.

3RD LINE (9) o

When the clarity of intelligence is abundantly covered by veils, you see no more at noon than in the middle of the night. Being incapable of acting is not a fault.

4TH LINE(9) ++

When the clarity of intelligence is covered by a thick veil, you see no more at noon than in the middle of the night. An accidental encounter with a supporter or a teacher who can be your complement will lead you to success.

5TH LINE (6) +++

If suppleness and gentleness guide you, you will attract recognition and praise, and will know success.

6TH LINE (6) ---

If you push abundance too far, darkness will steal the clarity of intelligence. You will have to search in vain, no one will come to you. This will lead to a long isolation and failure.

Constituting Trigram	*Nuclear Trigram*
(No. 56 The Traveler)	(No. 28 The Great in Excess)
Fire ☲	☱ Lake
Mountain ☶	☴ Wind

Symbols and Images

—Fire burns on the Mountain and does not stay in one place, forced as it is to find fuel.
— Fire in the upper trigram rises and Mountain in the lower trigram pushes down. The two elements get further and further away from each other.
—Outward clarity and inner restraint should characterize the regulation of criminal matters. Like a fire on the mountain, the proceeding and punishment should not carry on eternally.

General Situation

The situation will be favorable and presage success under the single condition that you employ supple adaptation. You are like a traveler going from place to place, with nowhere to call home. A traveler is vulnerable because he does not have the support of those close to him and he needs to find shelter. That is why he must be correct, discreet, agreeable, and flexible, as well as useful and attentive to others. This way he will arouse sympathy and benevolence, which will help him to quickly meet good companions on the way and to easily find secure places to stop and restore his strength.

The voyager should advance prudently. Times are not propitious for great undertakings. On the other hand, small actions will lead to success if they are carried out with humility, discretion, and care.
Finally, this hexagram also concerns those who have to regulate litigation or proceedings or those who have to take sanctions. It is necessary for them to clarify the situation with the light of intelligence, all the while remaining inwardly firm and just. Then, the decisions and sanctions will be prompt, equitable, and clear.

Predictions and Advice

—Favorable for the reasonable, humble, and prudent.
—Times are not propitious for great enterprises, however actions of small scope presage success.

Notes on Interpretation

The position and evolution of the traveler are very dependent upon circumstances and people; that is why everything rests upon his interior qualities.

Hexagram 56/Interpretation of the Lines

Ruler of the Hexagram: 5th Line.

1st Line (6) --

As a traveler, being weak, superficial, or inconsequential only brings problems and disagreements.

2nd Line (6) ++

As a traveler, you approach a rest stop or a shelter where you can protect your belongings and find discrete and effective help assistance to help restore you. You should not be discouraged, but persevere.

3rd Line (9) --

As a traveler, showing too much pride, passion, or energy will destroy your shelter, distance you from those who would support you, and presage danger.

4th Line (9) o

As a traveler, you have the use of shelter, possesions, and recognition, but your heart is not satisfied because you cannot really make good use of these advantages.

5th Line (6) ++

Thanks to your qualities and uprightness, you can attain your goal in spite of some losses. This will be the source of praise and the promise of future responsibilities.

6th Line (9) ---

If you are inconsequential, superficial, or impetuous, you will lose your shelter. At first, you might believe that this is not serious and laugh about it, but in the end you will be sorry. Losing humility and flexible adaptation will bring on failure.

THE GENTLE WIND/HEXAGRAM 57

Constituting Trigram	*Nuclear Trigram*
(No. 57 The Gentle Wind)	(No. 38 Opposition)

Wind  Fire

Wind Lake

Symbols and Images

—Wind in the upper and lower trigrams symbolizes the continuous and persevering action of wind.
—The first Wind disperses and dissolves obstacles, the second gently diffuses luminous principles and penetrates darkness.

General Situation

With an attitude endowed with gentleness and suppleness, you will be able to dissolve the last obstacles and advance with good effect. It is not worthwhile to throw yourself into audacious adventures or great enterprises. On the contrary, you must avail yourself of actions of small scope accomplished with perseverance.

Time is on your side, as it is with the Wind. Wind owes its power to a modest but unrelentingly repetitive force. Thus, even if the wind is weak, its constancy is capable of bending great trees; let the nature of your action be like this constant wind.

This image also indicates that your action and influence should be subterranean, without spectacular effect, but also without being calculated or having ulterior motives. The dark force of powerful emotions would be harmful to a clear and just motivation and spirit. By proceeding calmly you can obtain profound and enduring results.
If you show suppleness, gentleness, and docility, you will distance yourself from all systemization and rigidity. You will be receptive to changes and the necessities of the moment while remaining true to your objectives.

This hexagram also indicates that it is important to tirelessly explain the motivations and objectives you hold in common with those who depend upon you so that they understand and execute their tasks with ease. Lastly, it would be worthwhile to seek the advice and support of someone with authority whose force has greater external influence than your own.

Predictions and Advice

—Favorable for small actions conducted with gentleness.
—Pursuing a clear goal and consulting with someone great and powerful is advantageous.

Notes on Interpretation

An excess of gentleness and humility can create a character that is too malleable and inconstant. In addition, fear or the desire to flatter engenders excess humility while pride and egoism entail the lack thereof; this is what the changing lines address.

Hexagram 57/Interpretation of the Lines

Constituting Rulers: 1st and 4th Lines.
Governing Ruler: 5th Line.

1st Line (6) +

If you continually advance and retreat, in the grips of hesitation, only sincerity coupled with a quasi-military determination will be profitable.

2nd Line (9) ++

Excessive humility and flexibility will leave you unsettled; it would be good to seek the advice of experienced or wise people to guide you. This will lead to success and avoid fault.

3rd Line (9) -

Trying again and again to show suppleness and adaptation and not succeeding will lead to disagreements.

4th Line (6) ++

Your regrets disappear because humility and suppleness come to fruition.

5th Line (9) +++

The situation is presage to success. Errors of the past are erased. Even if in the beginning you have committed some faults, you will finally realize your goal. Prudence and vigilance are necessary before and after you act: beforehand in order to reflect deeply upon your action and afterward to follow its evolution and consequences. In this way, success is assured.

6th Line (9) --

Humility and suppleness pushed to the extreme will leave you unsettled and take away possessions and recognition. Continuing in this way is presage to a failure.

Constituting Trigram	*Nuclear Trigram*
(No. 58 Joyful Exchange)	(No. 37 Family)

Lake ䷹ ䷤ Wind
Lake Fire

Symbols and Images

—The doubling of Lake in the upper and lower trigrams imparts the image of joy and learning that inspires impulse and progress.

General Situation

The overall situation is favorable but demands the development of a cheerful and serene mood in order to foster a pleasant and propitious atmosphere for exchange.

The joy mentioned here is the joy you should develop within yourself as well as the joy you can arouse in others. That is why this hexagram insists on welcoming all beings with tolerance, gentleness, and humbleness, for this will give birth to their joy and satisfaction.

Joy is not superficial, without strength or value. On the contrary, its strength is such that it inspires men to go into battle without fear of suffering or death. During times of peace, it can move mountains, for joy, friendliness, and gentleness attain goals more surely than constraint or force. This power should imperatively be guided by integrity and sincerity, otherwise it could degenerate into superficiality, dissipation, and futility, and would serve only to manipulate others or be put to use in selfish interests.

Allied to virtue, justice, and perseverance, joy is also the strength of character that is manifested by amiability and emotional stability. Lastly, joy is linked to the mouth, exchange, communication, knowledge, and teaching. It is the exciting joy of learning together, interdependence, and mutual encouragement. All of this creates a sympathetic climate that you should cultivate and preserve to eliminate disagreements and conflicts.

Predictions and Advice

—Joy, mutual helpfulness, and conviviality allow you to create favorable circumstances.
—Showing perseverance is favorable.

Notes on Interpretation

Joy can be more or less polluted by emotions or temptations which have nothing to do with the true joy born of interior strength and integrity; this is addressed by the changing lines.

HEXAGRAM 58/INTERPRETATION OF THE LINES

CONSTITUTING RULERS: 3RD AND 6TH LINES.

GOVERNING RULERS: 2ND AND 5TH LINES.

1ST LINE (9) +++

If you develop a joy born of humbleness and equity, it will lead you to success.

2ND LINE (9) +++

If you develop a joy that rests upon integrity and confidence, it will lead you to success and regrets will fade away.

3RD LINE (6) ---

If your joy is based on looking for external satisfaction and is born of an inconstant and easily influenced mind, this will lead to failure.

4TH LINE (9) - OR ++

If your joy does not originate from your inner strength and it is troubled with futile motivations, it will bring restlessness. Abandoning these motivations will make room for true joy.

5TH LINE (9) -

If you make compromises and let yourself be seduced by inferior joys, these will harm you in the end. Danger lurks.

6TH LINE (6) o

If you do give more firmness to your character, you will be insatiable, incessantly seeking new forms of satisfaction.

DISSOLUTION/HEXAGRAM 59

Constituting Trigram	*Nuclear Trigram*
(No. 59 Dissolution)	(No. 27 Nourishment)

Wind/Wood  Mountain

Water Thunder

Symbols and Images

—Wind above Water: the gentle penetration of the Wind agitates the surface of the Water and disperses it into fine droplets. In this way, the boundary between the two elements is dissolved.

—Wood floats upon the Water and supports the undertaking of great things.

General Situation

In order to turn the situation to your advantage and apply yourself in great endeavors it is essential to dissolve obstacles and reunite things and people that have been split apart.

When people are estranged it is always because they lack a common, light-associated objective. Gathering their hearts in religious celebrations or reuniting them in great enterprises revives the communal sentiment and restores each person to his or her place and role.

The emulation and mobilization thus created will erase differences and disagreements to the advantage of sharing and communication. You will then be able to see the commonality between people and that will allow you to rise above your own interests to offer whatever you can.

Dissolving stubbornness and the causes of separation demands determination and inner work. Sentiments such as egoism, pride, or the lack of compassion can only serve to increase dissent. On the other hand, love toward others and justice, along with a firm and serene character will abolish the boundaries.

Predictions and Advice

—Favorable for dissolving rigidity and reuniting whatever has been split apart.
—Gathering around a light-associated objective and taking on great endeavors with perseverance is favorable.

Notes on Interpretation

It is important to find may have been a point of tension, rupture, or demobilization, and to remedy it.

Being cold, distant, or staying on the defensive is not the proper attitude. On the contrary, it is necessary to foster reconciliation, communication, and harmony.

Hexagram 59/Interpretation of the Lines

Ruler of the Hexagram: 5th Line.

1st Line (6) +++

Putting an end to the disunion as soon as it manifests, by acting energetically with "the strength of a horse" will lead to success.

2nd Line (9) +

When disunion is manifest, quickly finding a place of peace and rest will make all your regrets disappear.

3rd Line (6) ++

If you do your best to dissolve your rigidity and selfishness, you will have no regrets.

4th Line (6) +++

Dissolving obstacles in a non-partisan spirit for the good of the entire community will lead you to great success. Through dissolution you will experience increase, although the ordinary man cannot understand this.

5th Line (9) ++

Proposing ideas and dissipating misunderstandings will dissolve the obstacles, in the same way that sweat dissipates a fever. You will then be able to assert yourself and commit no fault.

6th Line (9) +

Dissolution of obstacles will avoid great misfortune and allow everyone to reside far from danger. In this way, no fault will be committed.

Constituting Trigram	*Nuclear Trigram*
(No. 60 Moderation)	(No. 27 Nourishment)

Water   Mountain
Lake Thunder

Symbols and Images

—Lake in the lower trigram should be moderated because it cannot receive more Water (the upper trigram) than it can contain.

General Situation

The situation will be favorable if you know how to moderate and contain yourself and respect rules and precepts.

Moderation takes on different aspects according to the domains in life to which it is applied. If it is a financial matter, moderation is economy and measure; on a moral plane, it is virtue and detachment; facing an initiative, it is reflection and mastery; in one's love life, it is discretion and restraint; in character development, it is contentment and flexibility; in the political sphere, it is justice and uprightness.

Moderation should be sustained by freely agreed-upon limitations that allow you to manage your strengths and capacities. In fact, if there were no limits we would all be lost in the profusion of infinite experiences and we would exhaust ourselves even before attaining our goals. Limitations are the guard rails that should be clearly respected, for rules that are too vague or fluctuating can have no positive effect.

You should also guard against excess moderation. This is an individual matter and depends on the demands of the times. Excessive limitation can be manifested by overly strict discipline; this quickly becomes resented and disobeyed and is harmful for growth, with the privation and frustration that it imposes. The second kind of excess is too much reserve or uncalled-for parsimony. These stances would cause you to fall short of the demands of the situation. Lastly, narrow-minded or egocentric viewpoints would also represent excesses that limit your field of understanding and action.

Predictions and Advice

—Favorable if you freely accept moderation. This should be clearly defined and should be based on previous reflection.
—Unbalanced or resentful moderation will lead to an insupportable impasse.

Hexagram 60/Interpretation of the Lines

Rulers of the Hexagram: 5th Line.

1st Line (9) o

If you know how to contain and limit yourself, you will commit no fault.

2nd Line (9) --

Narrow or egocentric limits will prevent you from establishing valuable contacts with the outside world, which would be a failure.

3rd Line (6) o

A lackadaisical attitude or without moderation, can only lead to disappointment. By being aware of this and knowing that you alone are responsible, you will avoid committing fault.

4th Line (6) ++

Peaceful, just, and sage moderation is favorable.

5th Line (9) +++

A just and measured moderation will lead to success and recognition.

6th Line (6) o

Hard and restrictive limitations are presage to failure. Lifting those that are excessive will dispel regrets.

Constituting Trigram	*Nuclear Trigram*
(No. 61 Inner Confidence)	(No. 27 Nourishment)
Wind	Mountain
Lake	Thunder

Symbols and Images

—The shape of this hexagram shows a central emptiness that symbolizes the humility and absence of prejudice, which give birth to inner confidence.
—Wind above Lake: the Wind ripples the surface of the Water because it gently penetrates it. This is the image of true understanding that looks to penetrate the inner meaning of things.
—On high, Wind is gentleness toward inferiors. Below, Lake is the joy of following superiors.

General Situation

The situation described here demands a great opening of the heart and spirit and great adaptability so that you can cultivate an inner confidence that will allow you to progress successfully.

In unstable or blocked situations, or when dealing with changeable, stubborn, or temperamental people, success is possible only through the use of gentleness, which must be free of egocentric or ulterior motives. Try to sincerely listen to others and to understand them. Your receptivity will influence your interlocutor who will then be approachable and persuadable.

Your approach should rise above the simple view of reaching an objective; it should rest upon a true communion and a correct attitude. In this way, the bond you make with others will be durable and will prevail even when a common interest is lacking. By doing this, you will find circumstances propitious for success. You can persevere in them and take on ambitious projects.

Lastly, if you have to judge or impose sanctions, you should do so with tolerance in order to attain an understanding that rises above mere appearances. The forgiveness that flows from this will rest upon the clarity of intelligence and magnanimity and it will be an impressive example to the extent that recidivism will not occur.

Predictions and Advice

—Success if you show confidence, sincerity, understanding, and total and true inner openness.
—You can undertake great things.

HEXAGRAM 61/INTERPRETATION OF THE LINES

CONSTITUTING RULERS: 3RD AND 4TH LINES.
GOVERNING RULERS: 2ND AND 5TH LINES.

1ST LINE (9) ++ OR -

Being fundamentally confident and sincere will lead you to success. Anything premeditated or prejudicial will harm your inner calm.

2ND LINE (9) ++

Confidence, sincerity, and deep feelings bring people closer together in agreement. The image is a baby crane who responds to his mother's call even though she is hidden. Furthermore, feelings of sympathy and joy will foster communion and the sharing of the most precious qualities and good things.

3RD LINE (6) o

Confidence that is not born within but depends upon others will cause you to be victimized by alternating feelings of hatred and peace, sadness and joy.

4TH LINE (6) +

Confidence, when allied with humbleness, is like the moon that keeps itself from becoming full in order not to shine too brightly. Such qualities ensure that differences do not create dissent and do not prevent one from going forward. Thus, no fault is committed.

5TH LINE (9) ++

Confidence and sincerity will create extremely solid bonds. No fault is committed.

6TH LINE (9) ---

An excess of confidence can lead to credulousness or to untenable promises. This is presage to failure.

Constituting Trigram	*Nuclear Trigram*
(No. 62 The Small in Excess)	(No. 28 The Great in Excess)

Thunder ䷽ ䷛ Lake
Mountain Wind

Symbols and Images

—The weak yin lines are numerous and surround the strong yang lines. The "small ones" (yin) are in excess with respect to the "great ones" (yang). This calls for prudence.
—Thunder grumbles at the summit of the Mountain and is heard from afar. The fear that it arouses inspires the examination of conscience.
—The shape of this hexagram evokes a bird: the strong central lines are the body and the light yin lines are the wings. The bird should not fly too high if it wants to return to its nest.

General Situation

This hexagram promises success on the condition that you only undertake small things, for when the small has the advantage, nothing great or important can be envisaged.

The majority given to the yin lines indicates that you should be submissive. It is best to refrain from taking initiative and to act prudently, respectfully, and effectively. Your attitude might be judged to be mediocre, but do not let that bother you.

Whatever you wish to undertake or express, do so in a modest way; no great demonstration, great expense, or great pretense. Follow the example of the bird that never takes the risk of flying too high.

These choices should not be based on a false attitude. You need to truly, from within, accomplish a sincere retreat. In this way you will preserve your dignity, for it is humbleness and not degradation that is appropriate. It is also very prudent and favorable to conscientiously take on the duties that fall to you.

Predictions and Advice

—Anything small is favorable.
—Great things are impossible.
—Do not rise up; keeping a low profile will lead to success.

Hexagram 62/Interpretation of the Lines

Rulers of the Hexagram: 2nd and 5th Lines.

1st Line (6) ---

Acting with haste, energy, or ambition when restraint and modesty are called for will lead to failure.

2nd Line (6) +

Even if there is some excess in your objectives or comportment, if you do not go beyond what your functions and position demand, you will commit no fault.

3rd Line (9) o or ---

Without losing your integrity, an excess of prudence and precaution is necessary. Otherwise, you will be hurt and that will be a failure.

4th Line (9) o

If you do not commit any fault through excessive hardness or energy, you will succeed in finding a proper balance. Going forward will place you in danger. Great prudence and vigilance are imperative. While keeping your determination intact, do not act.

5th Line (6) o

When excess fosters the dark principle, nothing is favorable. However, you can attract a companion, although it will be in a very isolated place.

6th Line (6) ---

Extreme excess will lead you too far or too high. You will be trapped and destined for failure. A lack of due measure leads to difficulties and errors.

AFTER ORDER/HEXAGRAM 63

Constituting Trigram	*Nuclear Trigram*
(No. 63 After Order)	(No. 64 Before Order)

Water / Fire 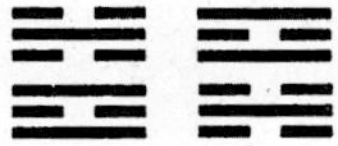 Fire / Water

Symbols and Images

—All the lines are in order, in their proper places.
—The upper trigram is Water, the movement of which is descending. The lower trigram is Fire, which rises. The two elements encounter each other but avoid getting too close because of the inverted positions of Water and Fire in the nuclear trigrams.
—Water is above Fire. Equilibrium between the two elements is possible but fragile and ephemeral; it is realized when Water ends up below Fire to create a new energy: steam.

General Situation

This hexagram indicates that the overall situation is at its maximum point of equilibrium. Success is only foreseeable by limiting yourself to small actions, for, when all the lines are in place, the smallest excess can throw the whole thing out of balance. At the same time, doing nothing will lead to the same result; that is why grand projects should be set aside in favor of small interventions that will make it possible to achieve or maintain order, down to the last detail.

This situation demands that you be very prudent and vigilant. If you allow yourself to be lulled by your success, you will soon become negligent and a general degradation will ensue. If, on the other hand, you remain attentive, you will be able to detect the smallest sign of trouble and rapidly take the necessary measures.

Predictions and Advice

—Success if you remain vigilant and concentrate on small actions.
—Trouble if you relax your attention or if you throw yourself into great enterprises.

Notes on Interpretation

As is shown by the text of the changing lines, it is difficult to remain at the summit.

HEXAGRAM 63/INTERPRETATION OF THE LINES

RULER OF THE HEXAGRAM: 2ND LINE.

1ST LINE (9) +

Containing yourself by checking your momentum and showing great vigilance and prudence will prevent you from committing faults.

2ND LINE (6) ++

In losing what was protecting you, you cannot advance or show yourself publicly. Do not persist; be patient and preserve your integrity. In this way, you will reach your goal.

3RD LINE (9) o

Once the summit is attained, showing energy and initiative is dangerous and difficult. The noble man is capable of this, the ordinary person is not.

4TH LINE (6) o

A perfect situation can transform into its opposite. That is why you should be extremely vigilant and prudent in order to foresee these reversals.

5TH LINE (9) ++

Once the summit is attained, the only things that matter are great sincerity and uprightness whether in religious offerings or in character development. This will lead to happiness.

6TH LINE (6) o

At the peak of the summit, disorder and troubles appear. Only extreme vigilance can ward off danger.

Constituting Trigram	*Nuclear Trigram*
(No. 64 Before Order)	(No. 63 After Order)

Fire / Water  Water / Fire

Symbols and Images

—Fire in the upper trigram has a naturally ascending movement. Water in the lower trigram has a naturally descending movement. The two elements increasingly distance themselves from one another.
—All of the lines are in incorrect positions (strong lines in weak places, and vice-versa). This is a time of disorder.
—Disorder precedes order. Order is foreseeable because each line of one trigram is the complement of the corresponding line in the other trigram (yin with yang and vice-versa). Furthermore, the nuclear trigrams are also Fire and Water, but in a favorable relationship.

General Situation

The situation that you face is full of disorder, confusion, and uncertainty. That is not favorable for any initiative. In the first place, you will have to shed some light on it and put it in order before envisioning anything.

Clarity will come through reflecting upon discovering the balancing factors that are germinating within the chaos. By doing this you will avoid falling into hastiness and each thing and each person will find a suitable place.

You should develop prudence and perspicacity, and be like an old fox whose long experience and extreme vigilance saved him from all traps. The young fox shows prudence in the beginning, but becomes excited and impatient upon approaching his goal, thereby annihilating all of his efforts. The old fox, on the other hand, does not rejoice once an objective is obtained and before he arrives there nothing can distract his concentration.

In such times, great actions are impossible. On the other hand, actions of small scope led with perseverance, simplicity, and humility will be favorable.

Predictions and Advice

—Favorable if you contain yourself and act prudently with forethought.
—Failure if you rush ahead.

HEXAGRAM 64/INTERPRETATION OF THE LINES

RULER OF THE HEXAGRAM: 5TH LINE.

1ST LINE (6) -

If you act without prudence or without balancing your strengths and capacities, you will plunge into hasty or thoughtless activities. This will lead to disagreements.

2ND LINE (9) ++

Containing yourself by reducing your momentum and initiatives is presage to success.

3RD LINE (6) - +

While order and equilibrium are not established, advancing will lead to an impasse, but daring to dissolve obstacles and restoring order will be advantageous.

4TH LINE (9) +++

There is a presage of success and past errors will be erased if you energetically go forward to conquer the obstacles, even the greatest ones. This will demand time and effort but will bring recognition and reward.

5TH LINE (6) +++

There is presage of success and past errors will be erased, with no lingering regrets if you deploy all the qualities of an accomplished person. The excellence of your qualities and your integrity will lead to success.

6TH LINE (9) O OR -

Relaxing and rejoicing when action is no longer required is without fault. But excessive confidence that makes you heedless and sink into negligence will cause you to lose what has been gained.

APPENDICES

I. DIVISION OF THE HEXAGRAMS IN TWO BOOKS[3]

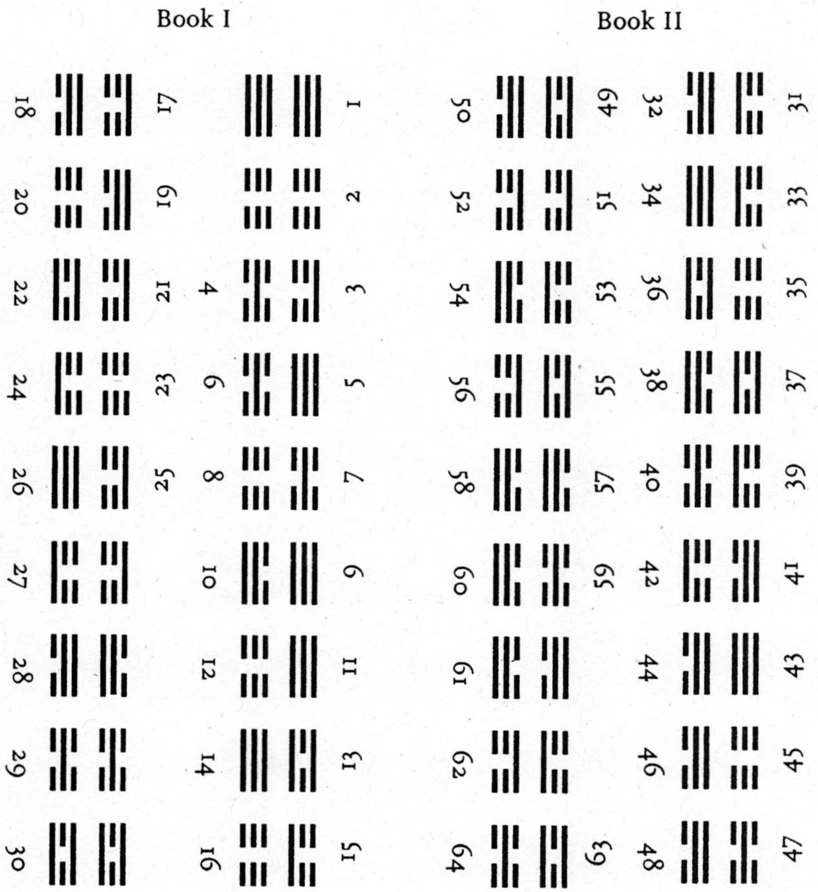

[3] Alice Fano, *Question de: Les Mutations du Yi King* (Paris: Editions Albin-Michel, 1994).

II. SEQUENCE AND CONNECTION OF THE HEXAGRAMS

BOOK I

Hexagram 1 HEAVEN is strong.

Hexagram 2 EARTH is malleable.

Hexagram 3 DIFFICULTIES OF BEGINNING: After the union of Earth and Heaven, the world is replenished, but things are in a state of confusion. The newly born is visible, but not autonomous. Such are the difficulties of beginning, the difficulties of birth.

Hexagram 4 IMMATURITY follows the torpor that envelops the newly-born. It follows the original chaos and precedes clarity.

Hexagram 5 WAITING is necessary because the very young still need to attend to the nourishment that will allow growth and advancement.

Hexagram 6 CONFLICT and animosity are inextricably tied to procuring nourishment.

Hexagram 7 MOBILIZING THE ARMY is inevitable when conflict has reached the point of an uprising. It is a source of distress.

Hexagram 8 SOLIDARITY is necessary for the people. It is the source of joy.

Hexagram 9 THE SMALL TAMES: Thanks to solidarity, the small (or the gentle) can accomplish its work and tame others.

Hexagram 10 TREADING CAREFULLY: Walking along the correct path fosters proper understanding between people and reinforces solidarity.

Hexagram 11 PROSPERITY comes with careful treading that has instituted union and prevented obstruction.

Hexagram 12 DECLINE follows prosperity, which cannot last indefinitely.

Hexagram 13 CONCORD AMONG PEOPLE fosters community and puts an end to decline.

Hexagram 14 GREAT POWER OF ACHIEVEMENT is rendered possible through the concord among people.

Hexagram 15 RESTRAINT affords possession of greatness while staying within the limits of accumulation. In this way, everything is easily accomplished.

Hexagram 16 JOYFUL ENTHUSIASM comes from remaining modest, even in greatness. Enthusiasm will make it possible to follow movement.

Hexagram 17 Joyful enthusiasm brings about FOLLOWING without resentment or ulterior motive.

Hexagram 18 RESTORING WHAT HAS DETERIORATED is possible with the assistance of the followers.

Hexagram 19 BENEVOLENT ATTENTION permits one to watch others and oneself attain greatness.

Hexagram 20 One can give CONTEMPLATION to that which is great, and the great is contemplated.

Hexagram 21 CUTTING THROUGH SEPARATION allows access to the union that is born of contemplation.

Hexagram 22 REFINEMENT is the nature and form in which union adorns itself.

Hexagram 23 USURY occurs when one gives too much importance to appearances and refinement.

Hexagram 24 RETURN OF THE LIGHT happens naturally after the break-up instigated by usury. It permits recovery from errors.

Hexagram 25 INNOCENCE comes when error has been recognized. Innocence helps one to serenely face unexpected external obstacles.

Hexagram 26 THE GREAT TAMES: Candor gives power to the great. One must use patience take advantage of this moment.

Hexagram 27 NOURISHMENT results when the great is divided according to the nature and needs of each person.

Hexagram 28 THE GREAT IN EXCESS: nourishment allows one to attain great heights.

Hexagram 29 DANGER: the abyss follows great heights.

Hexagram 30 CLARITY: In the depths of the abyss, the clarity of fire comes from the fuel on which it depends.

BOOK II

Hexagram 31	INFLUENCE OF ATTRACTION: after the union of Heaven and Earth (Book I), there is a quickening of the attraction between the fiancé and his beloved.
Hexagram 32	CONSTANCY is the quality that unites two people in marriage.
Hexagram 33	RETREAT allows one to withdraw in the face of obstruction to constancy.
Hexagram 34	GREAT STRENGTH: the end of the retreat engenders the accumulation of great forces.
Hexagram 35	ADVANCEMENT is the manifestation and expansion of strength, and not simply its accumulation.
Hexagram 36	DARKENING OF THE LIGHT comes after the manifestation of strength in daylight. Progress cannot be unlimited; it will be impaired or wounded.
Hexagram 37	One turns to FAMILY when everything is darkened. It is the occasion of turning inward.
Hexagram 38	OPPOSITION and misunderstanding are inevitable within the family.
Hexagram 39	OBSTACLE and difficulty come from opposition.
Hexagram 40	DELIVERANCE from tension and détente follow obstacles.
Hexagram 41	REDUCTION: too much relaxation can cause something to be lost. But reduction is the dawn of a blossoming, an augmentation.
Hexagram 42	AUGMENTATION comes after reduction. Increase is the beginning of decline.
Hexagram 43	Augmentation gives birth to the RESOLUTION to firmly follow the luminous way in order to prevent the return of darkness.
Hexagram 44	APPROACH OF THE MALLEABLE: even though one is firmly resolute, the malleable tries to approach.
Hexagram 45	GATHERING follows the approach of the malleable.
Hexagram 46	GROWTH: with gathering, everything pushes toward development.
Hexagram 47	EXHAUSTION is the lot of having reached maximum development. One should therefore look for support.

Hexagram 48 THE WELL: exhaustion leads one to seek the help of others. The well is the source of life and the place were people gather.

Hexagram 49 REVOLUTION is necessary to keep the well available to all. It refreshes the well's water.

Hexagram 50 THE CAULDRON collects the renewal brought about by the revolution and gives rise to an alchemical mutation.

Hexagram 51 SHOCK OF THUNDER is the luminous and revelatory impulse that comes with the new.

Hexagram 52 STILLNESS curbs the impulse of Thunder.

Hexagram 53 GRADUAL PROGRESS follows stillness. Advancement is made in small steps like a young bride-to-be waiting for her husband.

Hexagram 54 ERRONEOUS ENGAGEMENT: a step-by-step progression makes the young bride-to-be a willful spouse.

Hexagram 55 ABUNDANCE is provided by the spouse. It is the source of greatness, but also of worry and embarrassment.

Hexagram 56 THE TRAVELER: overabundance causes one to wander from the home and familial ties.

Hexagram 57 The supple docility of THE GENTLE WIND must be the traveler's primary quality, for if he wishes to be accepted he must be self-effacing.

Hexagram 58 JOYFUL EXCHANGE: accepted, the traveler becomes joyful and communicative.

Hexagram 59 DISSOLUTION of rigidity that isolates, as well as détente, are the effects of joy.

Hexagram 60 MODERATION is necessary to arrest dissolution and dissipation.

Hexagram 61 INNER CONFIDENCE comes from moderation, which gives birth to sincerity and authenticity.

Hexagram 62 THE SMALL IN EXCESS: inner confidence permits even the small to move; it operates a transition within small things.

Hexagram 63 AFTER ORDER: the accumulation of small acts has put everything in order and stabilized them.

Everything is accomplished.

Hexagram 64 BEFORE ORDER: if there is an "after order," there is a "before order," where everything remains to be done. The masculine yang aspect is exhausted in the sense that it cannot yet manifest.

III. SOME CHRONOLOGICAL LANDMARKS

Prehistoric

Circa 600,000–500,000 B.C.
• Yaunmou Man and Péking Man

Circa 200,000–100,000 B.C.
• Maba, Changyang, Digun, and Xujiayao Man

Circa 50,000–15,000 B.C.
• Heteao, Man, Laibin Man, Yunnan Man

Neolithic 10,000–4,000 B.C.
• The so-called Yangshao (West) and Longshan (East) cultures: black ceramics, polished stone, etc.
• Bronze Age of Gansu: figurative ceramics, jade, etc.

The Legendary Period

• Civilizing Sages:
Fuxi (4477–4363 B.C.), mythological creator of the trigrams
Shennong, the Divine Laborer (3217–3078 B.C.). He invented medicinal remedies.
Nuwa, wife and sister of Fuxi
Huangdi, the Yellow Emperor (2697–2599 B.C.), to whom we are indebted for acupuncture
Yao (2357–2258 B.C.), legendary emperor
Shun (2257–2208 B.C.), legendary emperor
Yu the Great, Founder of the semi-mythical Xia Dynasty
• Semi-mythical Xia Dynasty (2205–1767 B.C.)

Antiquity

• Shang or Yin Dynasty (1765–1122 B.C.): oracular inscriptions, appearance of writing.
• Zhou Dynasty, founded by King Wen: according to Tradition, the recording of the Ancient Text of the *Yijing*, the Zhou Yi.
• Western Zhou (1121–771 B.C.)
• Eastern Zhou (770–256 B.C.): the casting of iron, metal coins, etc.
The Spring and Autumn Period (722–481): Birth of Lao Tseu and Confucius.
Warring States Period (403–222 B.C.): multiple philosophical currents.
• Qin Dynasty (221–206 B.C.): Qin Shihuangdi created the first unified Chinese empire, constructed the Great Wall and burned the Classics.
• Han Dynasty (206 B.C.–220 A.D.) Confucianism becomes the official doctrine, commentaries on the Classics, opening of the silk route, fabrication of paper.

The Middle Ages

• The Three Kingdoms (220–280 A.D.): the kingdoms of Wei, Shu Han and Wu divide the country.
• Xi Jin Dynasty (Jin occidental): reunification.
• Northern and Southern Dynasties (316–589 A.D.): great invasions in China from the North; the country is divided into numerous and short-lived dynasties.
• Sui Dynasty (589–618 A.D.): construction of a network of navigable routes.
• Tang Dynasty (618–907 A.D.): Neo-Taoism, Empress Wu Hao tries to impose Buddhism as the state religion, first printed book.

The Modern Epoch

• Northern Song Dynasty (960-1126): Neo-Confucianism, moveable type, blossoming of porcelain.
• Southern Song Dynasty (1127-1279), annihilated by the Mongols.
• Yuan Mongol Dynasty (1271-1368): sojourn of Marco-Polo.

- Chinese Ming Dynasty (1368-1644)
- Sino-Manchurian Qing Dynasty (1644-1911): formation of the current *Yijing*.
- Republic of China (1912-1948)
- People's Republic of China (1949): Rehabilitation of Confucius (1978).

READING LIST

Blofeld, John, trans. *I Ching: The Book of Change.* London: Penguin/Arkana, 1991.

After Wilhelm's, this is probably one of the most well-known translation of the Yijing in English, first published by George Allen & Unwin, Ltd. in 1965. Blofeld's version, complete with background on the Yijing and his own commentary, is simpler than Wilhelm's and concentrates on the divinatory aspect of the Yijing while Wilhelm goes deeply into how the words of the text were derived from the Chinese ideograms and hexagrams. 228 pages, paperback, printed on ground-wood paper.

Huang, Alfred, trans. *The Complete I Ching: The Definitive Translation by the Taoist Master Alfred Huang.* Rochester, Vermont: Inner Traditions International, 1998.

A beautiful hardcover edition distinguished by a presentation and explanation of the ancient ideograms, as well as Master Huang's insight—emphasizing the union of Heaven and Humanity through the Tao of change—into the imagery of the text. Includes Confucius' commentaries on the text. 576 pages.

Javary, Cyrille J. D. *Understanding the I Ching.* Translated from French by Kirk McElhearn. Boston: Shambhala, 1997.

A compact guide to the history and development of the text of the Yijing, by a leading French authority on the subject. Includes instructions for casting hexagrams, and how to frame questions for the oracle. 156 pages, small format.

Karcher, Stephen. *How to Use the I Ching: A Guide to Working with the* Oracle of Change. Rockport, Massachusetts: Element Books, 1997.

Stephen Karcher's mystically poetic translation and original treatment of the trigrams, along with his commentary and focus on spiritual development, is easy to use for the novice and enchanting for those acquainted with the Yijing. 184 pages, paperback.

Lynn, Richard John, trans. *The Classic of Changes: A New Translation of the I Ching as Interpreted by Wang Bi.* New York: Columbia University Press, 1994.
The first English translation to include Wang Bi's commentaries on the Yijing, this is a thorough presentation (and beautiful hardcover edition) for a modern understanding of Wang Bi's ancient insight. 604 pages.

Secter, Mondo. *I Ching Clarified: A Practical Guide.* Boston: Charles E. Tuttle Company, Inc., 1993.
In addition to his straight-ahead interpretation (as opposed to direct translation) the author presents several revolutionary concepts, including "Hexagram Cards" (included in the book) that you use while casting your hexagram, the Evolutionary Hexagram, and a very enlightening way of dealing with multiple changing lines. The Hexagram Cards eliminate the need for pencil and paper, and reveal at a glance the resulting primary as well as nuclear hexagrams. 200 pages. Paperback.

Shaughnessy, Edward L., trans. *I Ching: The Classic of Changes.* New York: Ballentine Books, 1998.
This scholarly work is the first English translation of the newly discovered second-century B.C. Mawangdui texts. Presents the Chinese text alongside the translation, and includes the discovery of a commentary that quotes Confucius extensively on how he changed his earlier views of the Yijing. 358 pages, paperback, printed on ground-wood paper.

Whincup, Gregory. *Rediscovering the I Ching.* New York: St. Martin's Griffin, 1986.
Whincup's translation focuses less on the divinatory aspect of the Yijing than on the language, images and structure of the hexagrams—why they mean what they do. He is succinct in presenting his evidence for his interpretations. 150 pages. Paperback.

Wilhelm, Richard, trans. *The I Ching or Book of Changes.* Rendered into English by Cary F. Baynes. Princeton: Princeton University Press Bollingen Series XIX, 1967.
This is the classic English translation and the third edition includes C.G. Jung's introduction, the ancient text and the Commentaries. 802 pages, hardcover.

Wing, R. L. *The I Ching Workbook*. New York: Doubleday, 1979.
Wing presents a modern interpretation, instead of a word-for-word translation, of the Yijing in a workbook format so you can keep a record of the patterns of hexagrams that you cast. 184 pages, large format, spiral bound.

ANNOTATED BIBLIOGRAPHY

Translations of the Yijing

Groupe de travail du centre Djohi. Le Yi King mot à mot. Paris, France: Editions Albin-Michel, Collection Question de, 1994.
Translated by the Centre Djohi under the direction of Cyrille J. D. Javary, this translation is very interesting for those who are already a little familiar with the Yijing. The presentation of the ancient text by itself is poetically rich.

Philastre, Paul-Louis-Félix. *Le Yi King*. Cadeilhan, France: Editions Zulma, 1992.
Recently re-edited, this translation is absolutely essential. It also presents the ancient text in Chinese, and throughout the book are the Neo-Confucian commentaries by Tsheng Tse and Tshou Hi of the Song dynasty.

Wang, Dongliang. *Les signes et les mutations*. Paris, France: Edition L'Asiathèque, 1995.
This translation of the ancient is distinguished by a foreword containing a deep and interesting introduction to the Yijing.

Wilhelm, Richard. *Yi King—Le livre des transformations*. Rendered into French by Etienne Perrot. Paris, France: Editions Médicis, 1981.
The first translation initiated by a Chinese philosopher who was Wilhelm's "venerable Master." Note: The Yijing text is printed in large type while Wilhelm's own commentaries are in small type. This version is definitely the most accessible for the beginner.

General Works on the Yijing

Choain, Jean. *Introduction au Yi-King*. Monaco: Editions du Rocher, 1991.
Packed with information, this introduction includes very useful lexico-

graphical information (with Chinese phonetics and ideograms, which are often valuable pieces of information for non-scholars) The author is very reserved about the oracular aspect of the Yijing, and therefore does not tackle this subject.

Various authors. *Les mutations du Yi King*. Paris, France: Editions Albin Michel, Collection Question de, 1994.

A compilation of various articles, this 405-page book offers a large panorama of information on the Yijing and its applications: lots of facts and reflections. Among the authors are: Wang Dongliang, Cyrille J.D. Javary, and François Jullien.

All about the Yijing: Civilization, Philosophy, Text...

Cheng, Anne. *Entretiens de Confucius*, Paris, France: Editions du Seuil, Collection Points Sagesses, 1981.

Fong, Yeou Lan. *Précis d'histoire de la philosophie chinoise*. Paris, France: Edition Payot Le Mail, 1985.

A classic in the genre, even today, among more recent texts that explore the same terrain.

Fung, Yu-Lan. *A History of Chinese Philosophy, Volume 1: The Period of the Philosophers*. Derk Bodde, trans. Princeton: Princeton University Press, 1955.

Granet, Marcel. *La civilisation chinoise*. Paris, France: Edition Albin-Michel, Collection l'Evolution de l'humanité, 1988. (First edition, 1929.)

—— *La pensée chinoise*. Paris, France: Edition Albin-Michel, Collection l'Evolution de l'humanité. 1988. (First edition, 1934.)

For aficionados: a real delight due to the author's erudition, style, and humor. These fundamental works are very comprehensive.

Liou, Kia-Hway et Grynpas, Benedykt. *Philosophes Taoïstes: Lao Tseu, Tchouang Tseu, Lie Tseu*. Paris, France: Editions Gallimard, Bibliothèque de la pléiade, 1980.

TABLE OF THE 64 HEXAGRAMS

Upper ▸ / Lower ▾	☰	☳	☵	☶	☷	☴	☲	☱
☰	1	34	5	26	11	9	14	43
☳	25	51	3	27	24	42	21	17
☵	6	40	29	4	7	59	64	47
☶	33	62	39	52	15	53	56	31
☷	12	16	8	23	2	20	35	45
☴	44	32	48	18	46	57	50	28
☲	13	55	63	22	36	37	30	49
☱	10	54	60	41	19	61	38	58

Find the upper trigram of your hexagram in the top row and the lower trigram in the left column; where the column and row for each trigram meets represents the number of the hexagram you have cast.

OTHERS IMPORTANT NEW AGE BOOKS

MAGICAL TECHNIQUES OF TIBET (Secret Practices of Himalayan Magic)—*J.H. Brennan*

Learn about authentic Tibetan magical practices, including: tumo, the ability to stave of the cold by stimulating the chakras and energy channels of the body; light trance states to recall past lives; manipulation of energies via sound, rhythm, chanting, and drumming; and the spiritual practice of dream yoga. The book brings the ancient magical techniques of Tibet to the magicians of the West.

PRACTICE OF MAGIC (An Introductory Guide to the Art)—*Draja Mickaharic*

This book presents the study of magic as a special technology, rather than as an arcane mystery. It unfolds the intricacies of the magic. The basic tool to learning the art is to gain control of the mind. It will help you focus your conscious mental faculties, relax and quieten your body, and develop your spiritual ability to produce results in the physical world.

ISBN: 81-7822-063-6

LEARNING THE TAROT (A Tarot Book for Beginners)—*Joan Bunning*

The tarot can help you understand yourself better and teach you how to tap your inner resources more confidently. The book is a thorough—but never over-whelming—invitation to the beginner. Learn to use the tarot as a tool for inner guidance. Joan Bunning communicates the basic depth and beauty of each card, shows how the cards trigger psychological projection, enhance intuition, and improve communication with your Inner Guide.

ISBN: 81-7822-064-4

INTRODUCTION TO TAROT (Fundamentals and First-Steps)—*Anthony Louis*

Tarot Plain and Simple presents the Tarot in language that is exactly that—plain and simple—without confusing, arcane references. Plus, it is a proven method that is reliable and easy to use whether you want to do readings for yourself or for others. Whether you are a beginner who is trying to uncover the Tarot's symbolism for the first time, or you are an expert using it as a handy reference guide, *Tarot Plain and Simple* will help you get the most from your Tarot deck.

The Magic of Astral Voyages (The Art of Interdimensional Travel)—Bruce Goldberg

In *Astral Voyages*, Dr. Bruce Goldberg presents dozens of timetested techniques that train you to safely leave your physical body and explore other dimensions, near and far. Freedom from physical, mental, emotional, psychic, and spiritual entanglements is yours at last through astral travel. Get ready for the trip of a lifetime!

ISBN: 81-7822-089-x